ANGLESEY
THROUGH TIME

Warren Kovach

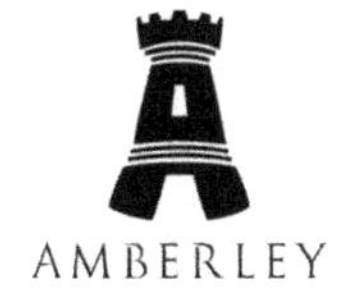

AMBERLEY

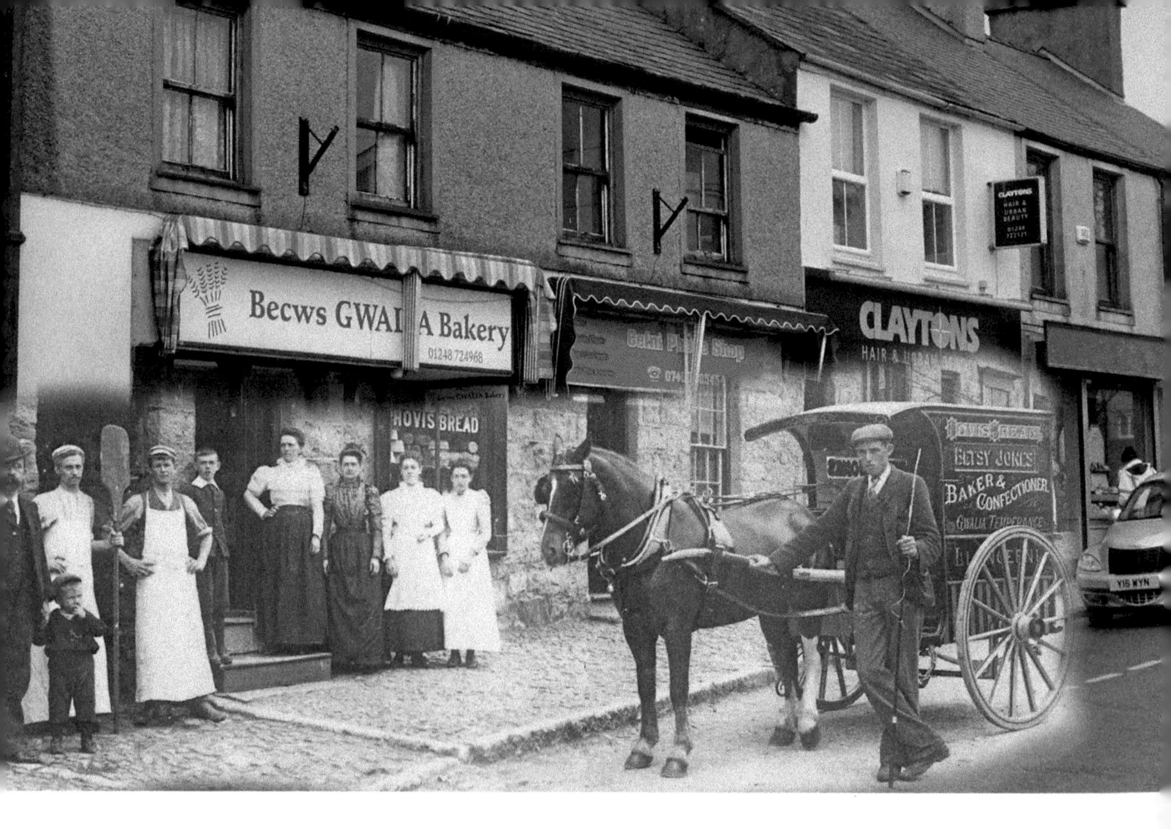

Gwalia Bakery, Llangefni

Knowledge of the past can bring the old days back to life. When you learn about the long history of the Gwalia Bakery, you can almost see owner Betsy Jones and her workers gathered outside the shop, hear the horse whinny and smell the freshly baked bread as you walk by.

First published 2013

Amberley Publishing
The Hill, Stroud, Gloucestershire, GL5 4EP
www.amberley-books.com

ISBN 978 1 4456 1652 0 (print)
ISBN 978 1 4456 1671 1 (ebook)

British Library Cataloguing in Publication Data.
A catalogue record for this book is available from the British Library.

Typesetting by Amberley Publishing.
Printed in Great Britain.

Introduction

Anglesey became an island around 5,000 years ago, as rising sea levels following the Ice Age eventually flooded the Menai Strait. Humans first arrived long before this, with the earliest evidence of them being around 7000 BC. These early inhabitants were hunter-gatherers, but around three millennia later they began to settle down and farm the land. They also started building the burial chambers and standing stones that abound across Anglesey. Industry arrived in the form of copper mining at Parys Mountain before 1600 BC, which fuelled trade with the wider world.

By the first century AD, the island was the stronghold of the Celts and their Druidic priests, standing against the Romans, who eventually conquered Anglesey. After the Romans left in the fourth century AD, there were raids and occasional settlements by the kings of Dublin, and later the Vikings. Through all this, the native Welsh remained dominant and were primarily ruled by the kings of Gwynedd.

Christianity arrived at this time, with churches being founded by the local saints across the island. They flourished in the twelfth and thirteenth centuries, when the older wooden buildings were replaced by stone-built structures. Many of these still survive today, either in their original form or as the heart of larger ones that have been expanded and rebuilt. This period also saw conflict with the English crown, culminating in the conquest of Wales by Edward I and his building of a ring of fortifications, including Beaumaris Castle on Anglesey.

From the eighteenth century, Anglesey became important for two reasons: copper and travel to Ireland. The mine in Parys Mountain was reopened at a time when copper was in demand for the production of guns, metal plating for ships and coinage. At one point it was the largest copper mine in the world and employed 1,500 people.

The many bays around the coast served as small ports throughout the ages, but by the eighteenth century Holyhead, the closest point to Ireland, had emerged as the main port. The building of the Menai Bridge and Telford's road across North Wales and Anglesey eased the hardship of the traveller, as did the later coming of the railways and the Britannia Bridge.

Throughout its history, Anglesey has been known as the breadbasket of Wales, and even today remains a mainly agricultural land. Those towns and villages that weren't developed to cater to the needs of travellers or miners were market towns and agricultural centres. In the past century, all have gone through numerous changes to meet the needs of increasing tourism and modern life in general.

The Photographs

This book aims to highlight Anglesey's past by comparing photographs of places as they are today to ones from a century ago or more. The majority of the pictures on the following pages show shops and houses, along with churches and other structures. In some cases, the buildings have changed little, while others have completely disappeared and been replaced by modern structures. In most you can see the same walls and roofs that previous generations saw, but they have been modified to reflect modern usages, tastes and promotional necessities.

At the turn of the twentieth century, most shops had small windows and simple signs. Some had more elaborate but tastefully designed shopfronts, surmounted by iron decorations, such as Manchester House in Amlwch (page 61). Today, the high streets in the towns are often a riot of large colourful signs and expansive plate-glass windows full of wares. In most cases, the original bare stonework, made of carefully dressed stones assembled in fine patterns, has been hidden behind plaster and paint, to the detriment of the overall character of the towns.

In smaller towns and villages, the trend often goes the other way; commercial premises are replaced by residences with no signs or show windows. The closure of small shops today is often attributed to the rise of supermarkets and chain stores, but this is a process that has been going on for a very long time. The village of Bodffordd had many inns and shops in the nineteenth century, but by the start of the twentieth century many of these had already been converted to homes. The building of the Menai Bridge and the new road to Holyhead (now the A5) led to the decline of many now bypassed villages along the old post road.

In selecting photographs and places to describe, I've tried to make sure the island has been evenly covered, with all the main towns and a selection of villages included. Many of the historical images have been provided by the Anglesey Archives. These are identified in the captions with the letters 'AA', followed by the document reference number. All other old photographs have come from my own collection, and all the modern ones were taken by me, mostly in 2012 and 2013.

When writing the captions, I've relied not only on the wide selection of Anglesey history books, but also my own research. In particular, I've scoured old Ordnance Survey maps, trade directories and the censuses to find out when buildings first appeared, who was living in them, and what trades were being carried out. Knowing the names of residents and shop owners (who may even be the ancestors of readers of this book) can enhance our personal connection with history.

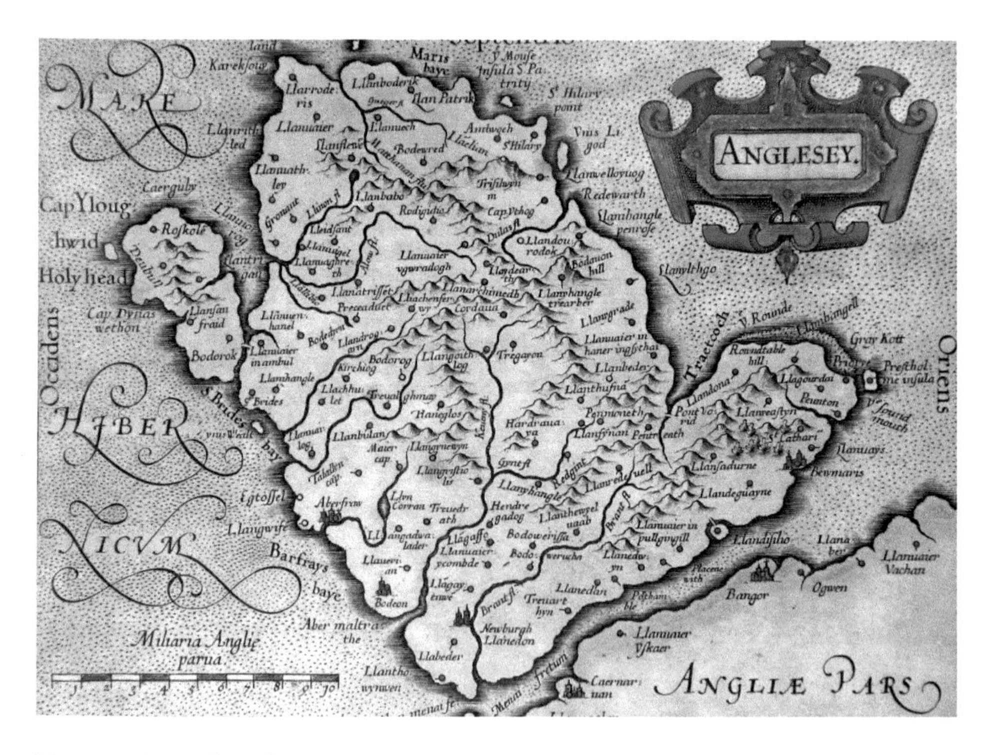

Mercator Map of Anglesey, *c.* 1595

This early map of Anglesey is by Gerard Mercator, the mapmaker who coined the term 'atlas' and gave his name to the Mercator projection. Advances in techniques at this time allowed for increasingly accurate maps, but modern-day technology (including the Landsat satellite, which took the picture below in December 2001) go beyond anything the early mapmakers could have imagined.

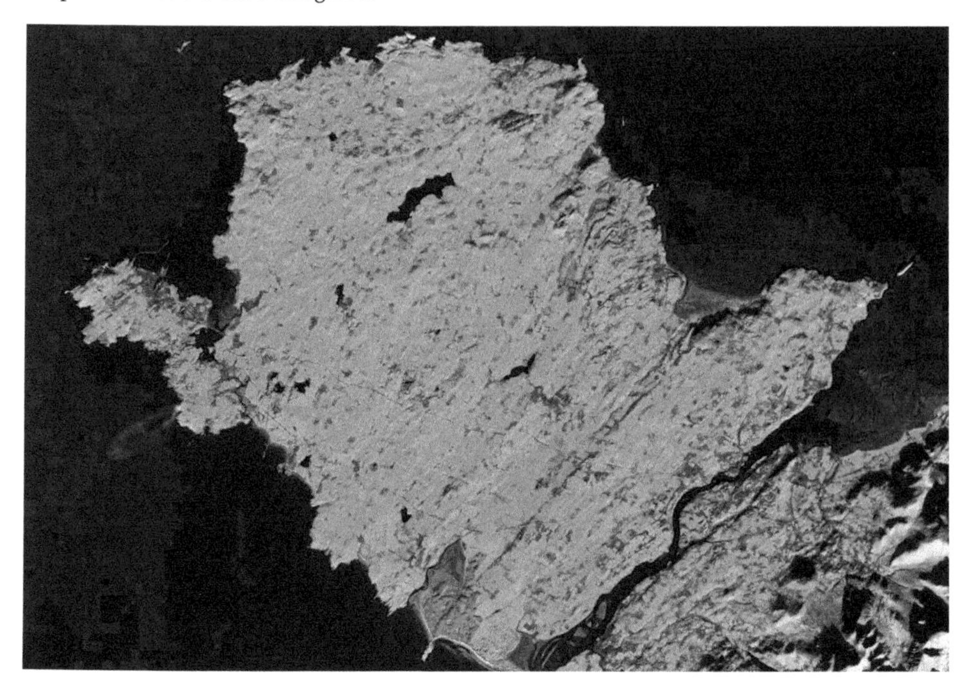

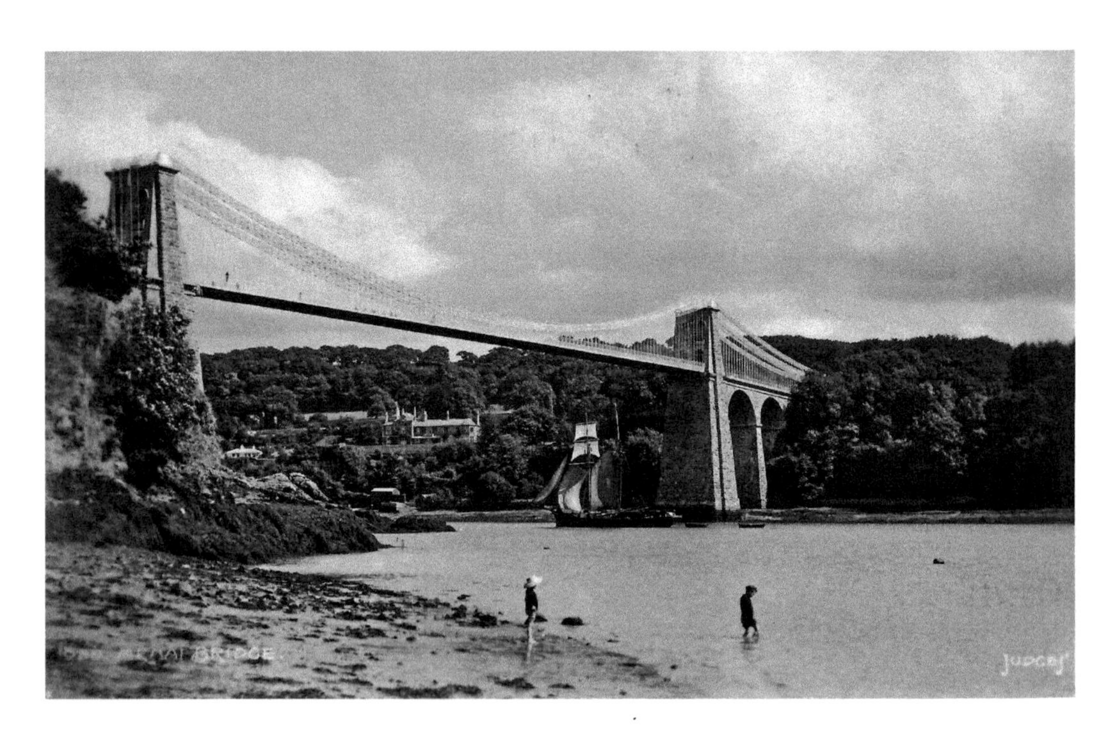

Menai Bridge, 1913

Probably the most iconic and recognisable structure on Anglesey, the Menai Bridge symbolises its status as an island. Designed by Thomas Telford, it was opened in 1826. Before this, travellers came to the island by one of the many ferries, which could be unreliable and dangerous. Many tragedies occurred with numerous lives lost. The older picture above shows the shore before the Belgian Promenade was built during the First World War. In this earlier period, this was a favourite bathing place, and beach huts lined the shore.

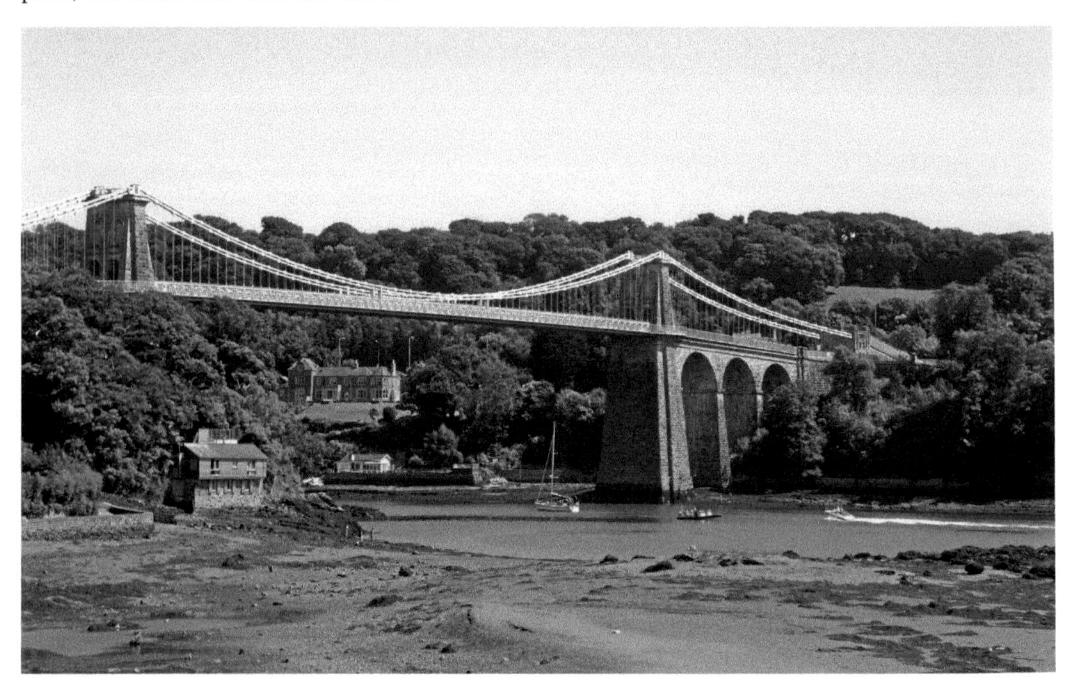

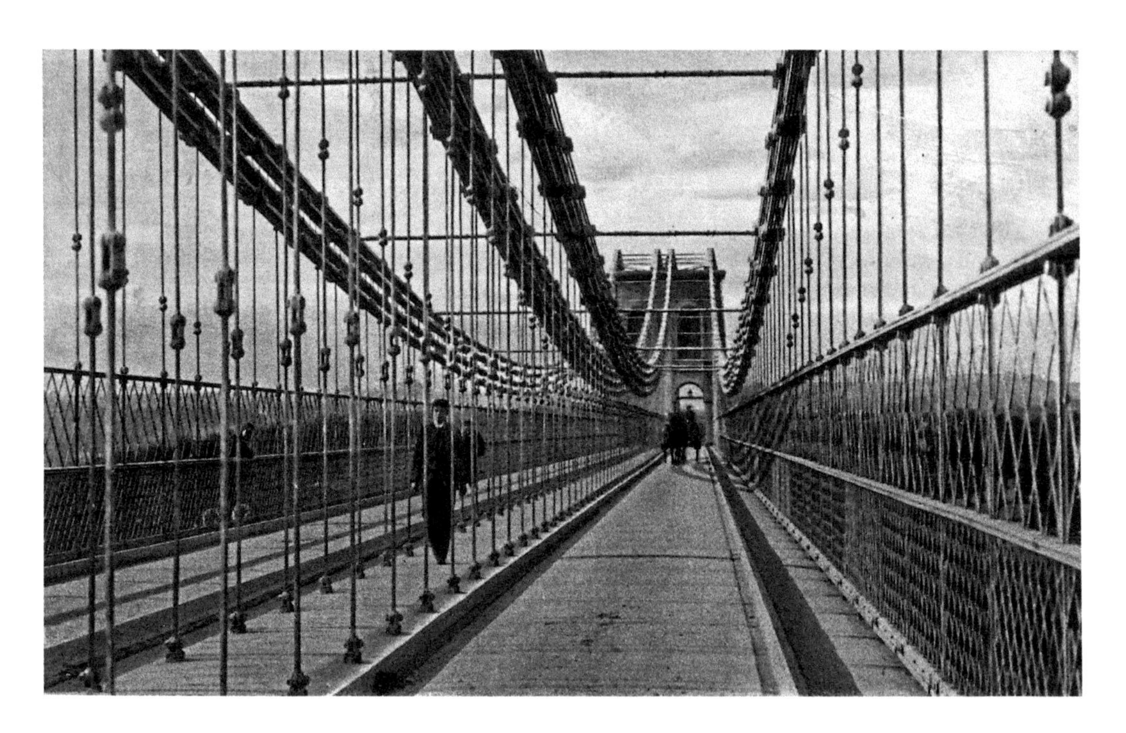

Menai Bridge, *c.* 1905

When completed, the Menai Bridge was the largest suspension bridge in the world. The road deck was 100 feet above the water, to let tall sailing ships pass underneath, and was supported by sixteen iron chains. The increasing popularity of motor vehicles in the 1930s meant the bridge needed to be strengthened. The iron chains were replaced by fewer steel ones, the arches were widened, and the walkway moved from the centre to either side. The photograph below was taken when it was closed for a mini-marathon, a rare time when you could safely walk down the middle.

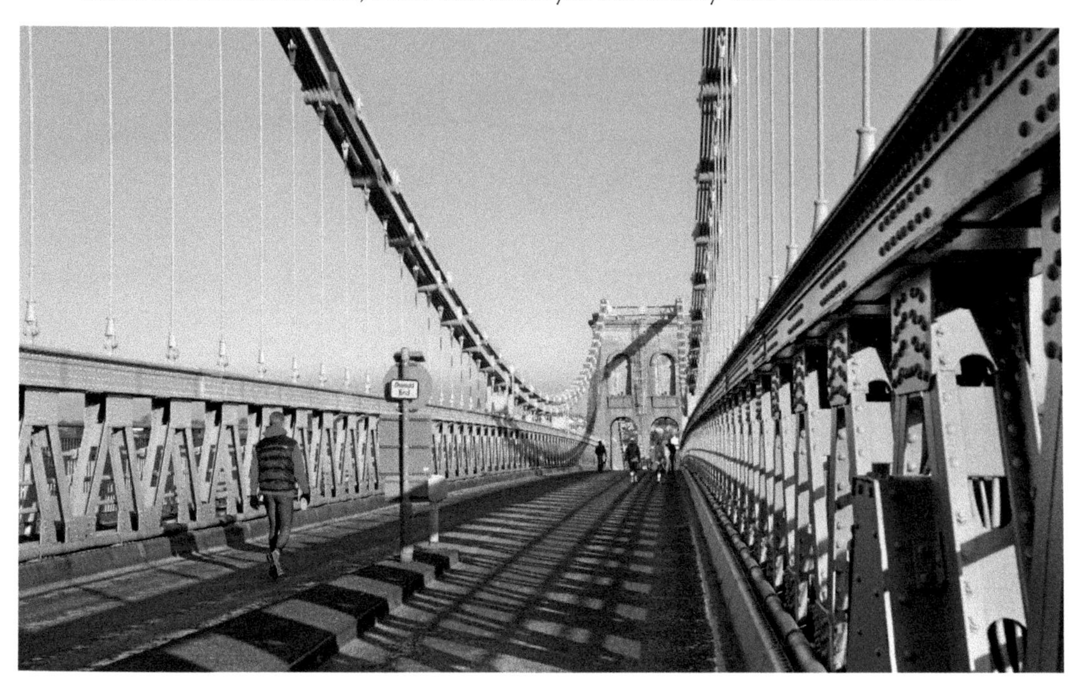

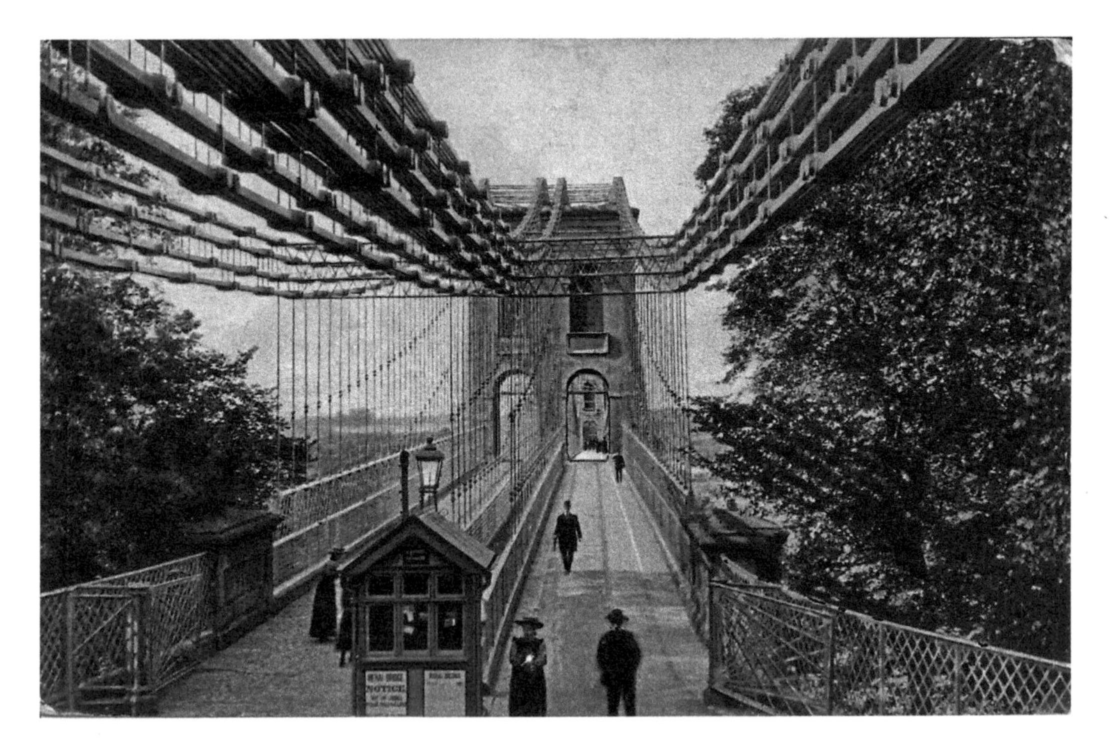

Menai Bridge, *c.* 1907

The final cost of building the bridge was £211,791 (about £19 million in today's money). This cost was recouped by charging tolls, collected at the tollbooth shown above. The charges ranged from 1*d* for a person walking across, 2*s* 6*d* for a stage or mail coach, and 1*s* for a score of cattle or oxen. The tolls were abolished after the reconstruction of the bridge, effective 1 January 1941.

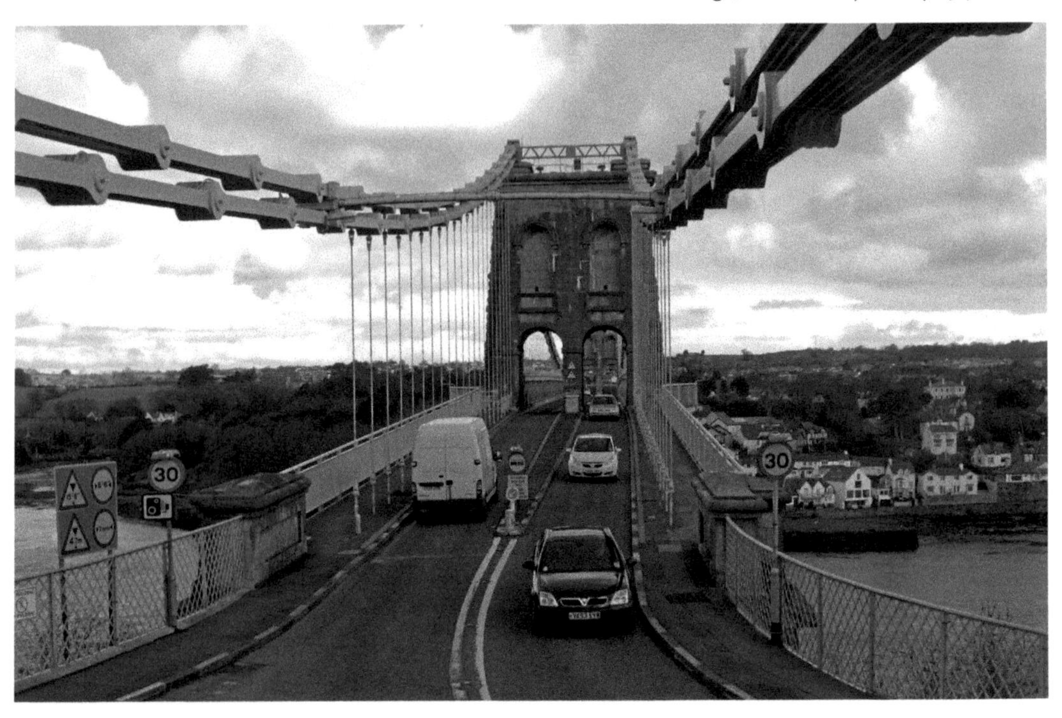

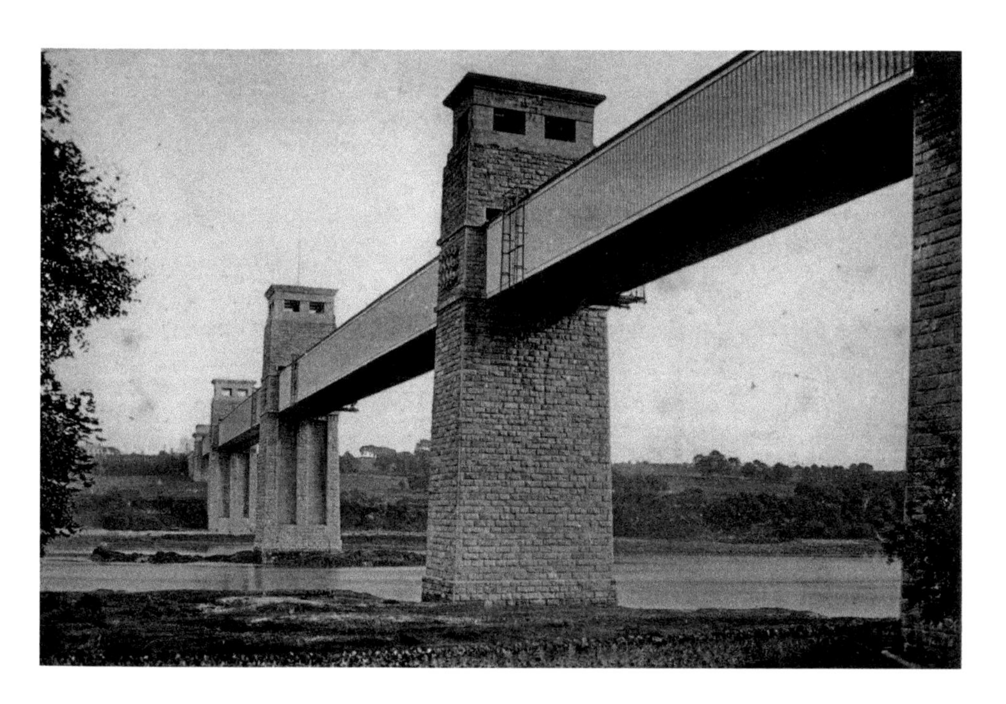

Britannia Tubular Bridge, Early Twentieth Century

With the coming of the railways in the mid-nineteenth century, another bridge was required to carry trains across the strait. Robert Stephenson was commissioned to build a new bridge, using an innovative tubular structure. Many doubted that the wrought-iron tubes would be strong enough to carry trains, and Stephenson initially planned to support them with chains through the openings at the top of the towers. However, tests on scale models showed it would easily support the weight. Construction began in 1846 and it was opened in 1850. (AA WSF-400)

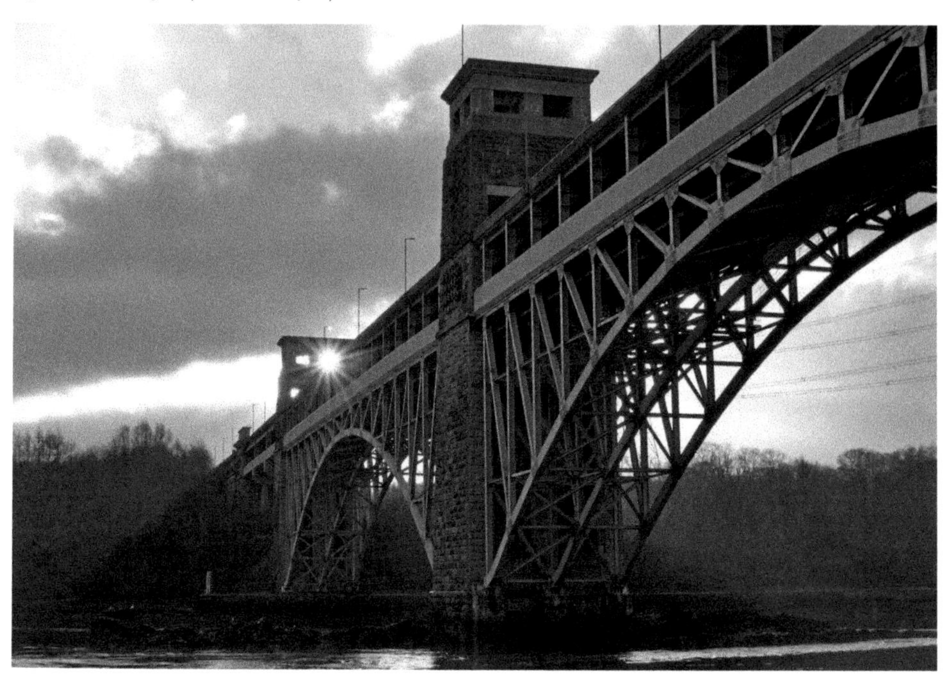

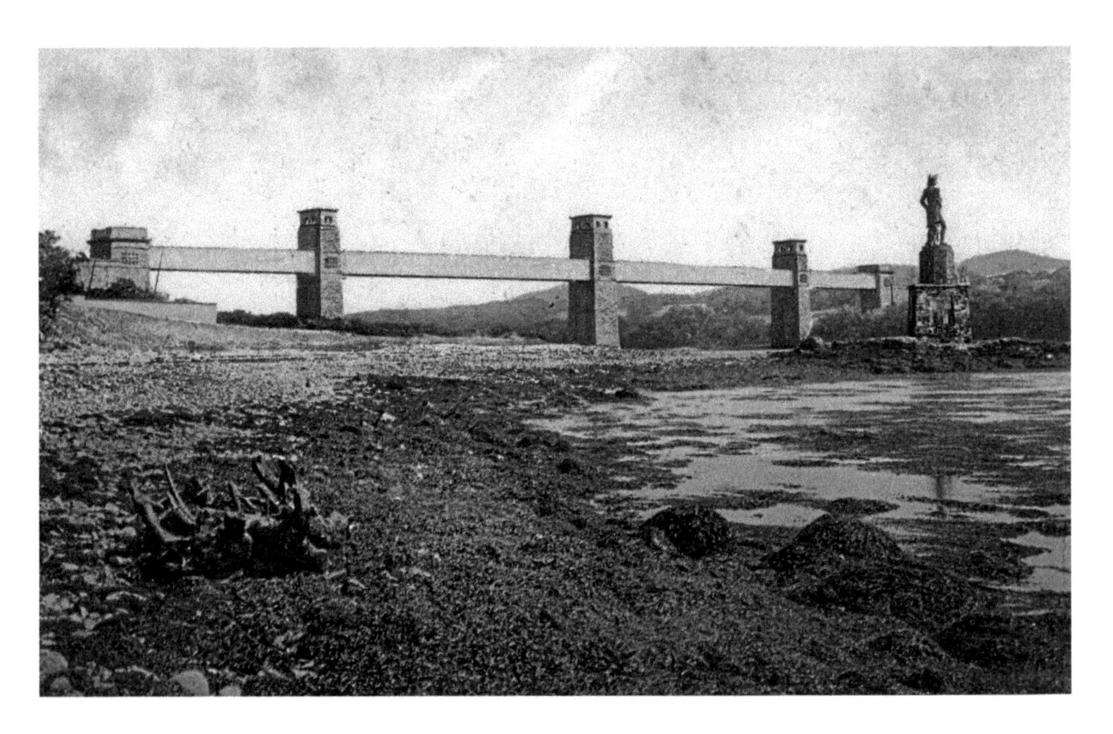

Britannia Tubular Bridge and Nelson's Statue, 1905

Disaster struck the bridge in 1970. A group of teenagers exploring the bridge with a makeshift torch accidentally started a fire that quickly engulfed the entire structure, warping the tubes beyond repair. It was decided to reconstruct the bridge as a dual-purpose one, with a roadway running above the railway. This required adding steel arches to support the weight. These pictures also show the statue of Admiral Horatio Nelson, erected in 1873, and carved by Admiral Lord Clarence Paget, amateur sculptor and son of the 1st Marquess of Anglesey. (AA WSG-4-92)

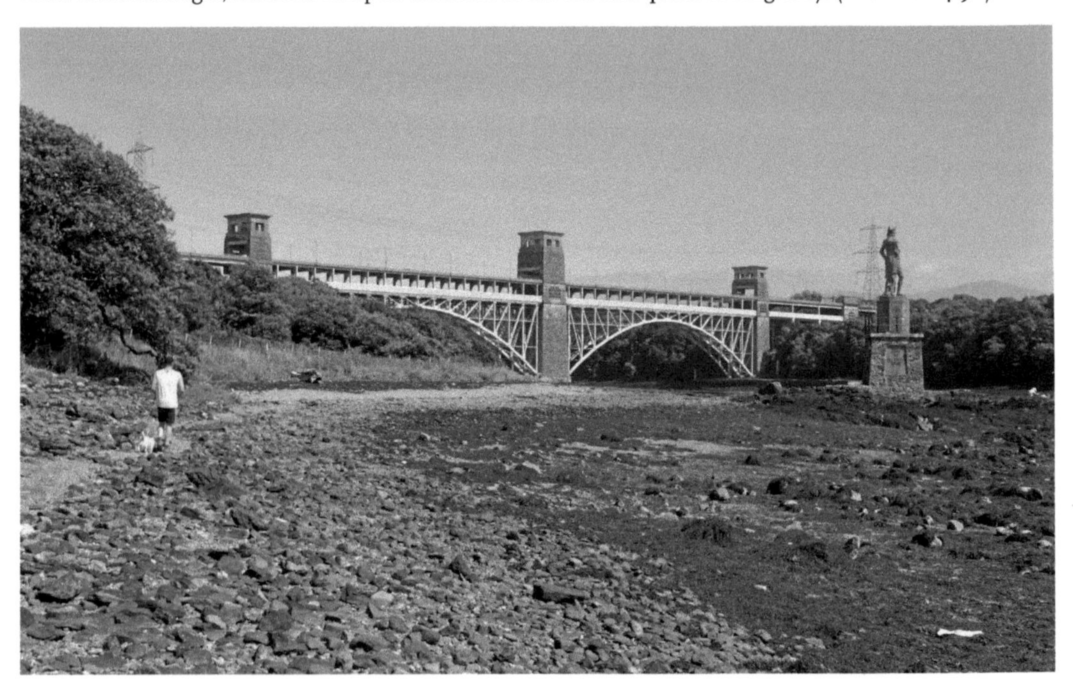

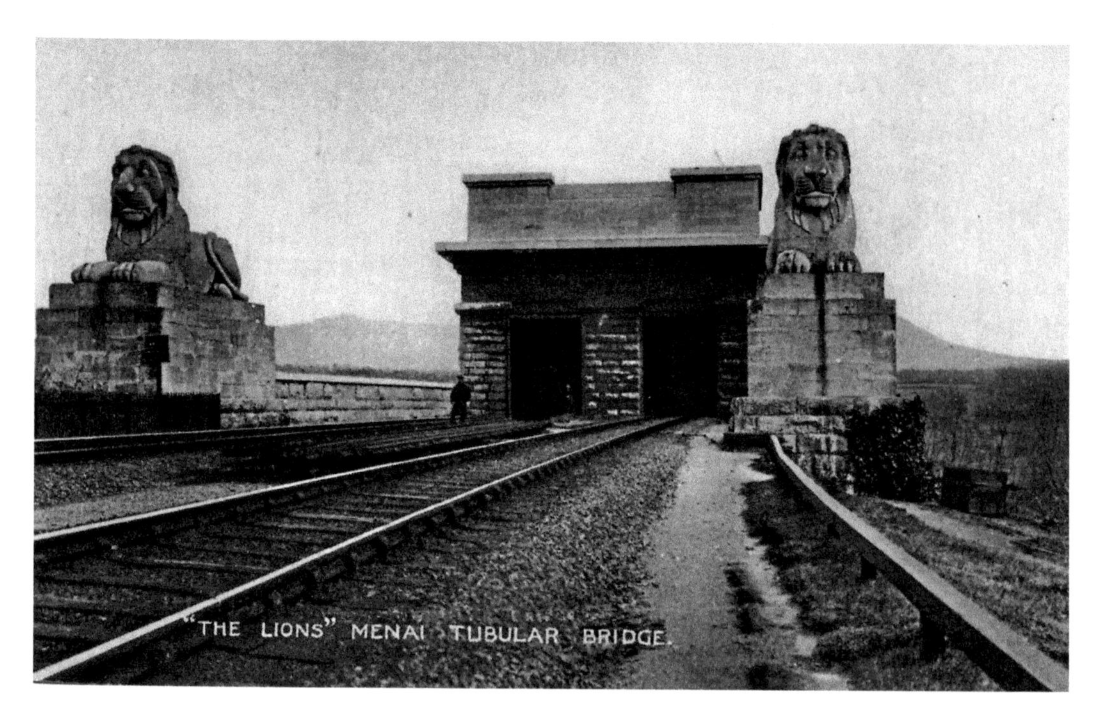

Entrance to Britannia Tubular Bridge, *c.* 1920
In addition to its innovative design, the Britannia Bridge was also distinguished by four stone lions, carved by John Thomas, who made many of the statues adorning the Houses of Parliament in London. It was also planned to have a 60-foot statue of Britannia with trident and shield on the centre tower, but cost limitations meant it was never added. After the fire and reconstruction of the bridge, the lions were left stranded below the road level, visible only to the curious who seek them out.

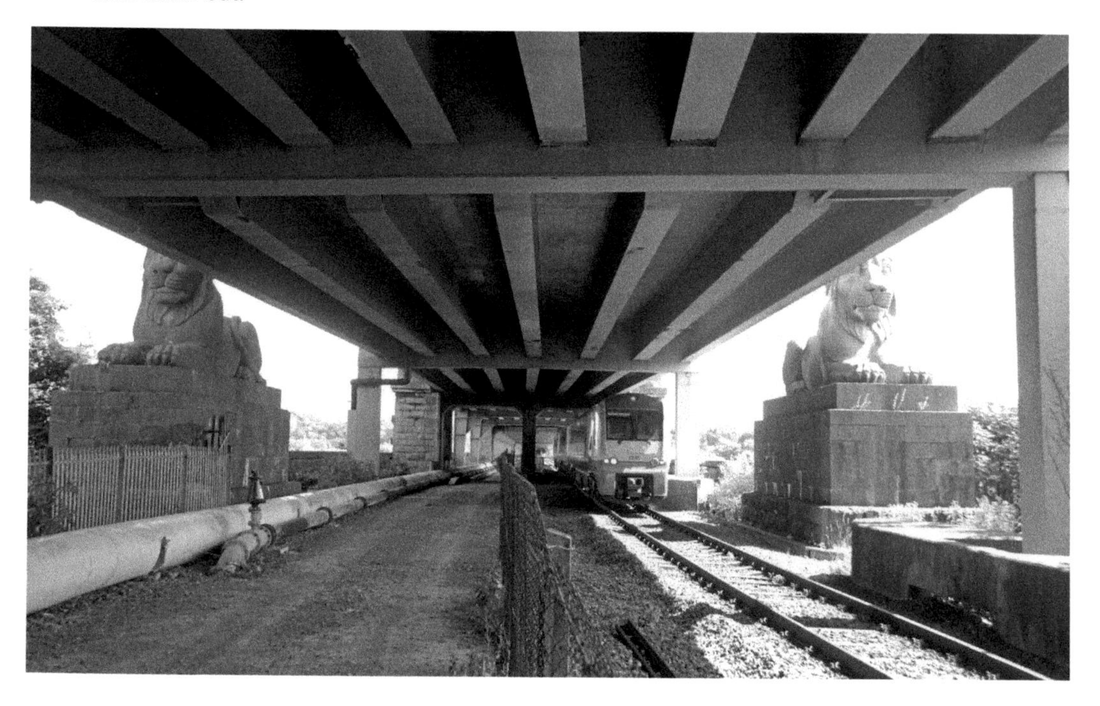

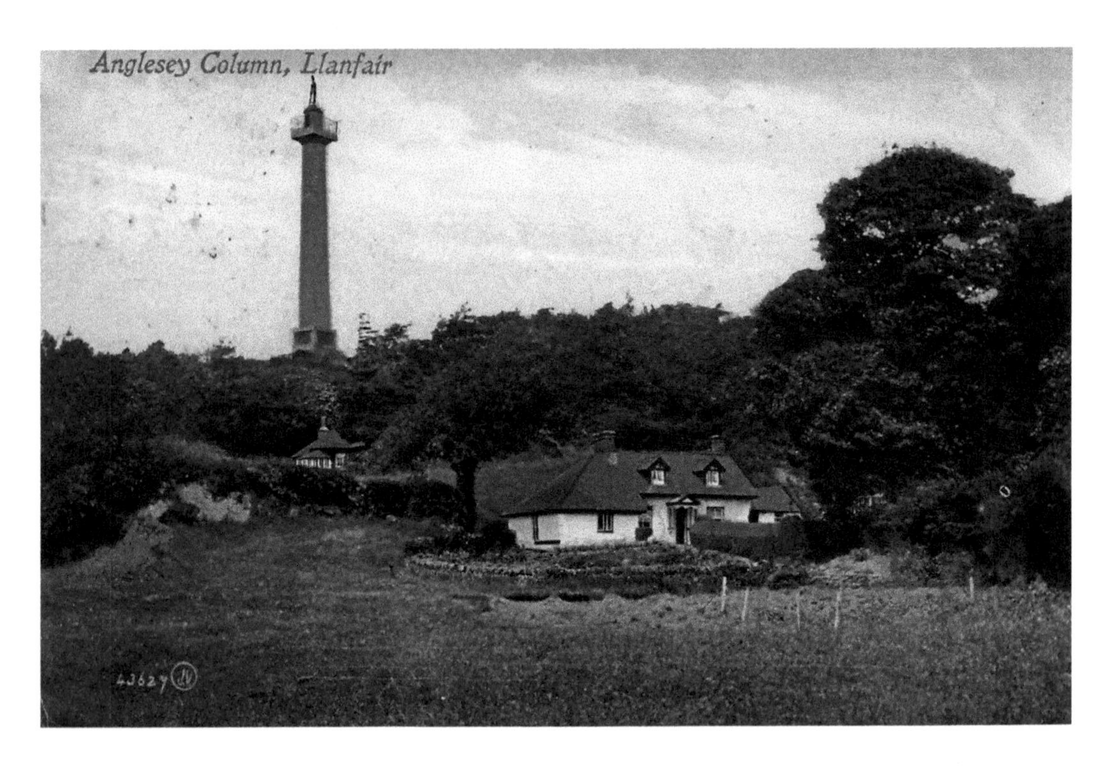

Anglesey Column, 1904

Standing 34 metres high, the Anglesey column was built in 1816 to commemorate Henry William Paget, the Earl of Uxbridge, the 1st Marquess of Anglesey, and the local landowner of Plas Newydd. He was a cavalry commander at the Duke of Wellington's side during the Battle of Waterloo and lost his leg to a cannonball. Initially, it was just a simple Doric column, but in 1860 it was topped by a 4-metre-high bronze statue of the Marquess.

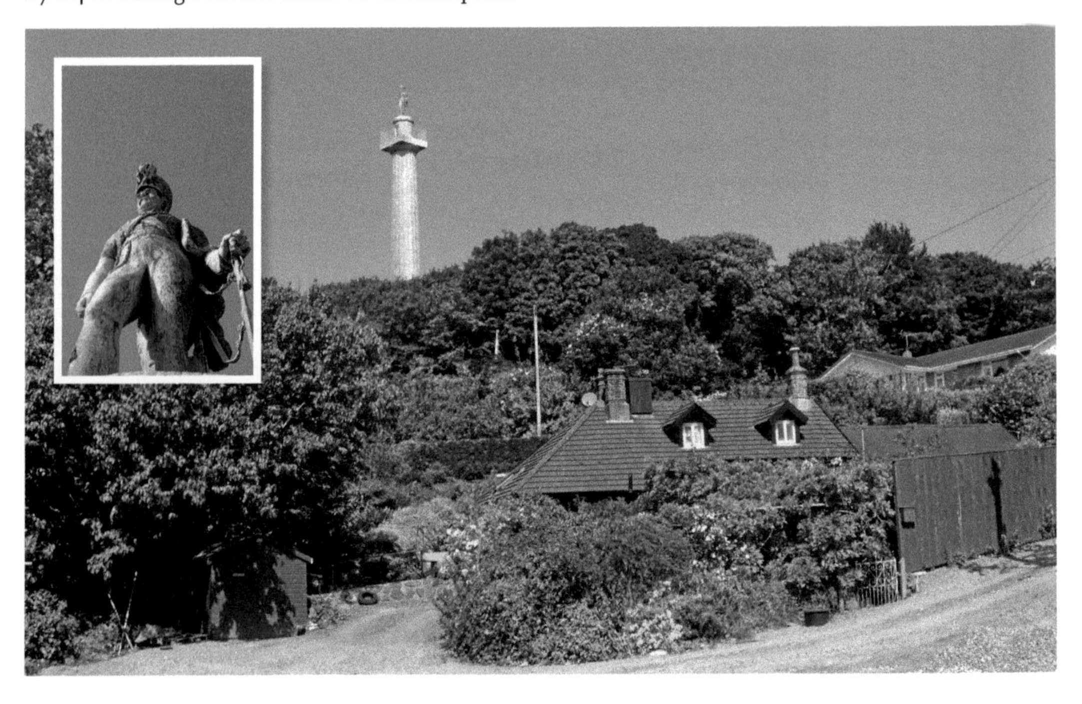

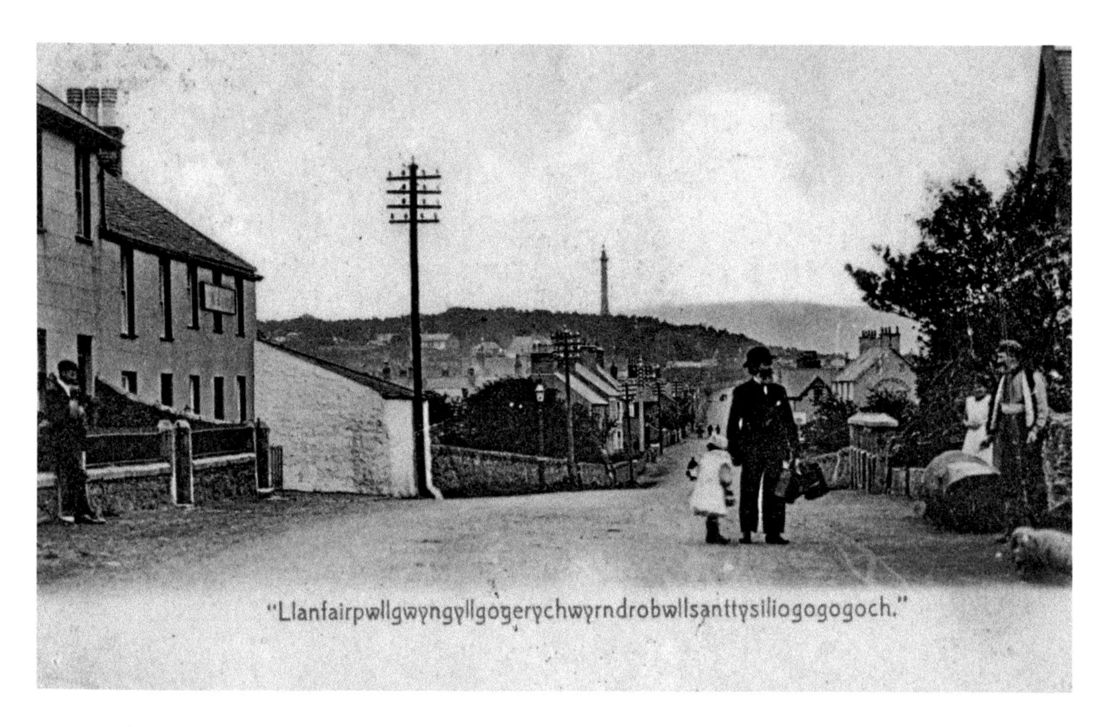

Holyhead Road, Llanfairpwllgwyngyll, 1904

The old main road from the Menai Bridge to Holyhead port runs past the Anglesey Column, seen in the distance above, and through Llanfairpwllgwyngyll village (or to give its famous full name, Llanfairpwllgwyngyllgogerychwyrndrobwllllantysiliogogogoch). In 1904, at the western end of the village, Capel Salem, the Wesleyan Methodist chapel (behind the trees on the right), faced the Butcher's Arms pub across the road. Today the pub is a residence, which stares across to a supermarket, the chapel having been demolished in the 1970s. (AA WSG-4-28)

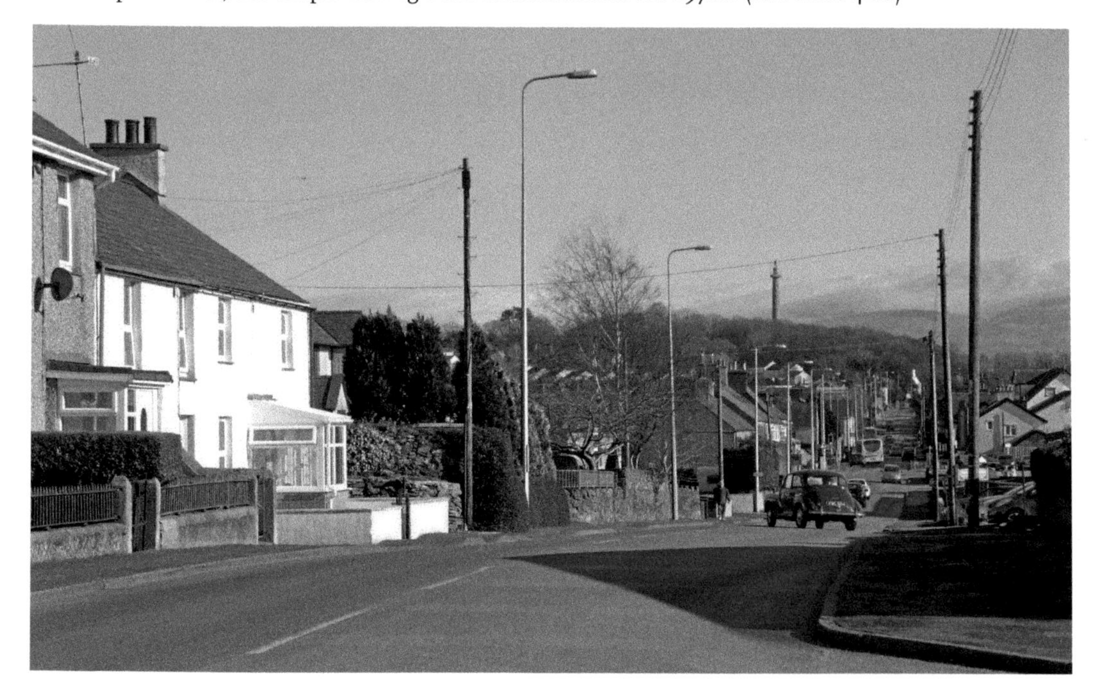

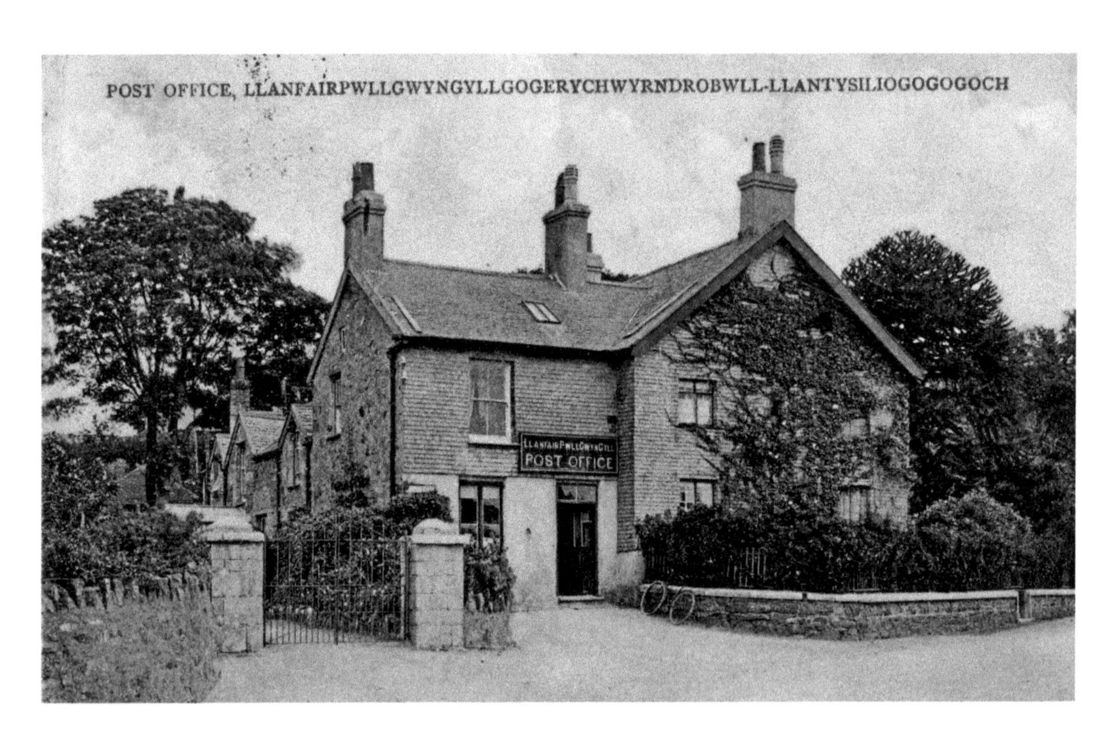

Llanfairpwllgwyngyll Post Office, *c.* 1908

Established in 1845, the Llanfairpwllgwyngyll post office was one of the earliest on Anglesey. It originally opened in the house pictured above, Tan-y-Coed, near the Anglesey Column and across from the tollbooth. In 1913, it relocated closer to the lower village centre, at what is now the Tafarn Ty Gwyn pub. It moved again, in 1935, to the building across from the railway station that today houses Menai Cleaning Services, then in 1978 to its current premises further east on the Holyhead road. (AA WSG-4-104)

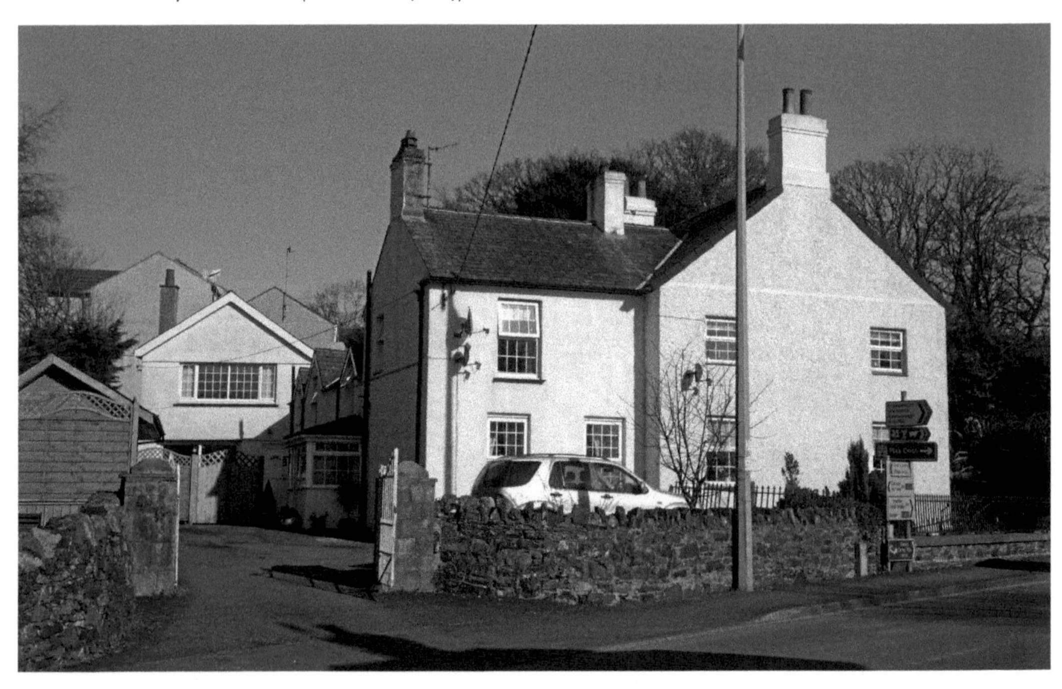

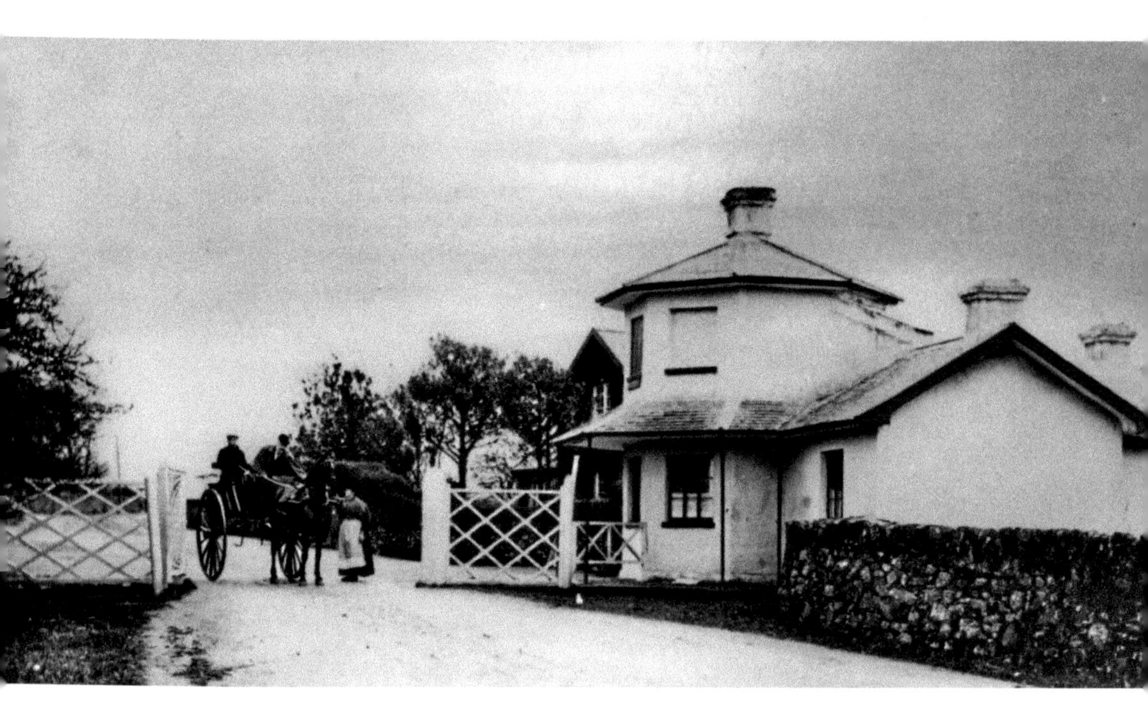

Llanfairpwllgwyngyll Toll Gate, Late Nineteenth Century

As well as designing the Menai Bridge, Thomas Telford built a new road, now called the A5, across the island to Holyhead. He also erected four toll houses along the way, with their distinct octagonal design and sunburst gates, which also provided housing for the toll collector and his family. This house has recently been converted into a museum about the toll houses and the history of the Women's Institute, which was founded in Llanfairpwllgwyngyll and held their first meetings in the toll house kitchen. (AA WSG-4-90)

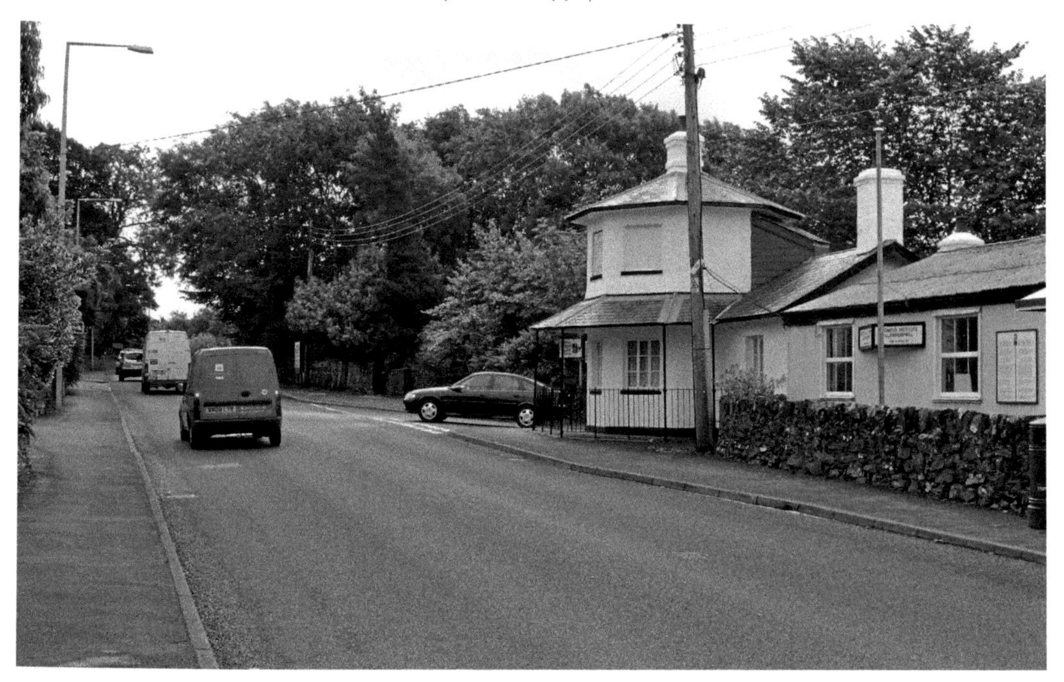

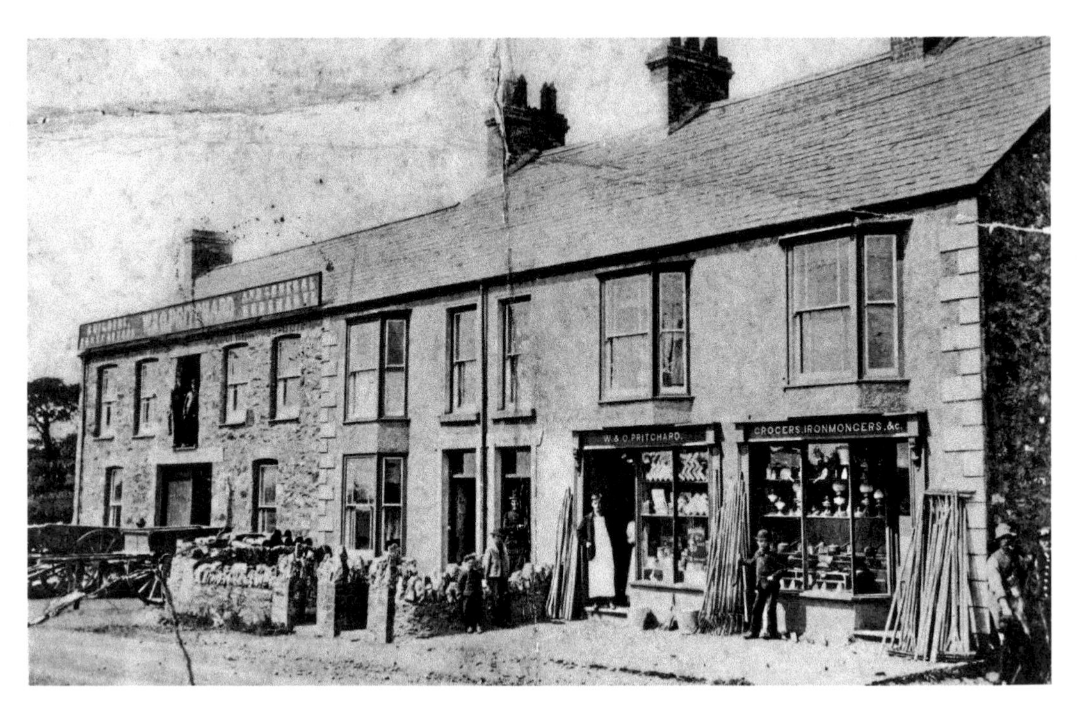

W. & O. Pritchard Shop, Llanfairpwllgwyngyll, *c.* 1890
One of the largest commercial enterprises in Llanfairpwllgwyngyll, this collection of businesses was run by brothers William and Owen Pritchard. The sons of joiner Lewis Pritchard, they set up their own business in the 1870s as builders in part of the Garnedd Wen terrace. They eventually expanded into the whole terrace, setting up a shop selling groceries, ironmongery and general goods, as well as photograph postcards of the village, including this one and the one on page 13. (AA WSG-4-56)

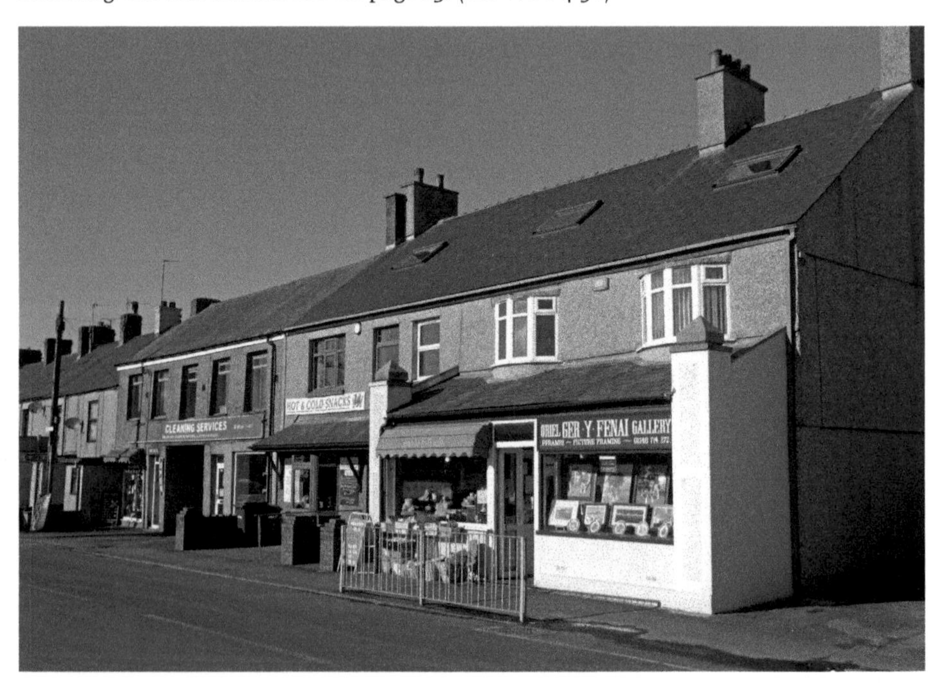

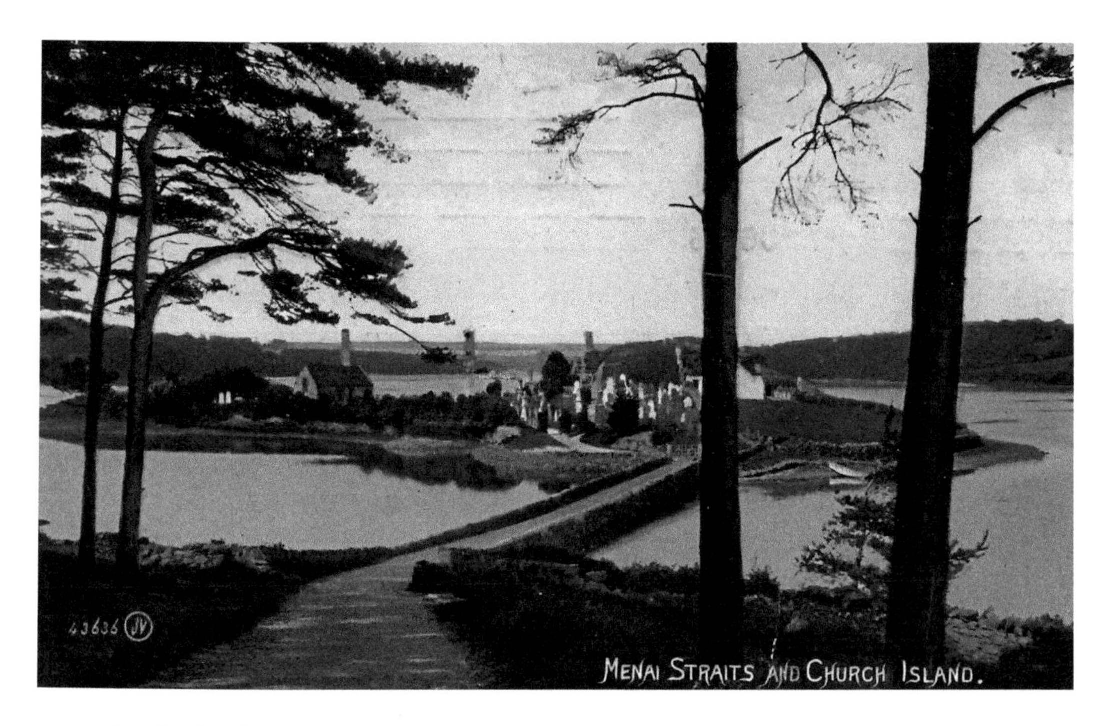

Church Island, Menai Bridge, 1904

Situated between the bridges and connected by a causeway, Church Island and its tiny church is a favourite place for walkers or those seeking peaceful reflection. The church was founded by St Tisilio around AD 630, and the current building dates to the fifteenth century. There is considerably more vegetation on and around Church Island today than there was in 1904. On the island itself, the magnificent Monterey cypress tree, just inside the gate, was just a small shrub 100 years ago.

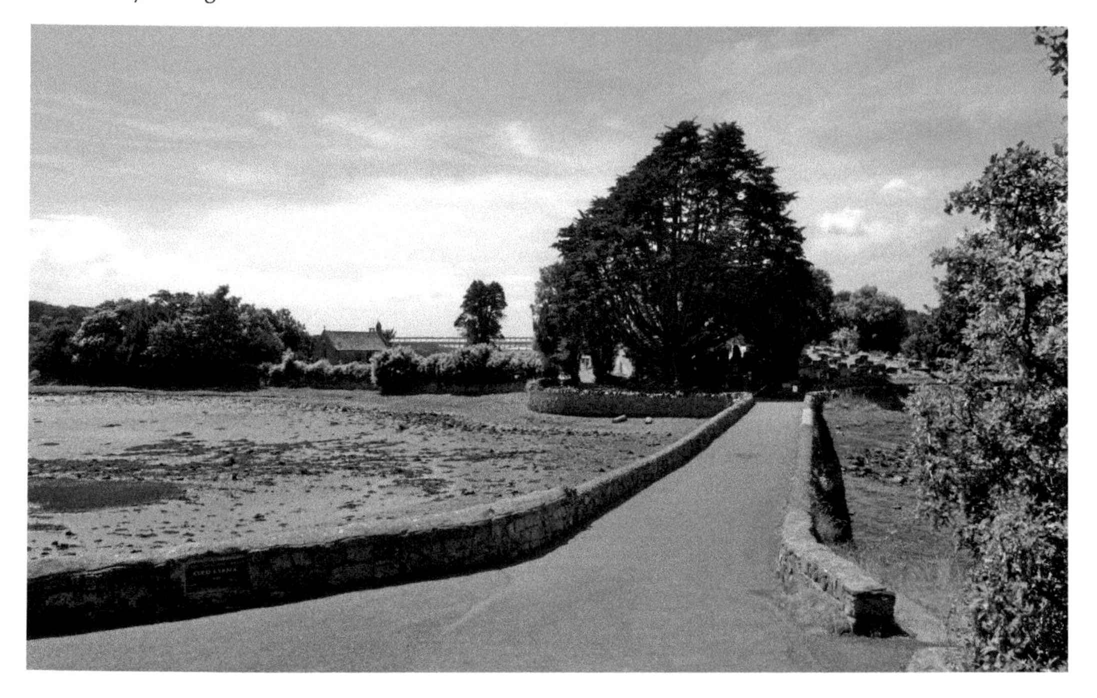

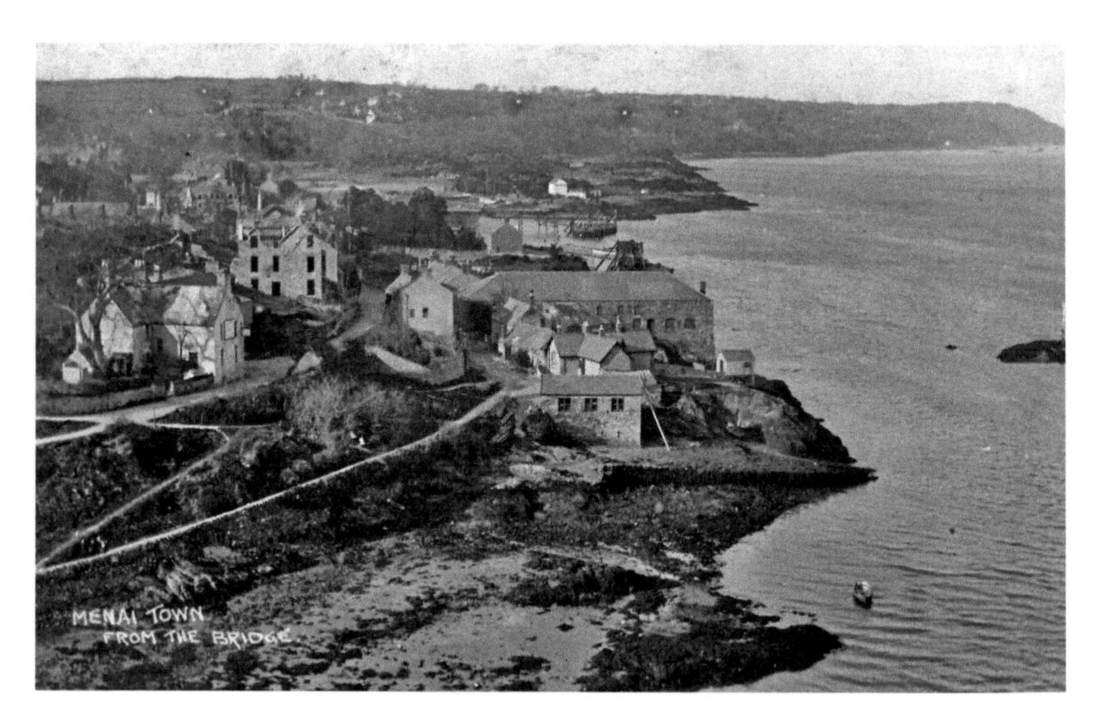

Menai Bridge Town from the Bridge, Before 1913
In the early twentieth century, the Cambria Inn, on the left in the photograph above, was one of the few buildings overlooking the shoreline in the shadow of the Menai Bridge. It is one of the oldest buildings in Menai Bridge, built around 1686, and originally housed the ferrymen. It later became an inn. By 1913, embankments had been built on the upper shore, extending Beach Road and allowing the houses now there to be built.

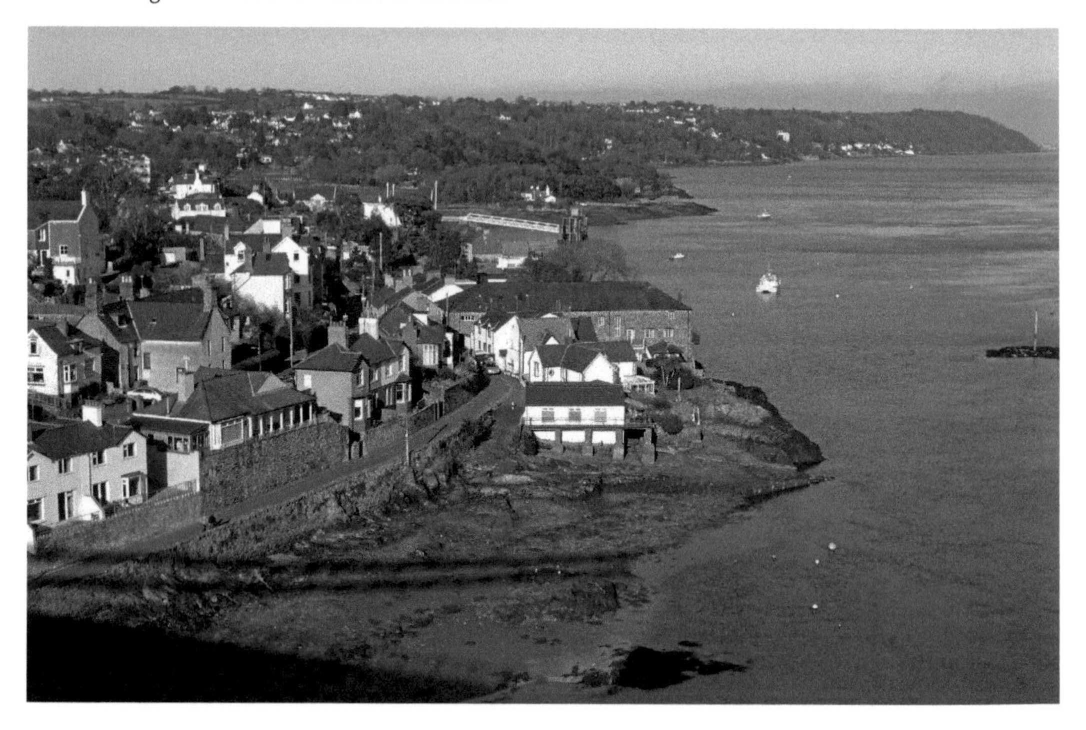

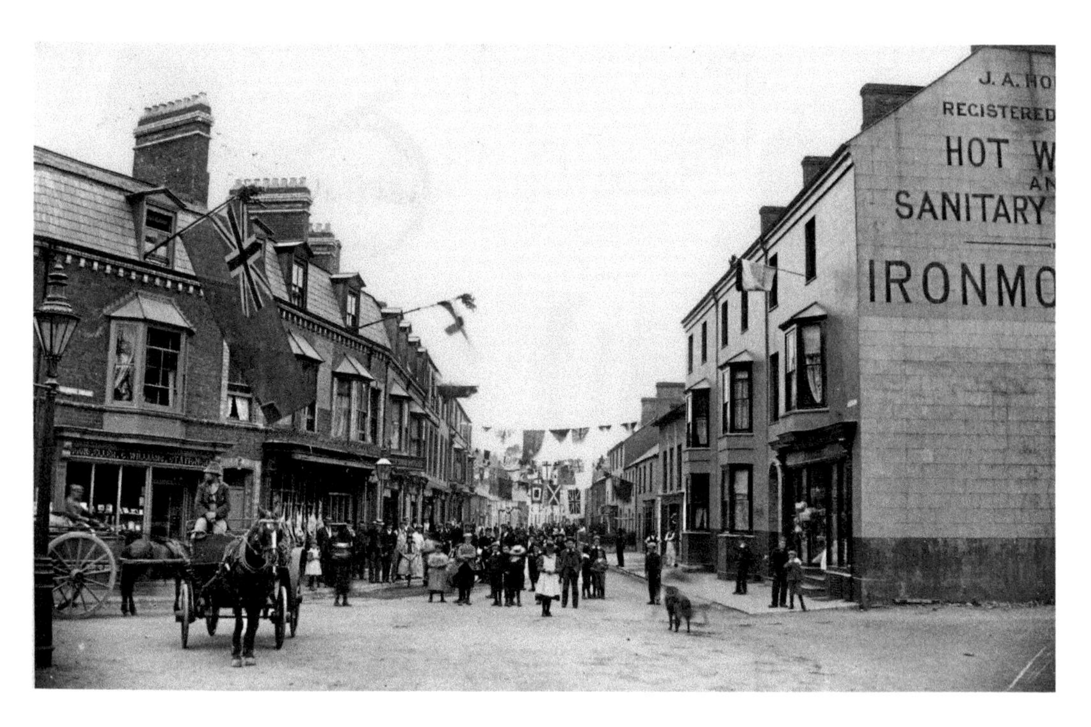

Uxbridge Square, Menai Bridge, 1890

The heart of Menai Bridge town is the square. It was originally called Bulkeley Square, after the landowning family from Beaumaris and the Bulkeley Arms Hotel at the square. In 1890, it was renamed Uxbridge Square in honour of the Earl of Uxbridge of Plas Newydd. In the photograph above, the townspeople are celebrating the coming of age (at fifteen years old) of the Earl of Uxbridge, the son of the 4th Marquess of Anglesey and the future 5th Marquess. (AA WSF-146)

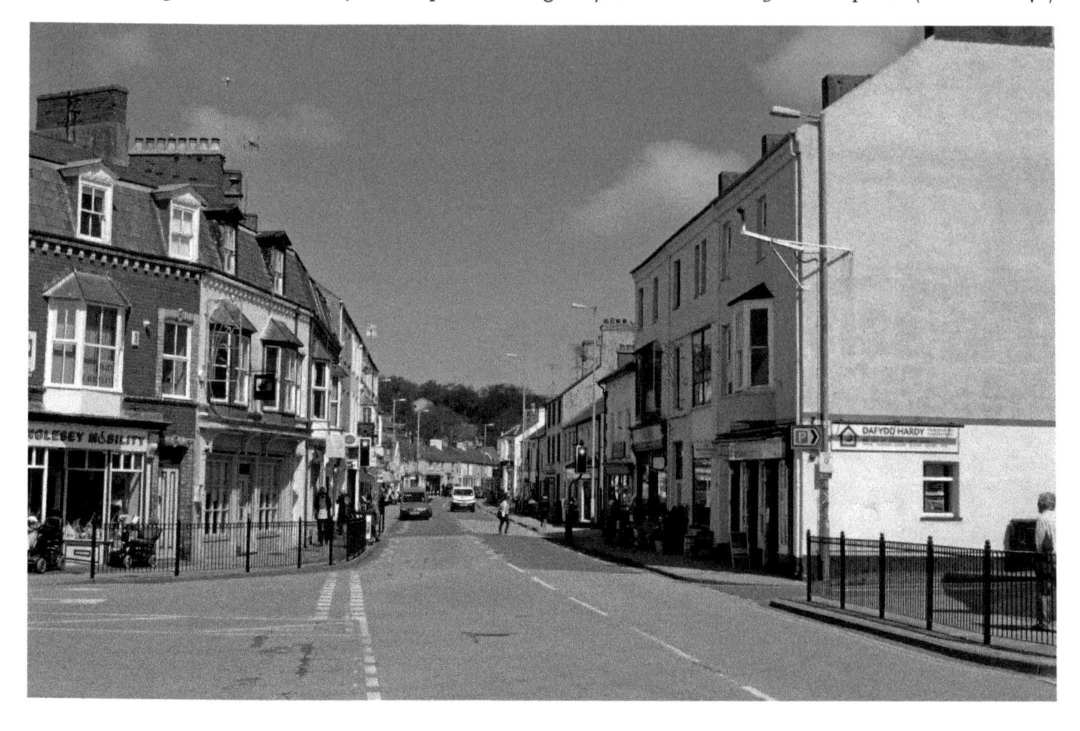

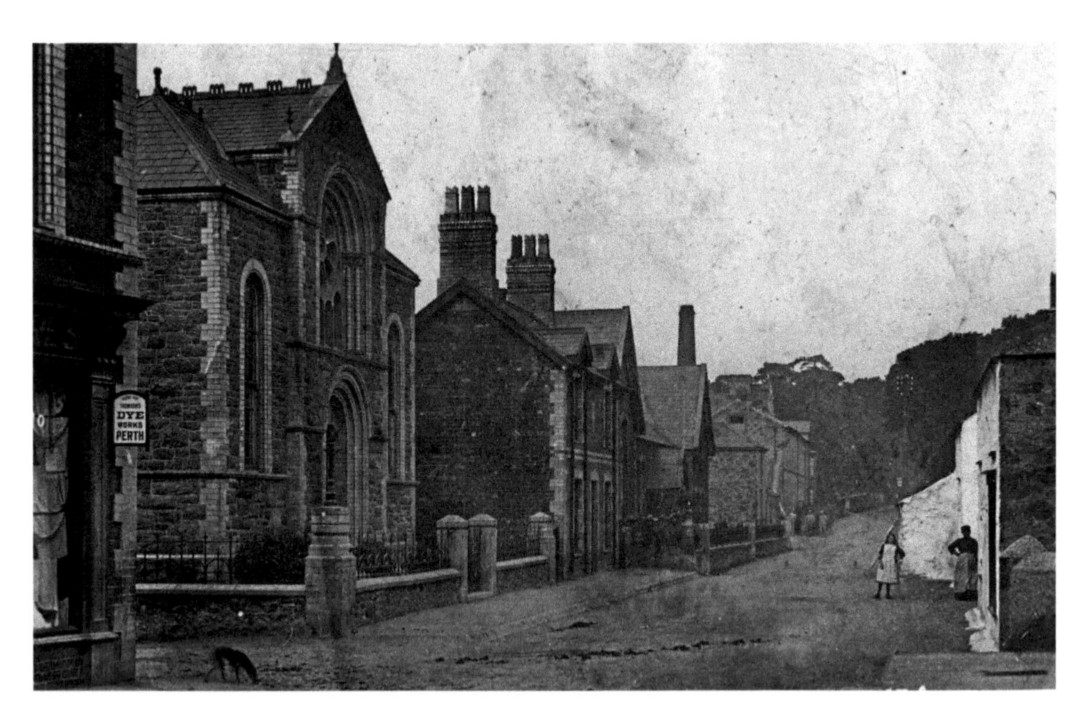

Dale Street, Menai Bridge, Early Twentieth Century

Built in 1884, the impressive Romanesque façade of the Welsh Baptist chapel, Capel Moreia, dominates Dale Street. It was designed by George Morgan of Carmarthen, South Wales, a leading architect whose chapels can be found all over Wales. It fell into disuse, and by the 1990s had become an antiques shop. The roof deteriorated greatly and the antiques were replaced by fruit and vegetables. The Baptist congregation still meet in the vestry to the rear of the building. (AA WSF-68)

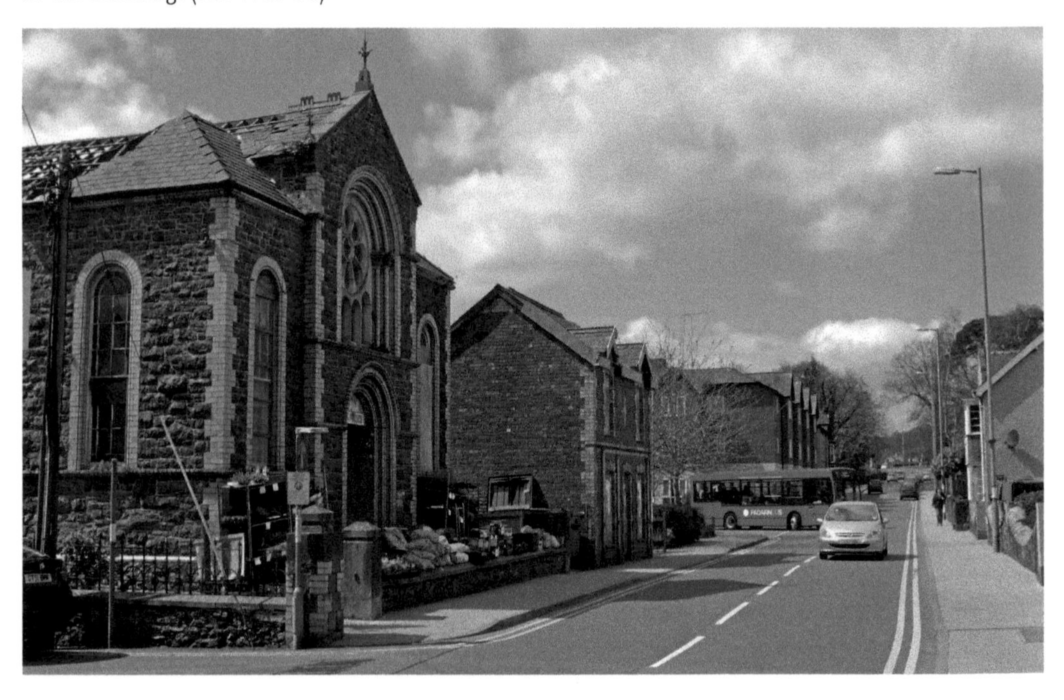

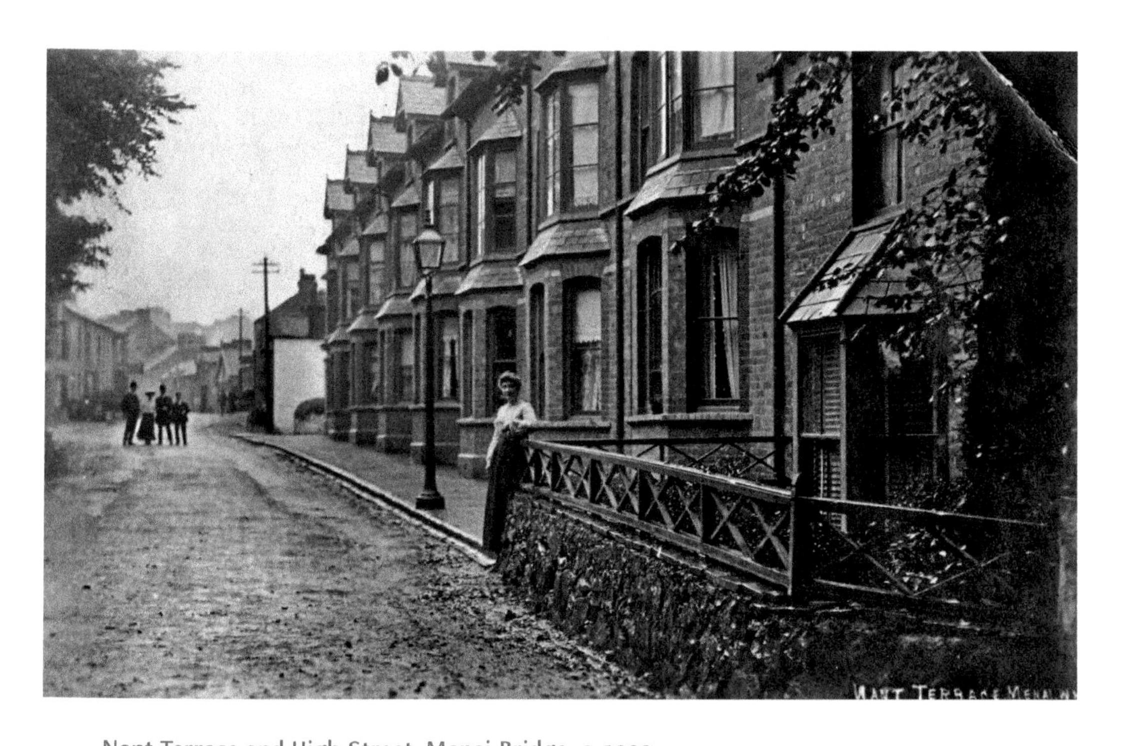

Nant Terrace and High Street, Menai Bridge, *c.* 1900
Built around 1880, this smart terrace extended the housing on the High Street further towards Beaumaris. At the time the above picture was taken, the second house from the right (No. 7) was occupied by Charles Cooke and his family. He was a coachman and often lived in New York, working for James Roosevelt, secretary of the US embassy in London and half-brother of the future president, Franklin Roosevelt. Five of his eleven children were born in the USA. (AA WSF-35)

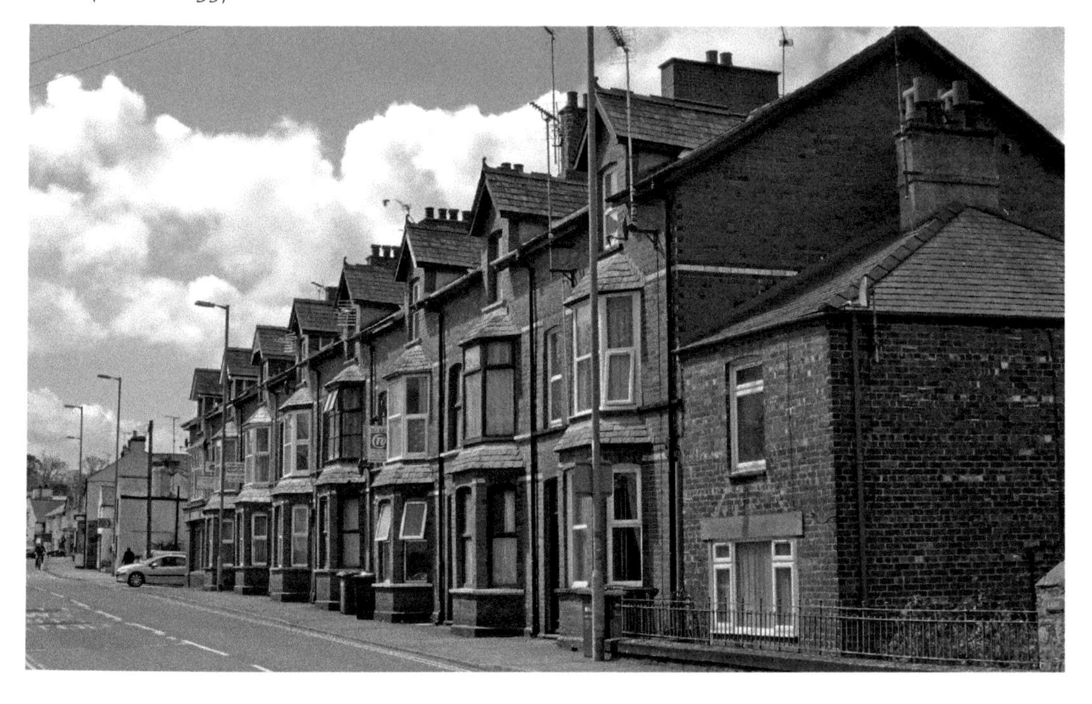

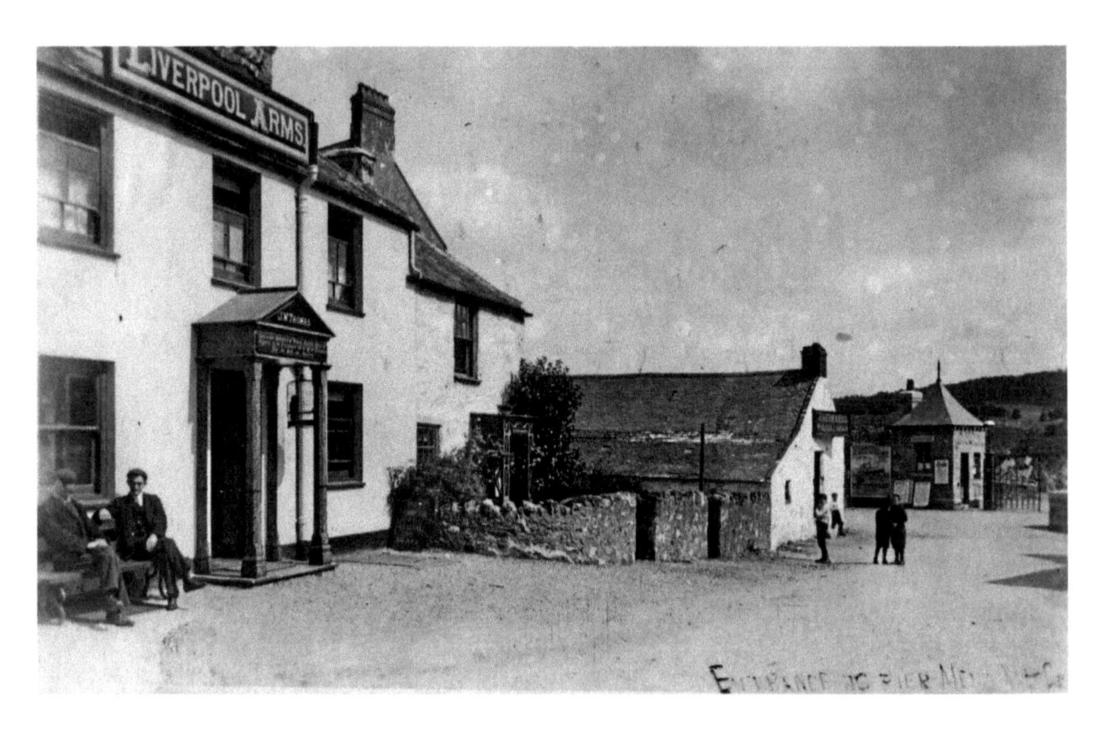

Liverpool Arms, Menai Bridge, *c.* 1905

This popular pub, known locally as the Livvy, was built in 1843 to cater for passengers arriving at the nearby St George's Pier from Liverpool. It used to be an old-fashioned pub, filled with maritime memorabilia and photographs, but after refurbishment in 2011 it has a more open and modern feel inside. The small building to the right in the photograph above was the ticket office for the steam packets to Liverpool. Through the gate was the newly opened promenade, which led to the pier. (AA WSF-149)

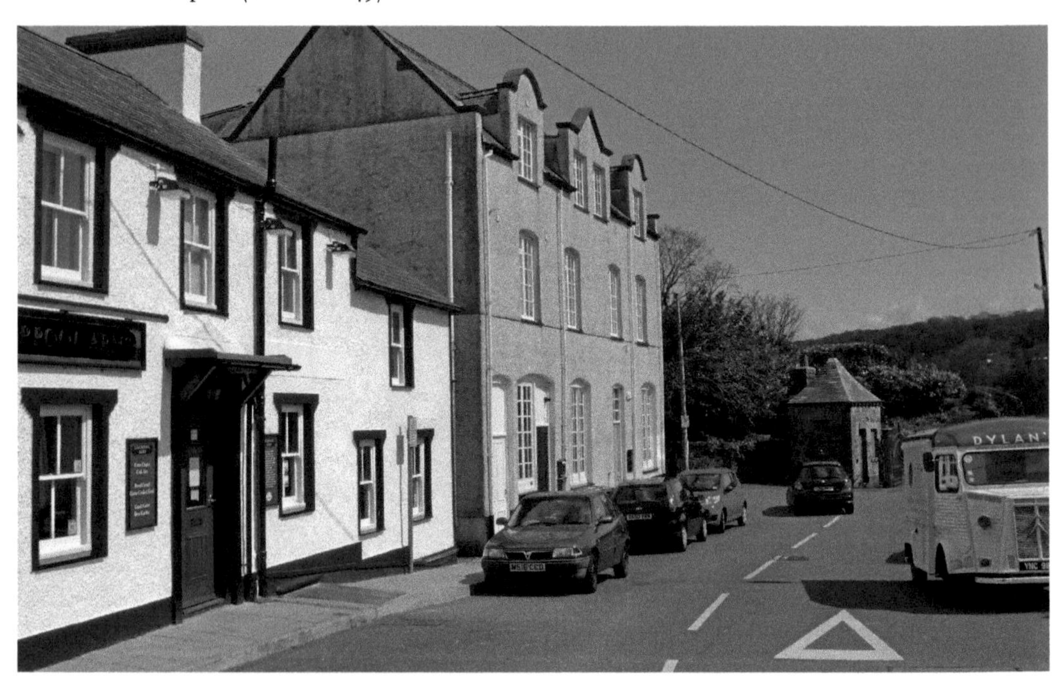

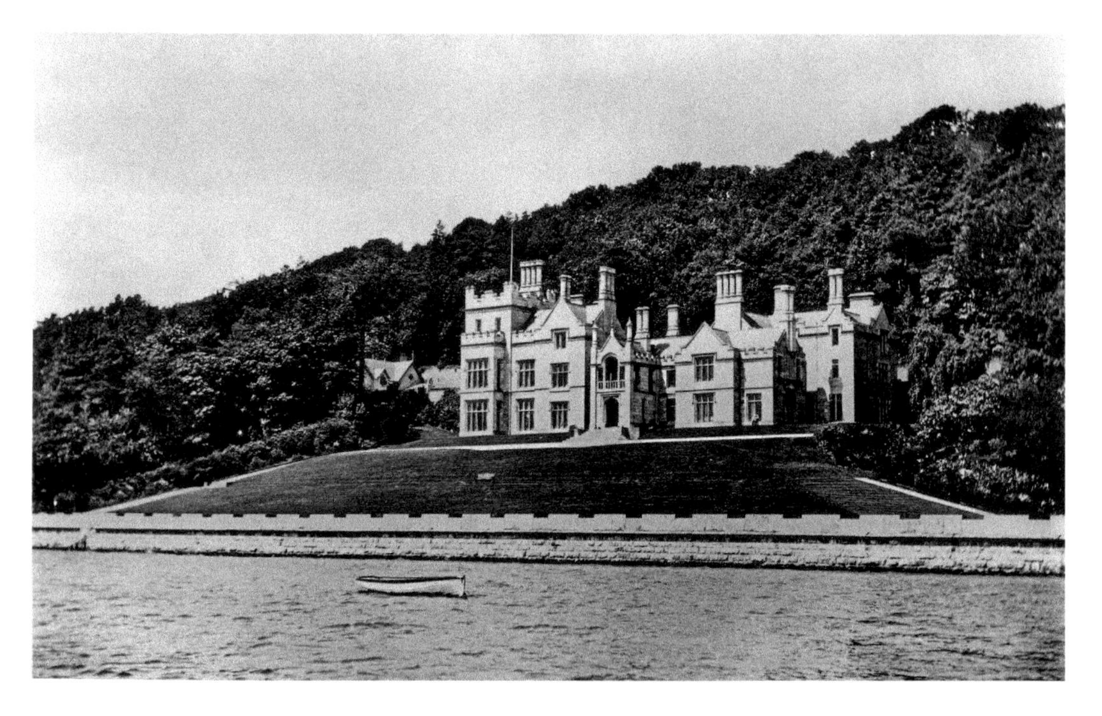

Glyn Garth, Menai Strait, 1898

This extravagant holiday villa was built in 1851 by the wealthy textile manufacturer Salis Schwabe. Born in Oldenburg, Germany, he moved to Lancashire in 1832 to make his fortune in the Industrial Revolution. He and his wife socialised with many famous musicians, artists and writers; Elizabeth Gaskell and Oscar Wilde reportedly stayed at Glyn Garth. It later served as the residence of the Bishop of Bangor, then as a Friendship Holidays Association property. It was demolished in 1964 and replaced by a block of flats in 1971. (AA WF-51)

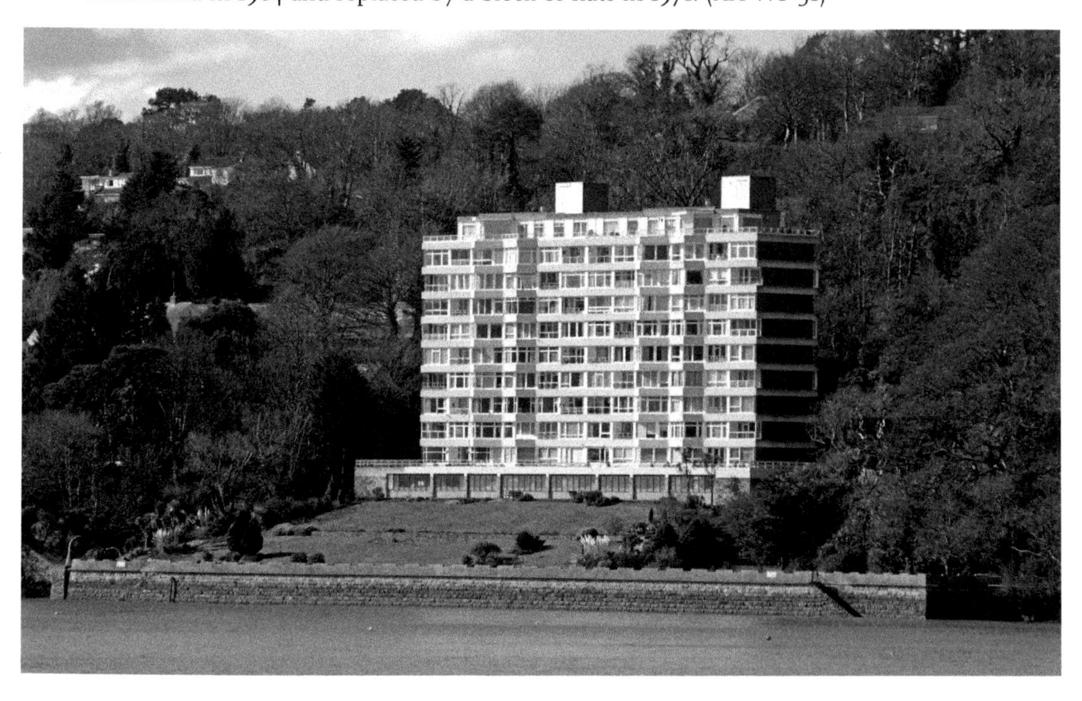

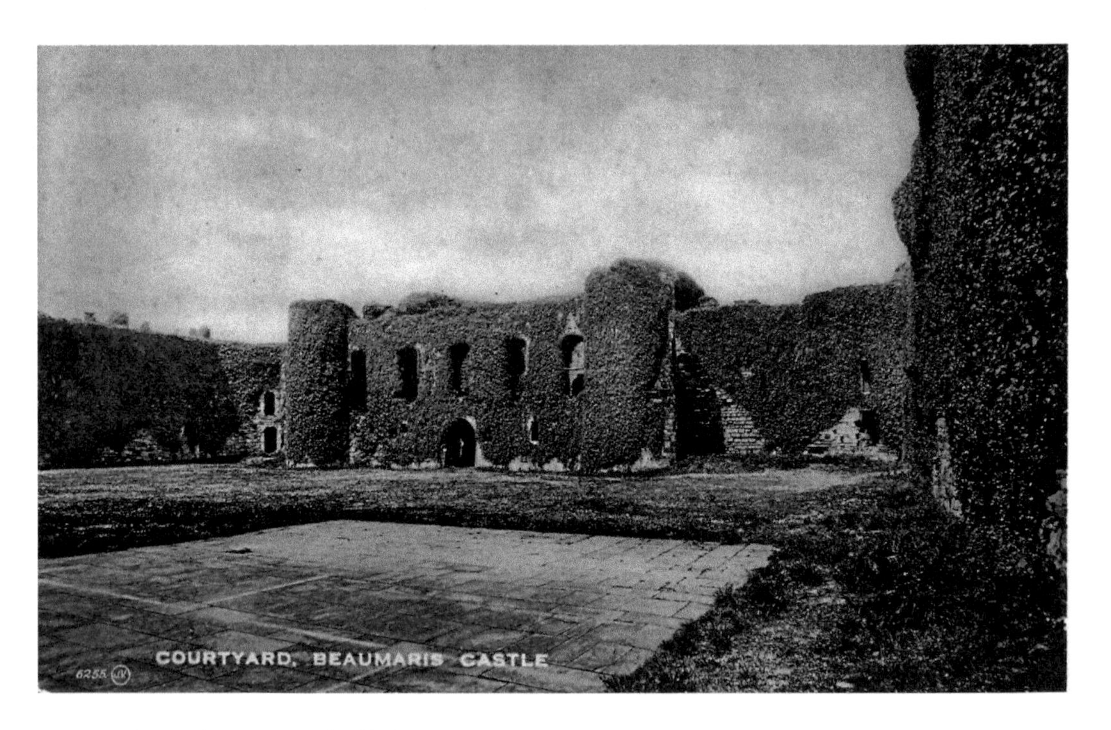

Beaumaris Castle Courtyard, 1886

After his invasion of Wales in 1282, Edward I built a series of castles to subdue the Welsh, including Beaumaris Castle. It was never fully finished and soon fell into disrepair. By the early nineteenth century it was owned by the Bulkeley family of Baron Hill, who later built tennis courts in the old courtyard. In 1925, they gifted it to the state. The vine-covered walls were restored and it became a popular tourist attraction, regularly hosting events like the medieval fair shown below.

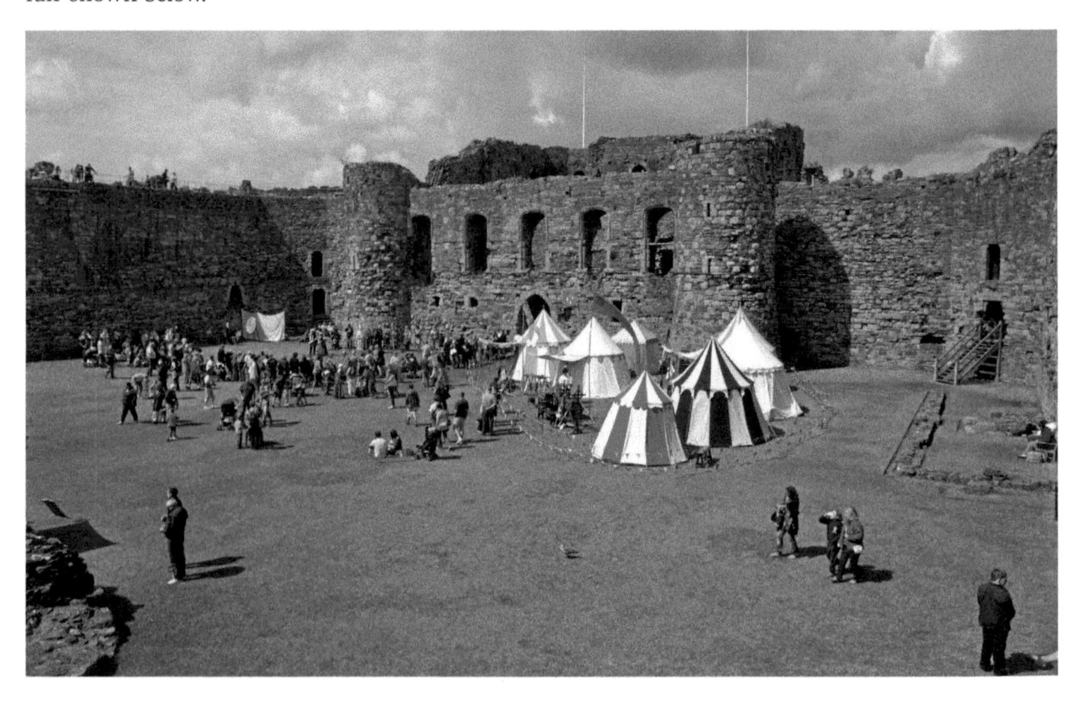

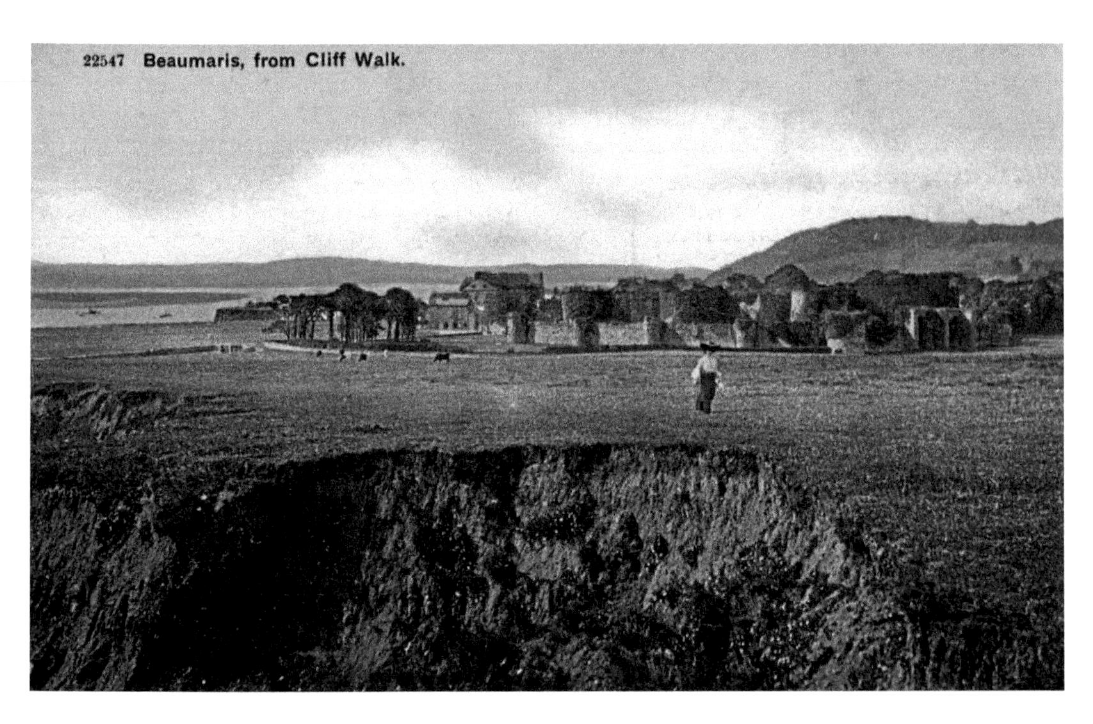

Beaumaris from the Cliff Walk, Early Twentieth Century
Edward I also granted a charter for a new town around the castle, Beaumaris. The residents of nearby Llanfaes, who were loyal to the native Princes of Wales, were forced to move to a new community in Newborough, and the new town was populated by incoming English settlers. It grew rapidly to become a major port and trading town, and today retains a number of buildings dating from the fifteenth to seventeenth centuries. (AA WSC-34)

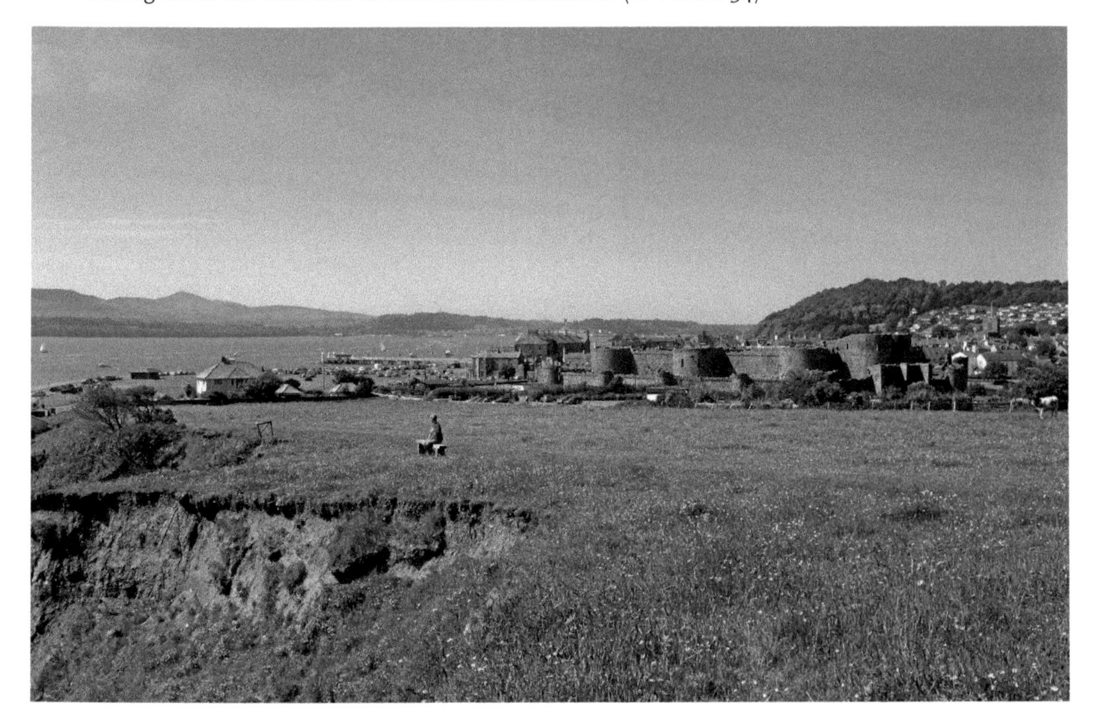

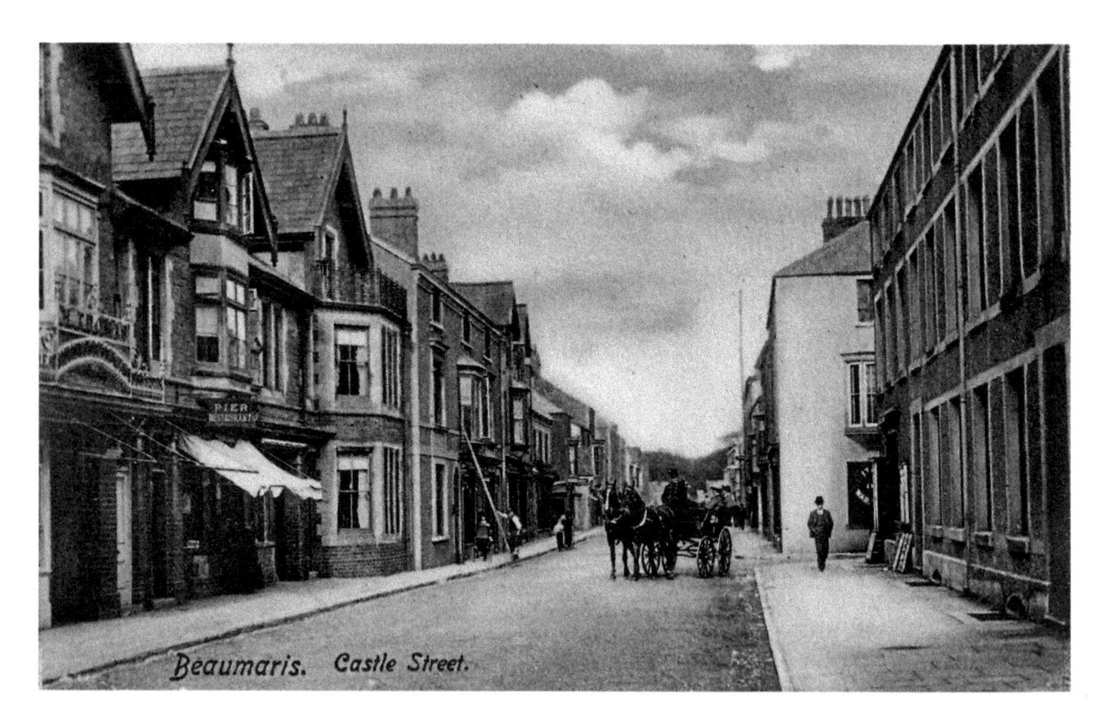

Castle Street, Beaumaris, 1906

Many of the earlier fifteenth- to seventeenth-century buildings were replaced in the nineteenth century. The buildings on the left were erected in 1892 by Sir Richard Henry Williams-Bulkeley, the 12th Baronet, whose initials are on a plaque on the wall. It housed Hugh Thomas's butcher shop and the Pier Restaurant, as well as William Delamere's provisions shop. Bulkeley Terrace, across the street, was built in the 1840s and included W. R. Hughes' shop on the corner, which sold books, stationery, fancy goods and postcards of Hughes' own photographs.

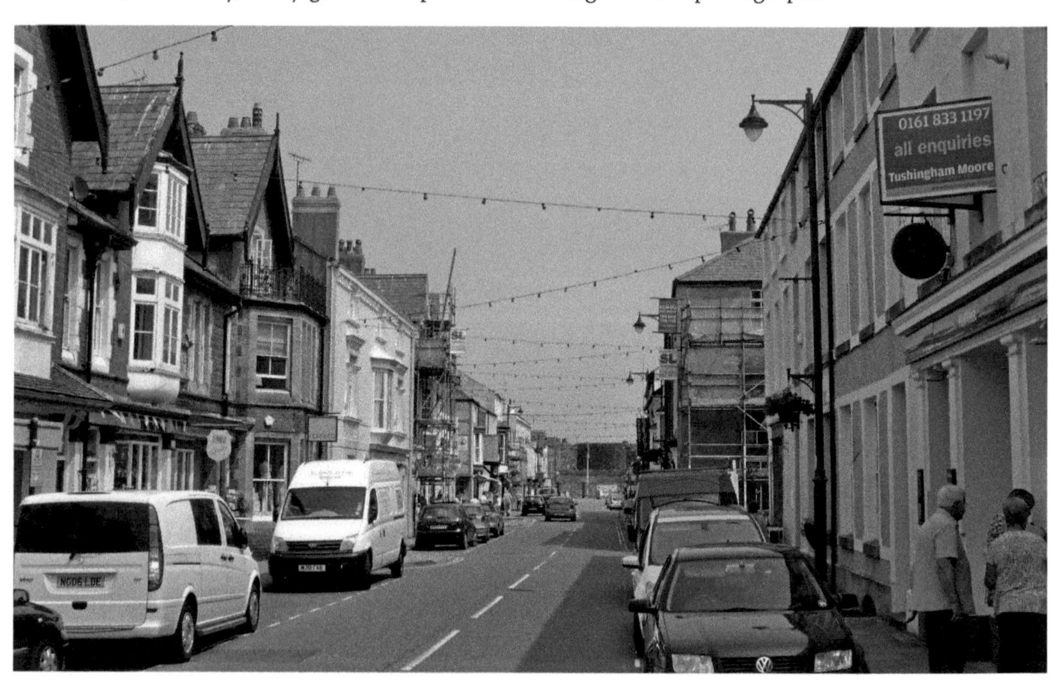

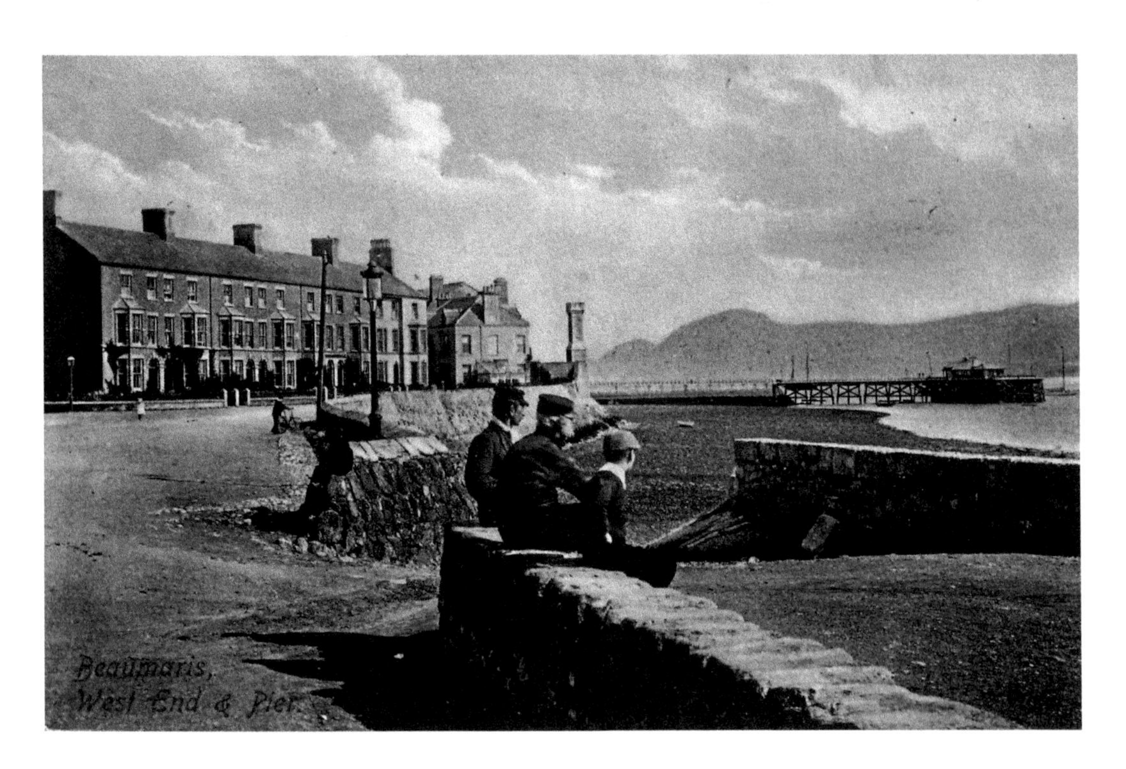

Beaumaris West End, 1905

The late eighteenth and nineteenth centuries also saw housing extend westward beyond Castle Street. The building of the West End terrace began in 1869, joining a handful of eighteenth-century buildings already at this end of town. This was an elegant part of town, with its views across to the mountains and seaside promenade. It was also close to the pier, bringing visitors from Liverpool, many of whom stayed in rooms rented out in these houses.

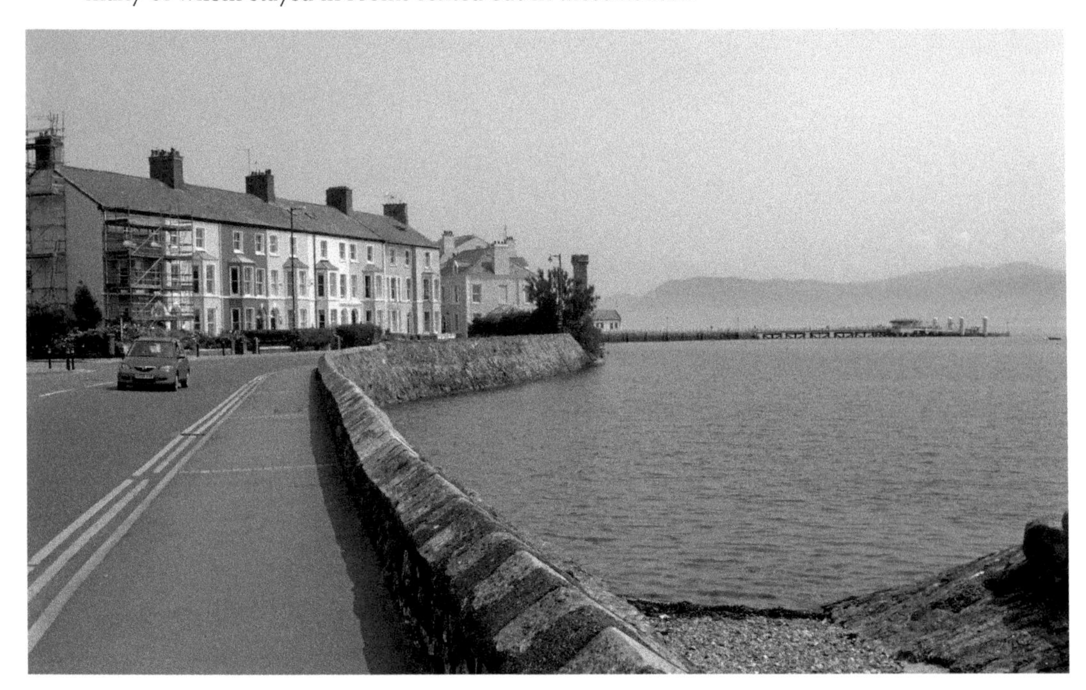

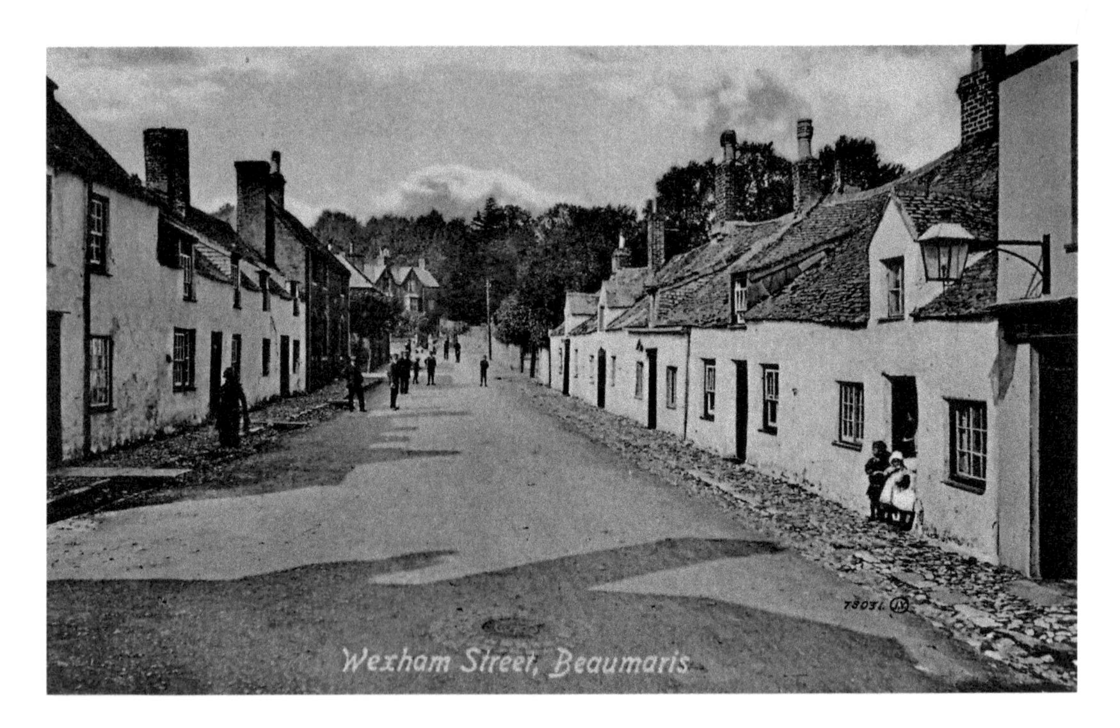

Wexham Street, Beaumaris, 1913

More modest housing was built on Wexham Street as the town expanded to the north-west from the seventeenth century. The single-storey cottages on the right above, which are now listed buildings, were built in the late eighteenth or early nineteenth centuries. The beams inside these houses are apparently made of ship timbers. When the above photograph was taken, these were occupied by mariners, plasterers, greengrocers and iron moulders, some with families of up to nine people.

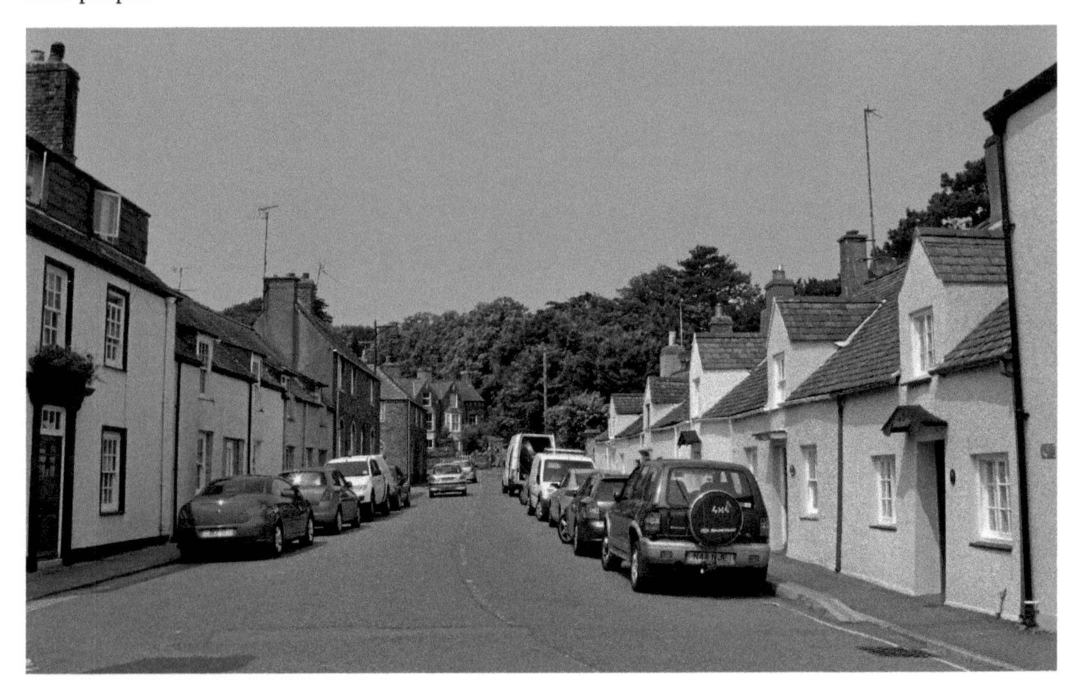

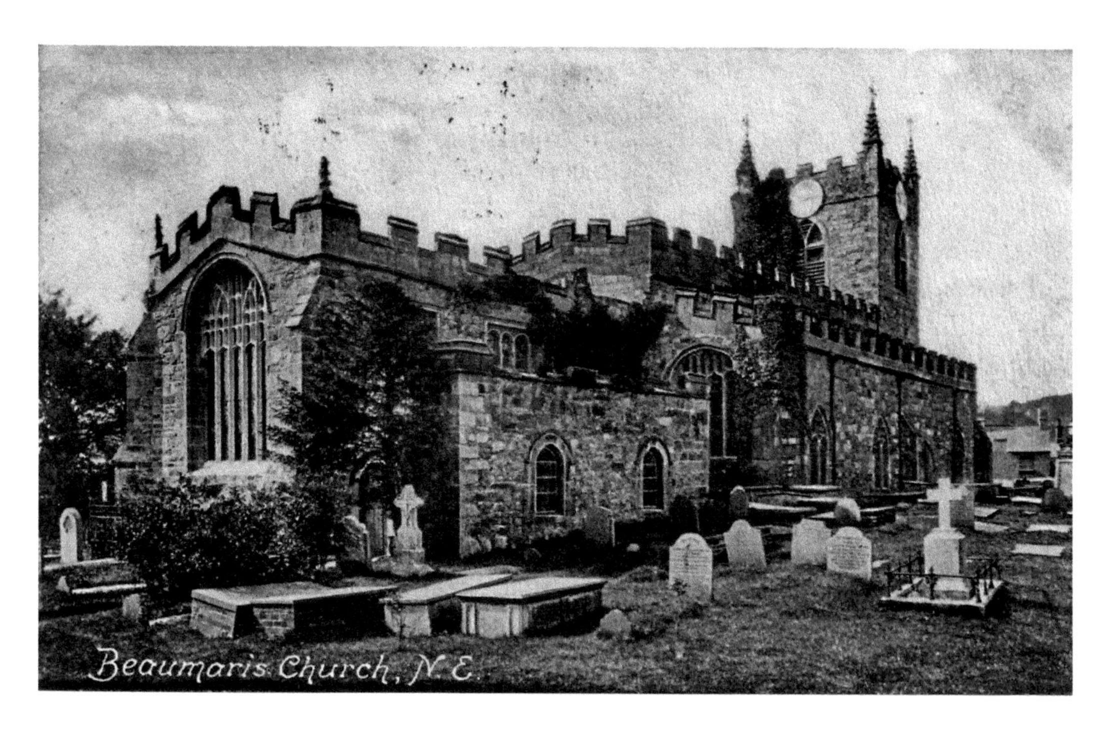

St Mary and St Nicholas Church, Beaumaris, 1905

Originally built as the garrison church for Beaumaris Castle, the main part of the building dates from the early fourteenth century. The chancel (to the left in these photographs) was added at the start of the sixteenth century; its large window was rebuilt in modern times. The church is renowned for containing the thirteenth-century stone coffin of Princess Joan, daughter of King John of England and wife of Llewellyn the Great, which had at one point been used as a horse trough before being rescued.

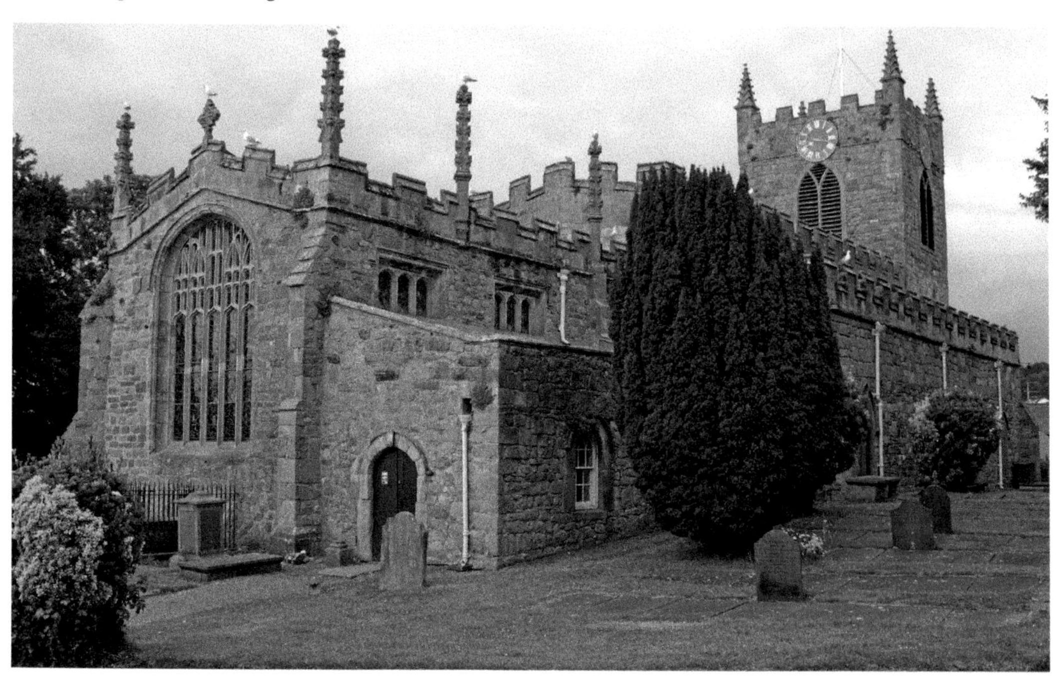

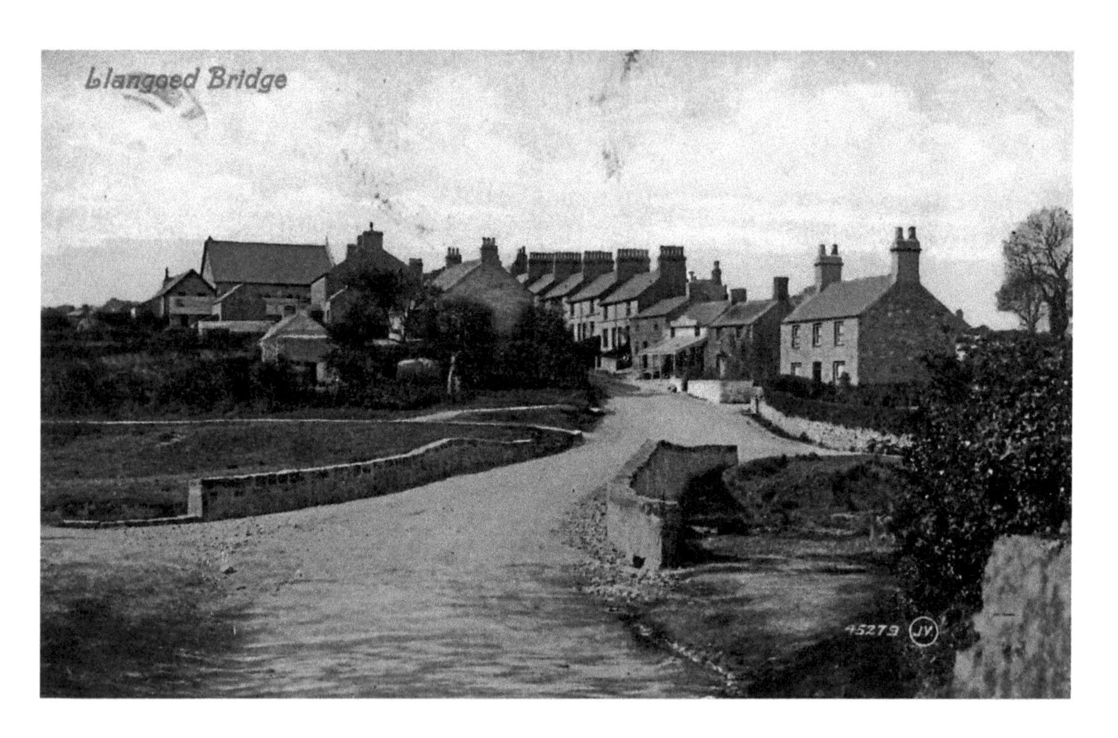

Llangoed Bridge, 1913

Crossing the Afon Lleiniog, the bridge at Llangoed leads uphill into the centre of the village. In the early nineteenth century there were just a handful of houses here, but many were built later in the century. The building with the blue awning above is Dublin House, which was a confectionery and tobacconist's shop owned by John Jones around this time. The police station was just to the right, and the Wesleyan Methodist chapel is across the street from Mona Terrace, which runs up the hill.

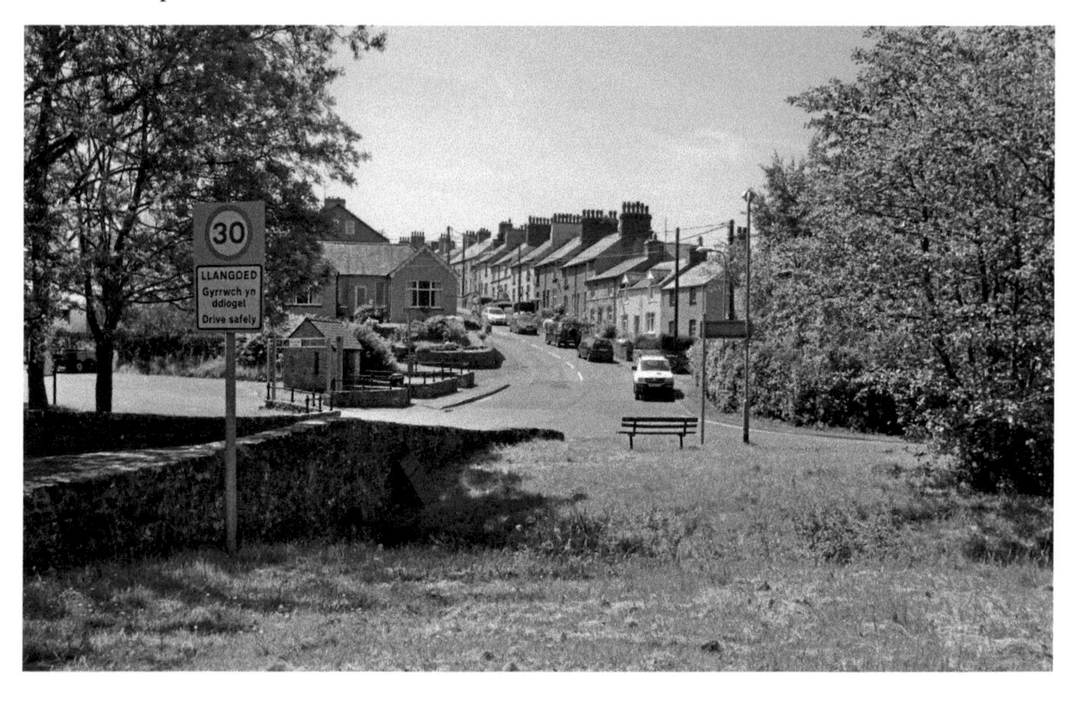

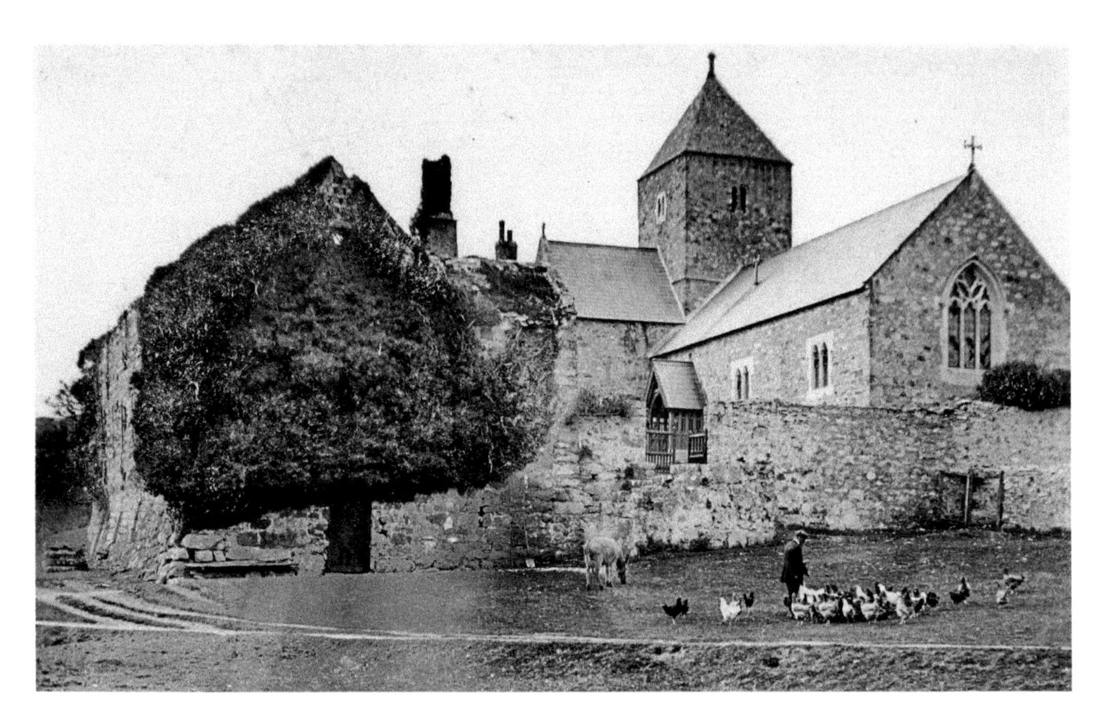

Penmon Priory, Early Twentieth Century
The first religious community at Penmon was founded in the sixth century AD by St Seiriol, supported by his brother King Cynlas of Rhos. Vikings destroyed the wooden buildings in 971, and the current church was erected in stages between 1140 and 1240. The ruined building at the left, which housed the monastic refectory and dormitories, was also built in the thirteenth century. The church houses two stone high crosses and a number of interesting architectural features. (AA WSG-9-34)

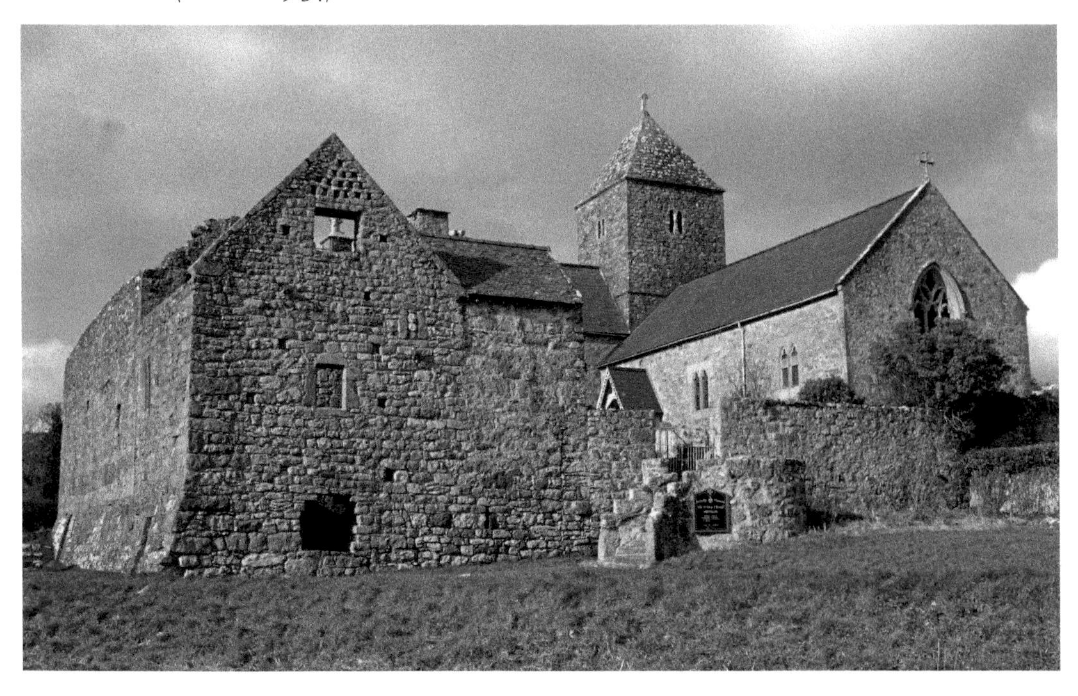

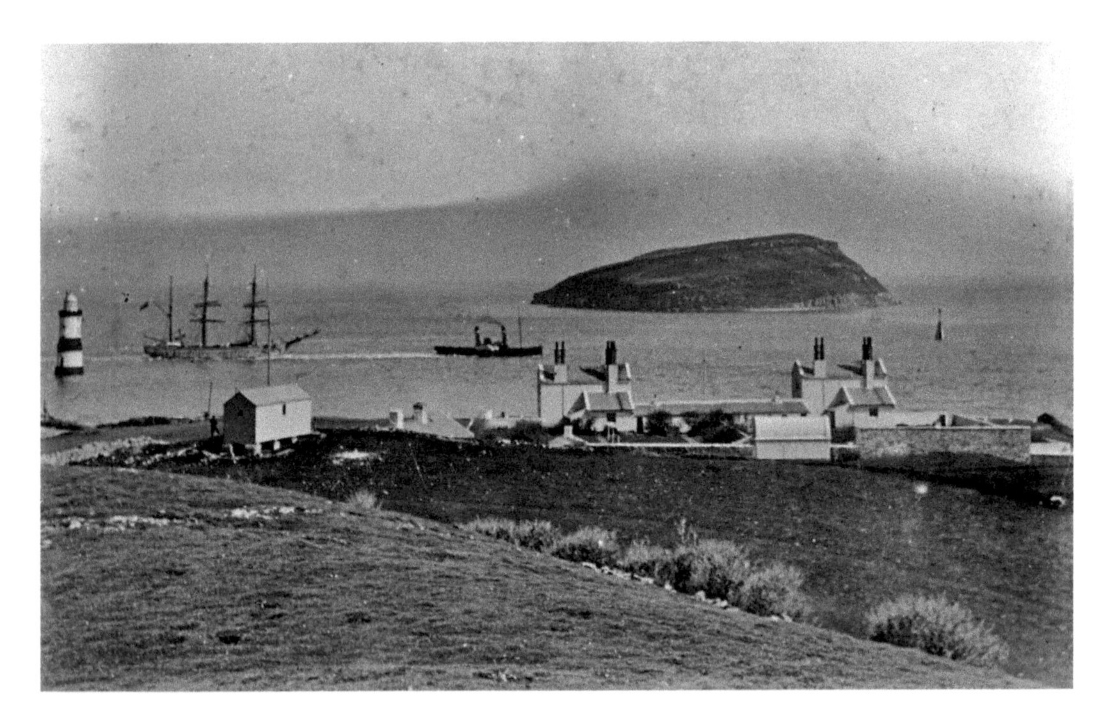

Puffin Island and Penmon Lighthouse, *c.* 1900
Half a mile from Penmon Priory is Puffin Island, or Ynys Seiriol, where St Seiriol also set up a religious community. He is said to be buried there. The sound between the island and the mainland is a regular passageway for ships, but is also treacherous. In 1831, the Rothesay Castle paddle steamer sank nearby, with the loss of 130 lives. The Trwyn Du lighthouse was built soon after, as were the keepers' cottages, shown in these photographs. (AA WSG-9-171)

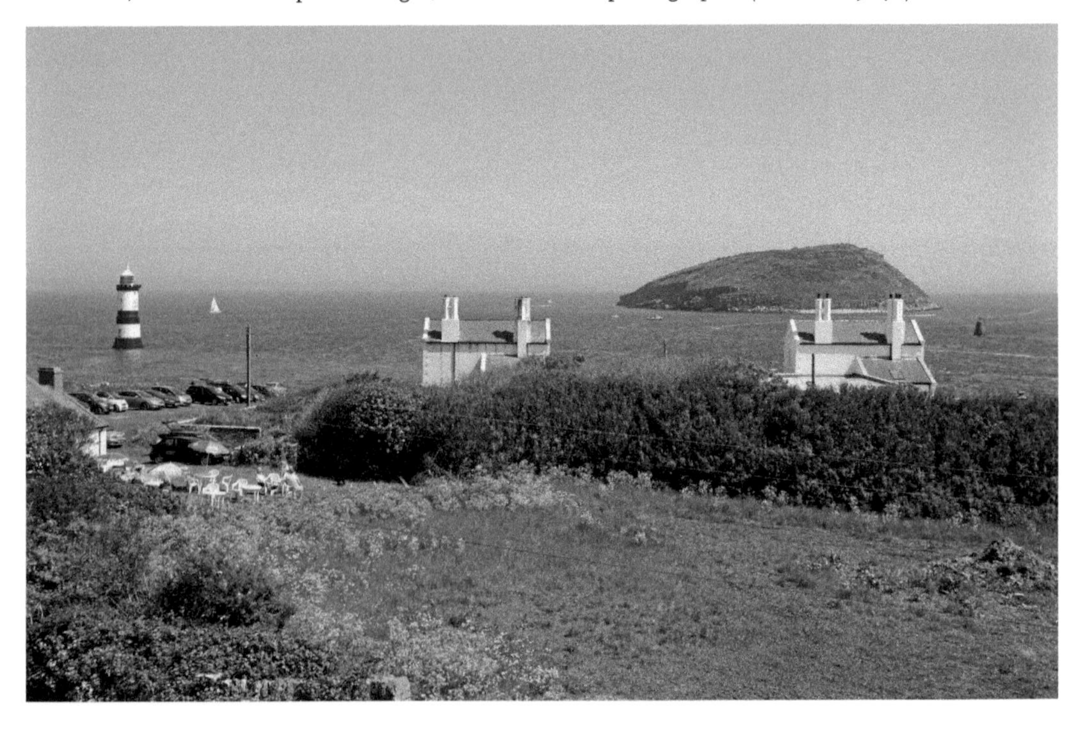

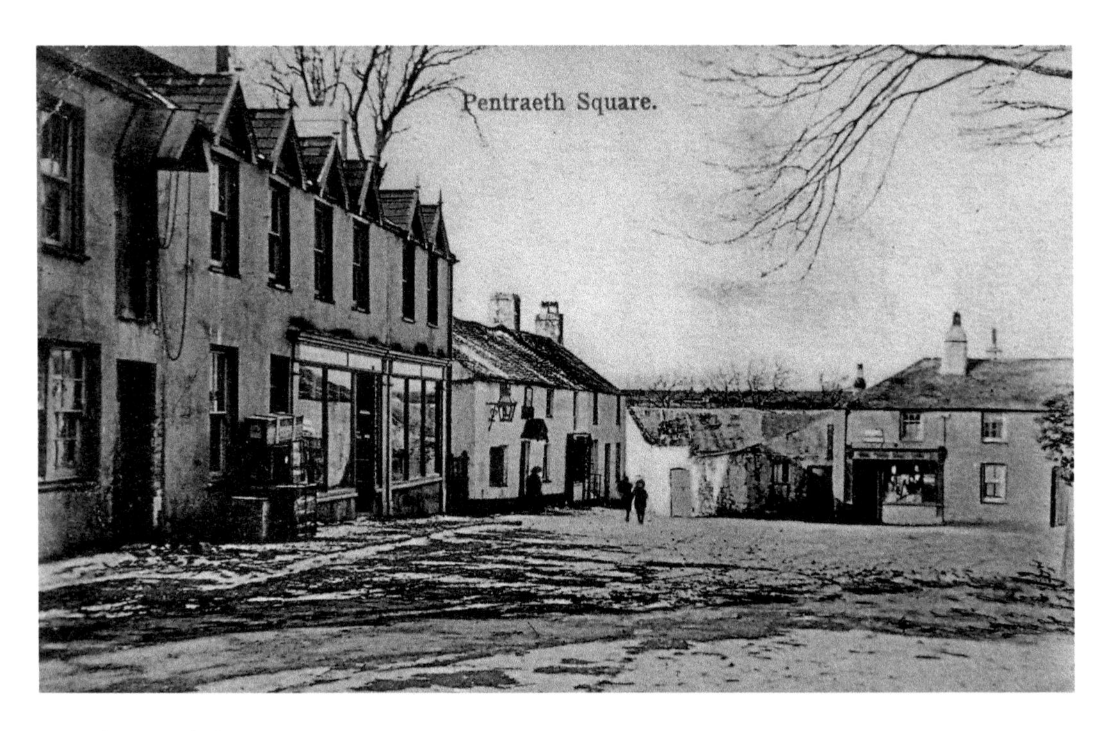

Pentraeth Square, 1905

The focus of Pentraeth village was, and remains, The Square. The main building on the left above is Cloth Hall, a general merchant shop selling groceries, cloth, hardware, and all sorts of other items for the rural community. It continued as a grocery store up until the 1990s, when it became a furniture shop and now a flooring supplier, with an adjacent party supplier and bakery. The building beyond it was the White Horse Inn, which was later rebuilt to become the post office and newsagent.

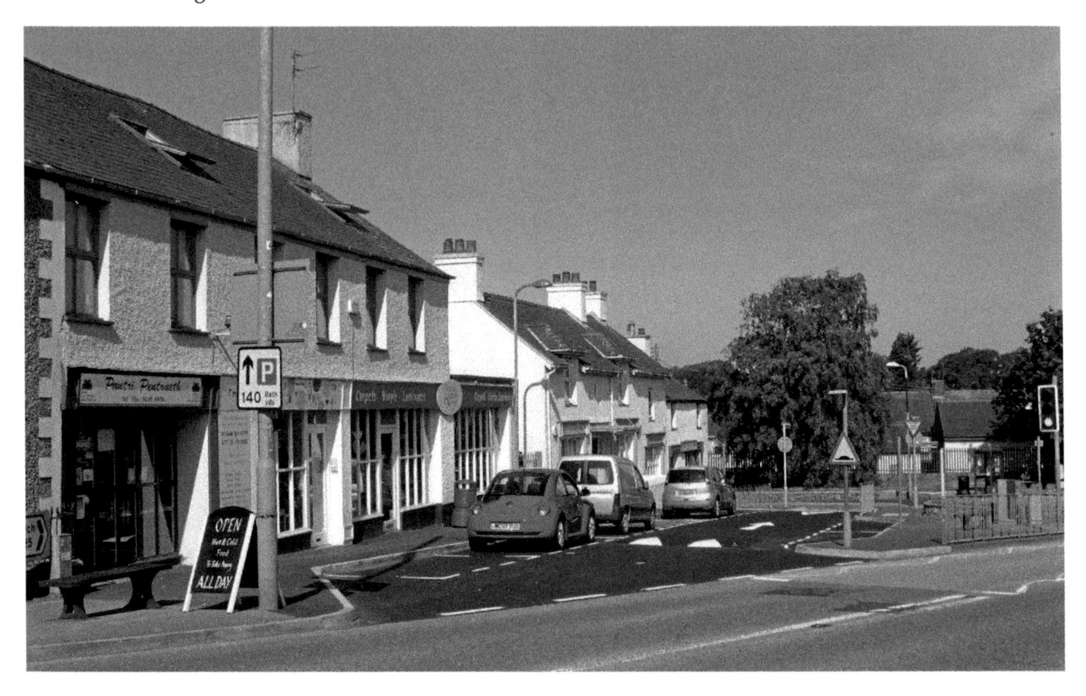

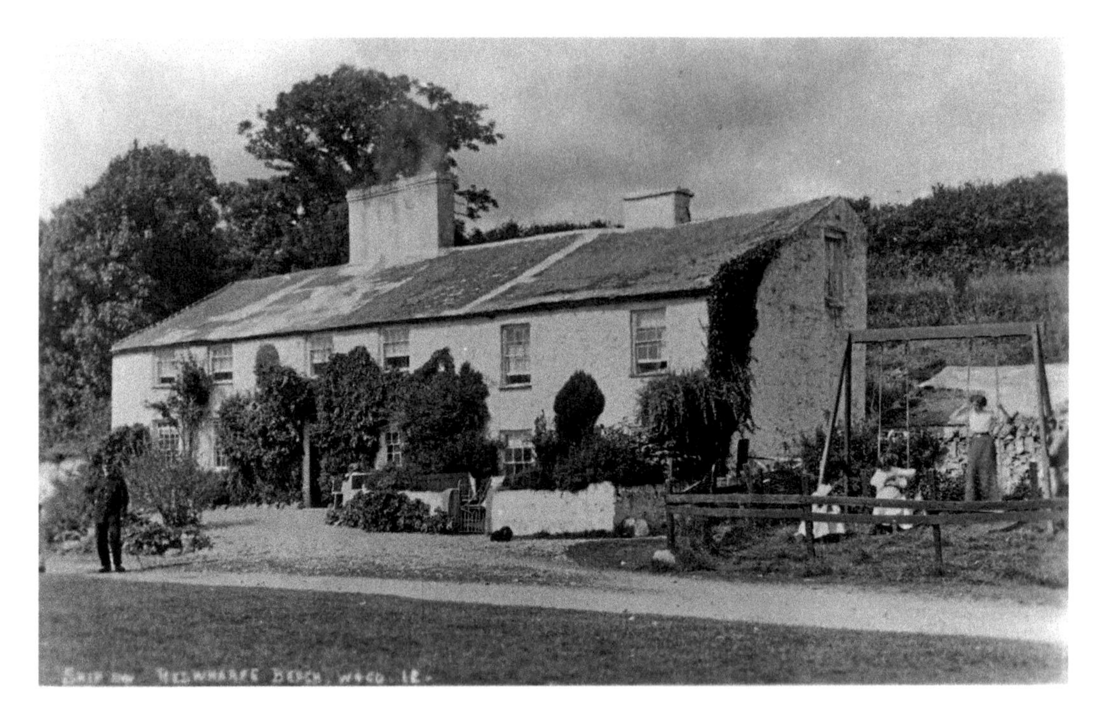

Ship Inn, Red Wharf Bay, *c.* 1915
Red Wharf Bay was a thriving port and shipbuilding area through the eighteenth and nineteenth centuries. The Ship Inn, built in the early nineteenth century, provided vital sustenance to the sailors and workers, as it does today for tourists and locals. Originally called the Little Quay, then later the Old Quay, it was renamed the Ship Inn by 1881. The inn initially occupied just the left two-thirds of the above building, with the rest being a cottage. Other buildings nearby housed coal and corn merchants, distributing supplies brought in by ship. (AA WSH-11-57)

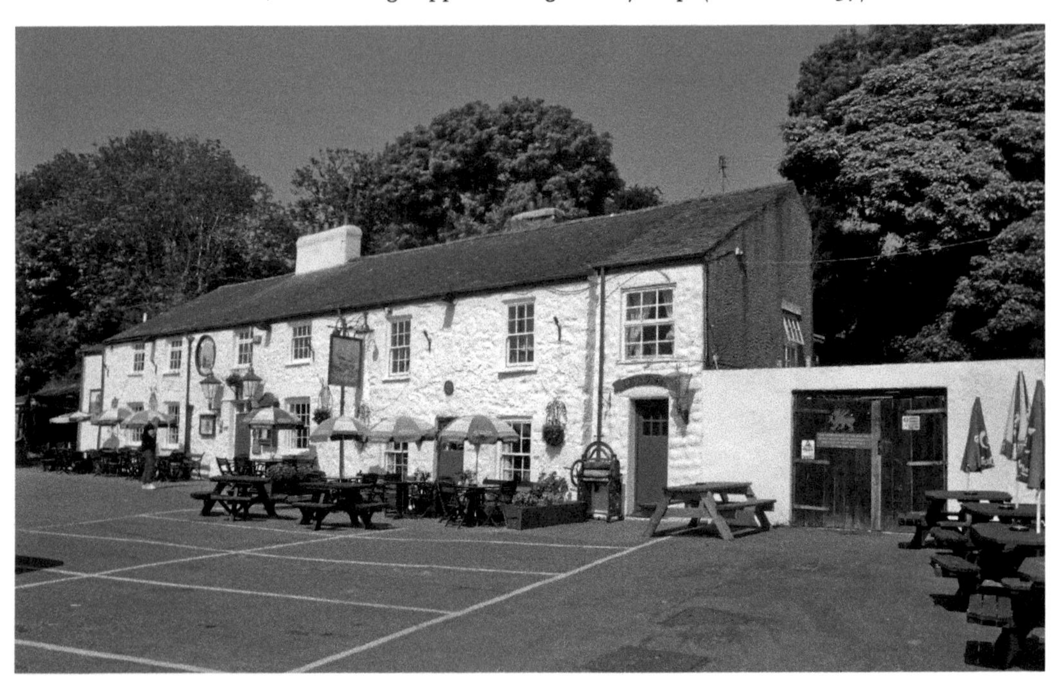

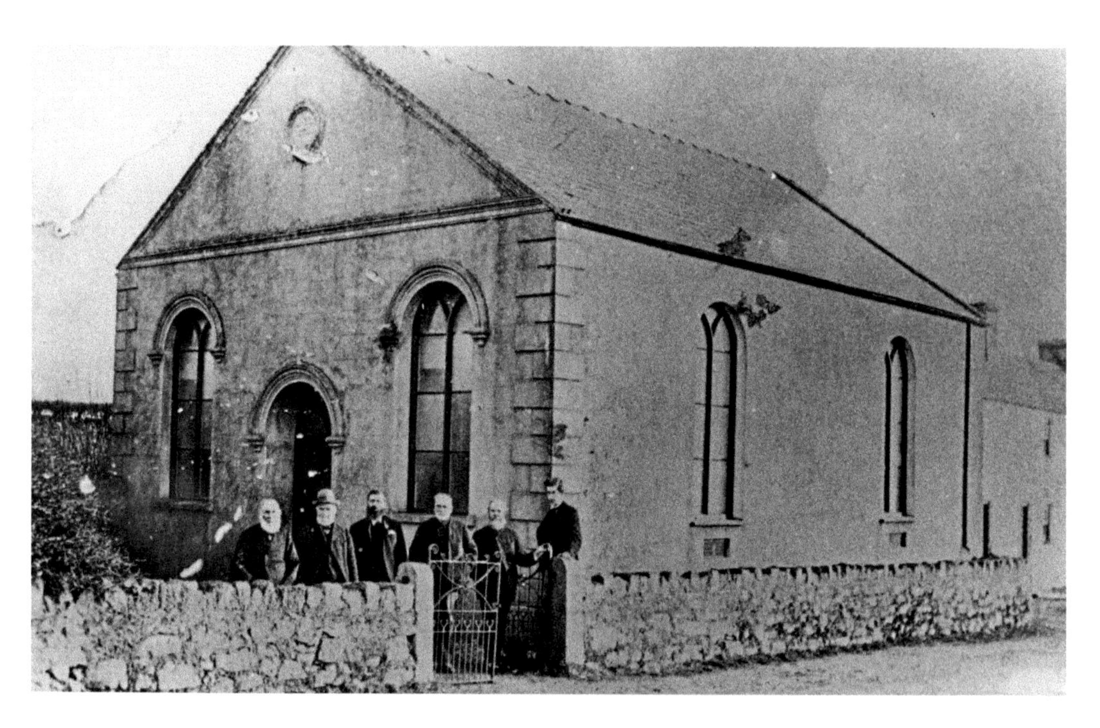

Siloam Chapel, Talwrn, 1898

A Welsh Independent chapel was built in the small village of Talwrn in 1841, and was rebuilt in its current form in 1880. It is known as Capel Bach (little chapel) to distinguish it from larger Capel Mawr (big chapel), the Methodist chapel on the hill. The five older men above were deacons of the chapel. The tall young man on the right was John Talwrn Jones, who was being supported financially by the chapel to study at the Bala-Bangor Theological Seminary. (AA WSH-6-2)

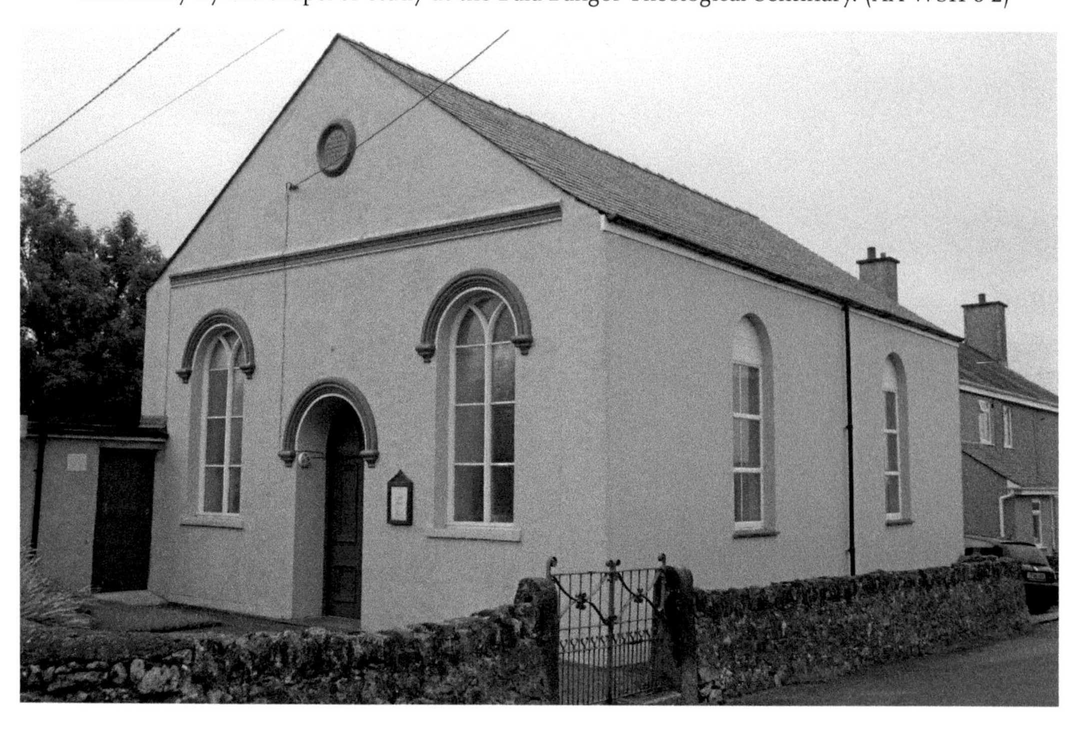

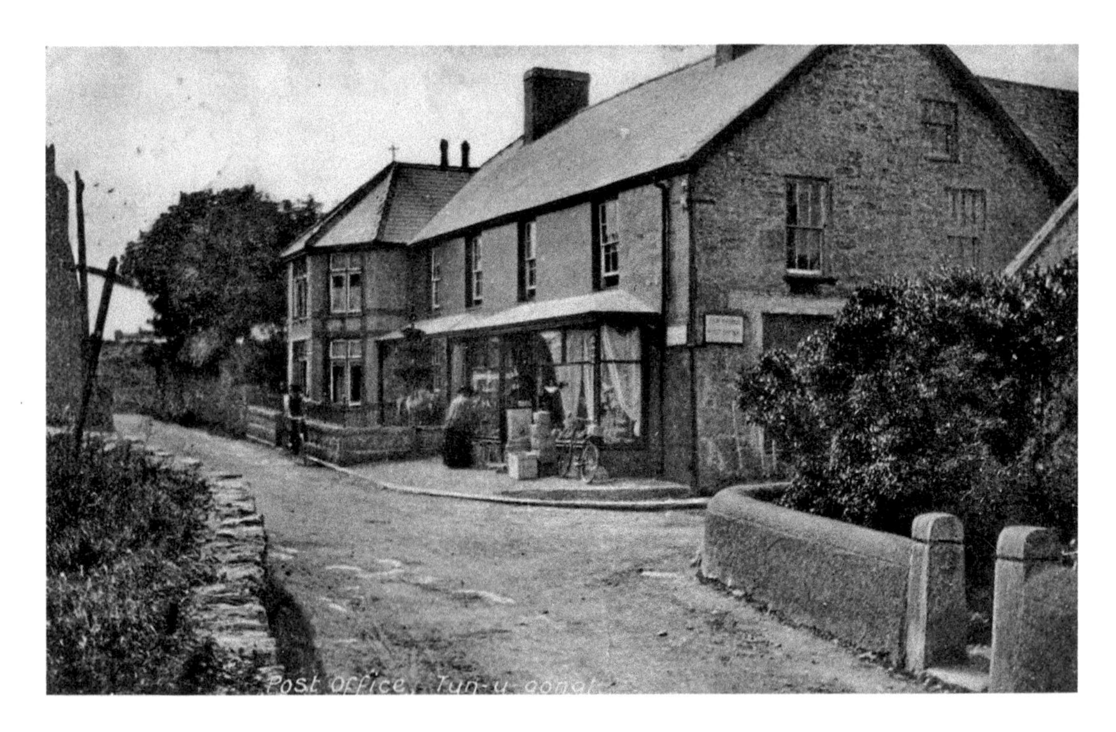

Tynygongl Post Office, 1909

The old post office and shop at Tynygongl was the focal point for the parish of Llanfair Mathafarn Eithaf in the nineteenth and early twentieth centuries. It was run by John Prytherch Williams for more than forty years, then from 1902 by his son, William, and sold groceries, draperies and general goods. The post office moved to the centre of Benllech later in the twentieth century, and the grocery shop eventually closed. It has been abandoned and boarded up for several years now. (AA WSH-11-112)

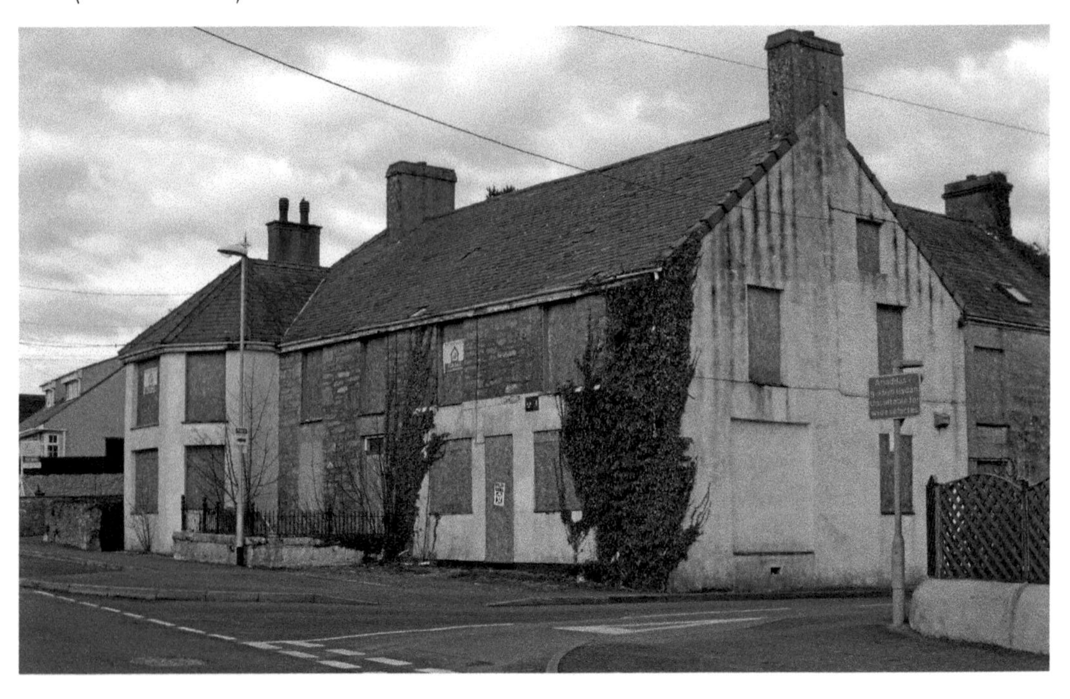

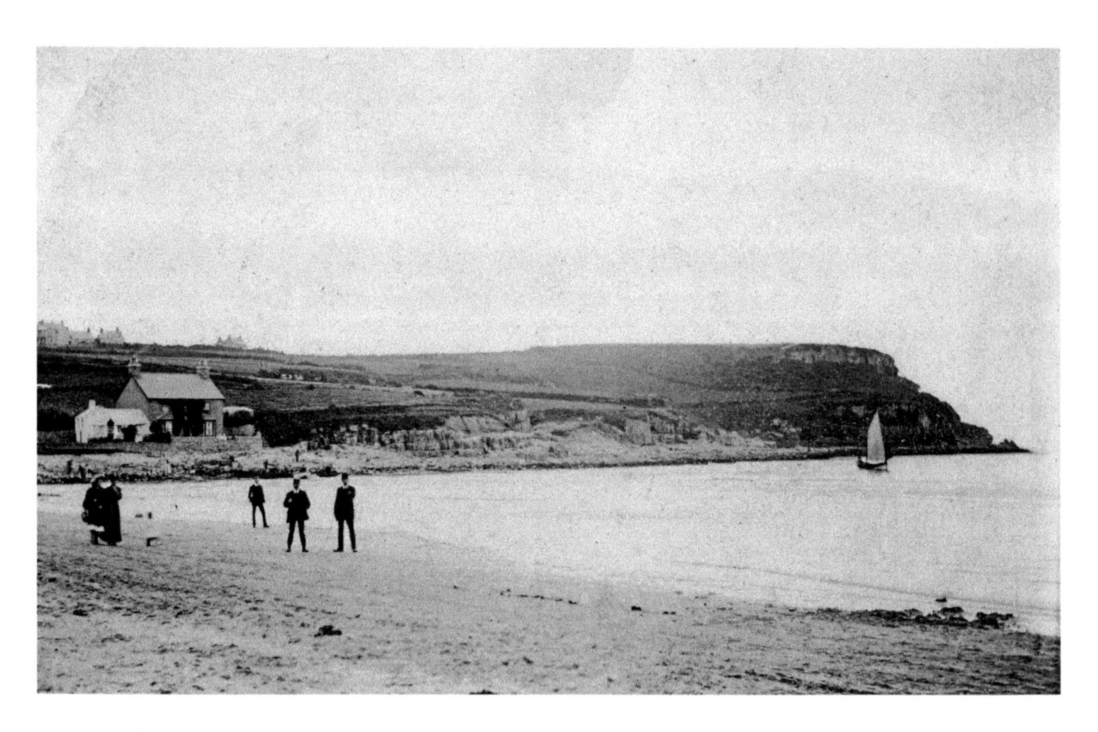

Benllech Bay, 1907

From the start of the twentieth century, Benllech Beach became an increasingly popular tourist destination. The relatively empty beach and hillside in 1907 contrasts with the sands crowded with sunbathers and the landscape full of caravans today. Behind the holidaymakers in the image above is Benllech Isaf, the home of stonemason Robert Parry, who around this time turned it into a lodging house. Today it is still a guest house with a café in the adjoining cottage. (AA WSH-11-18)

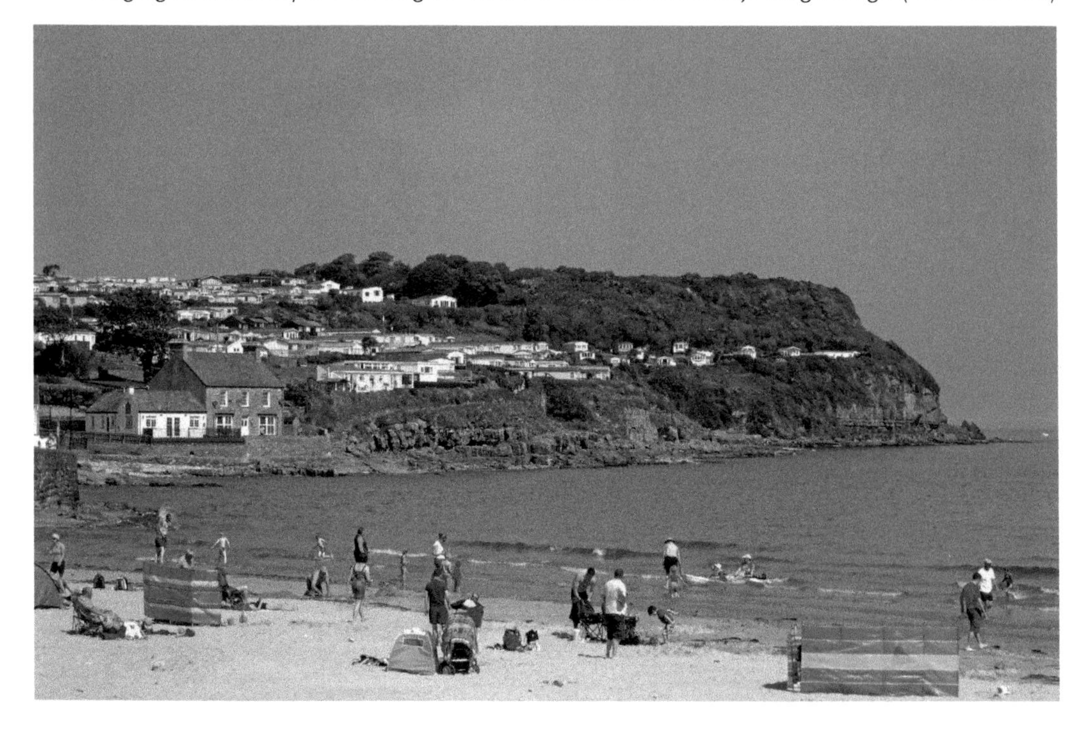

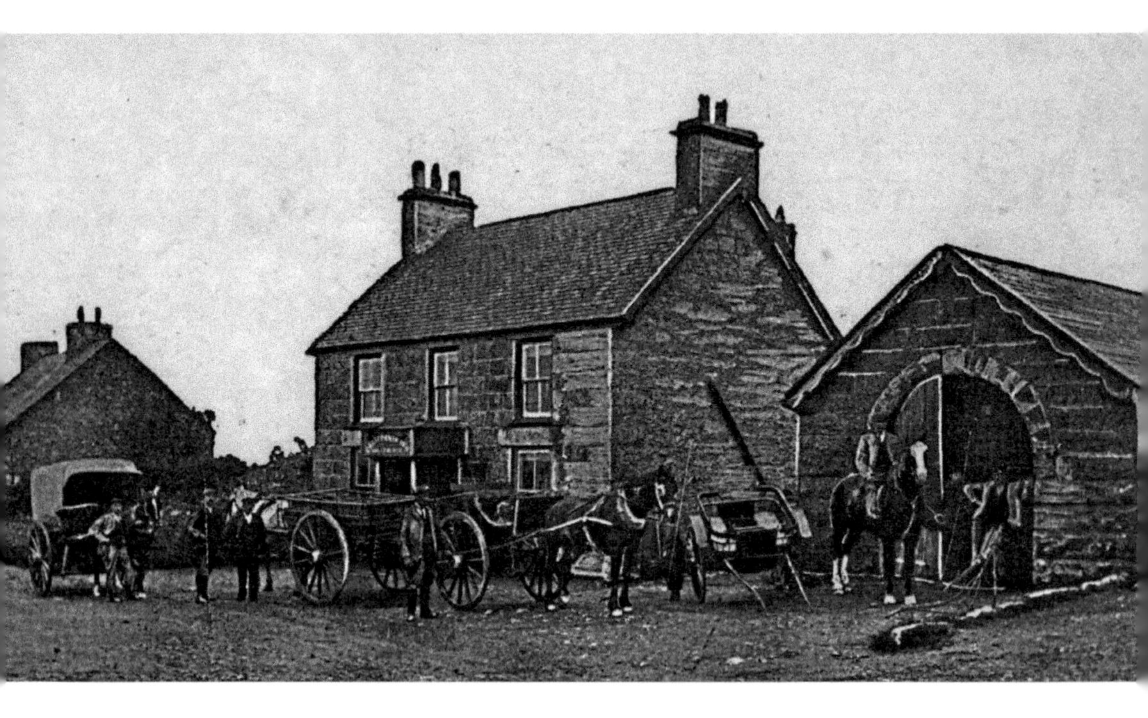

California Inn, Brynteg, Early Twentieth Century

When the sailor William Thomas returned to his native Anglesey with a pocket full of gold from the California Gold Rush, he built an inn at the crossroads in Brynteg, christening it the California Inn. In his book *Wild Wales*, an account of his 1854 tour around Wales, George Borrow recalls his astonishment at meeting a Spanish-speaking Welshman who was building a house after returning from Chile and California. That man, William Thomas, ran the inn for the rest of his life, after which his son, John, took it over. (AA WSH-11-3)

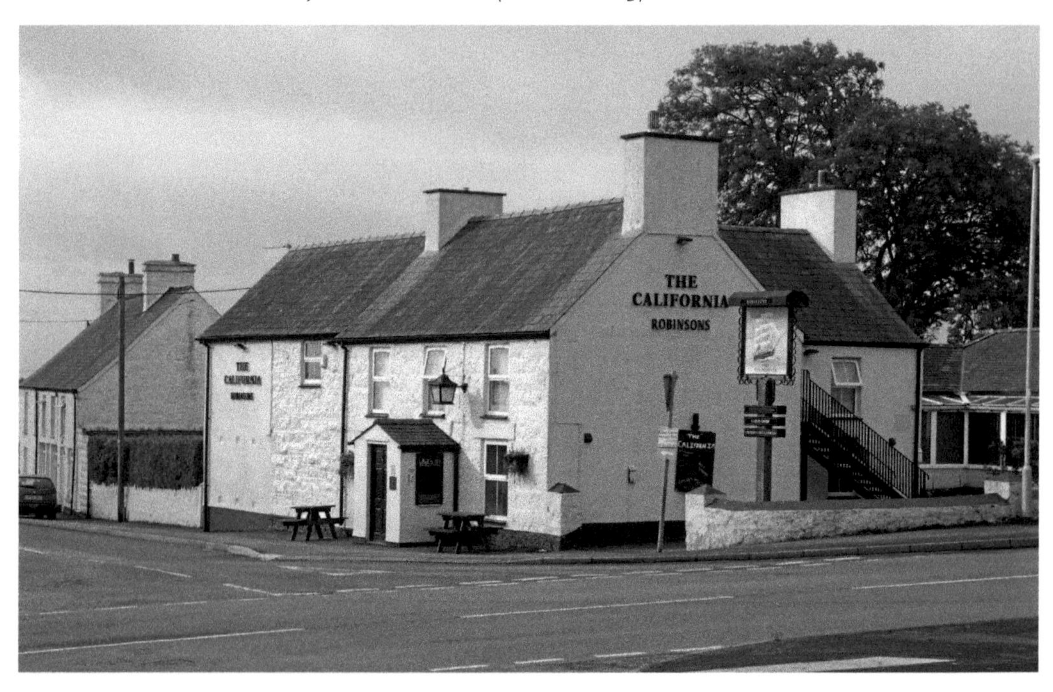

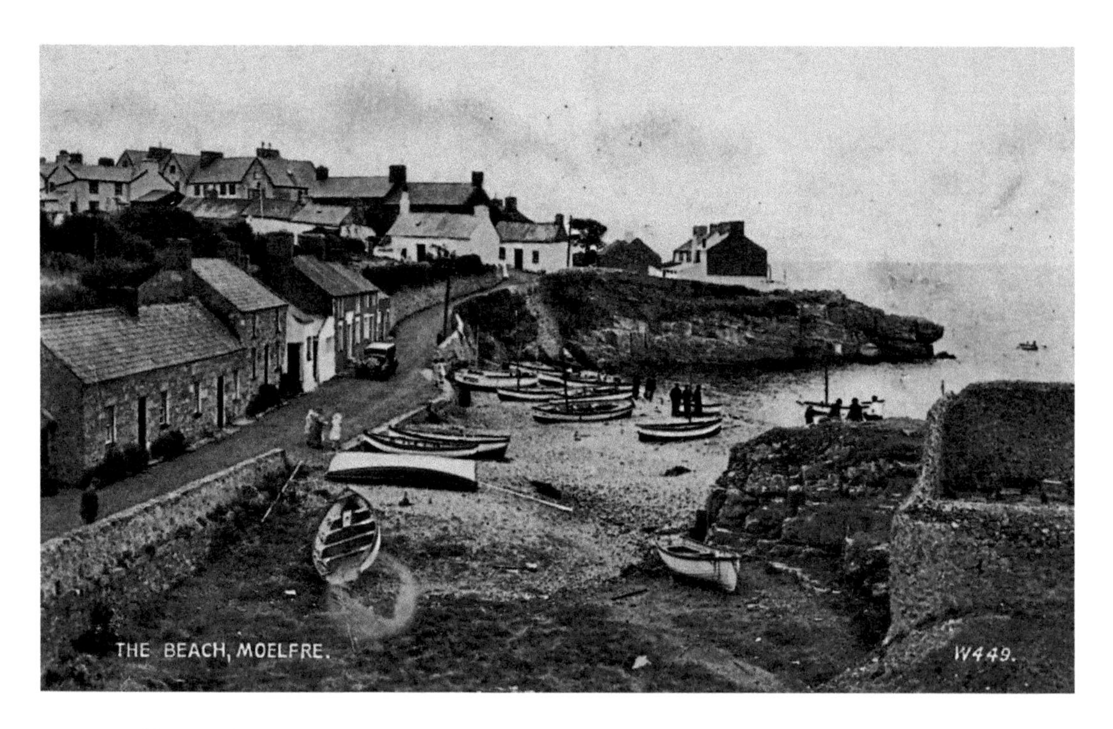

Moelfre Harbour, 1935

For centuries, Moelfre Harbour has been a safe place for inshore fishermen to launch their boats, with up to thirty landing daily, full of herring, at the end of the nineteenth century. In the twentieth century, it became a popular seaside tourist village. The building by the car above is the fifteenth-century Crown and Anchor Inn, which also served as the post office. It is now a pair of holiday cottages.

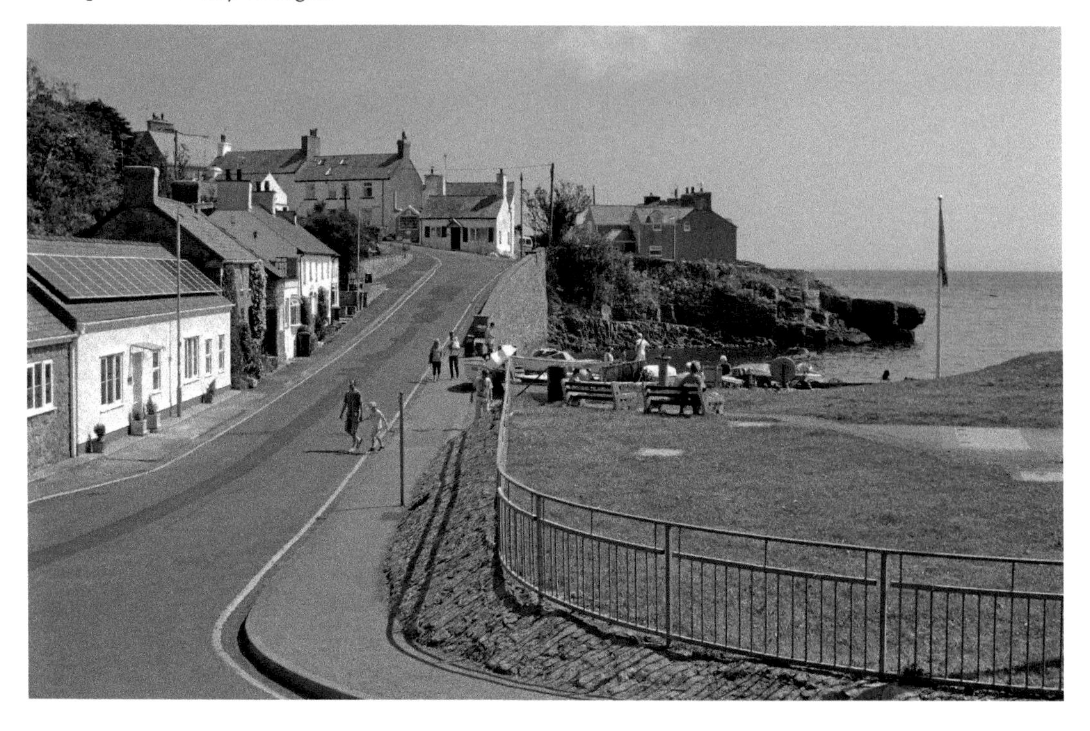

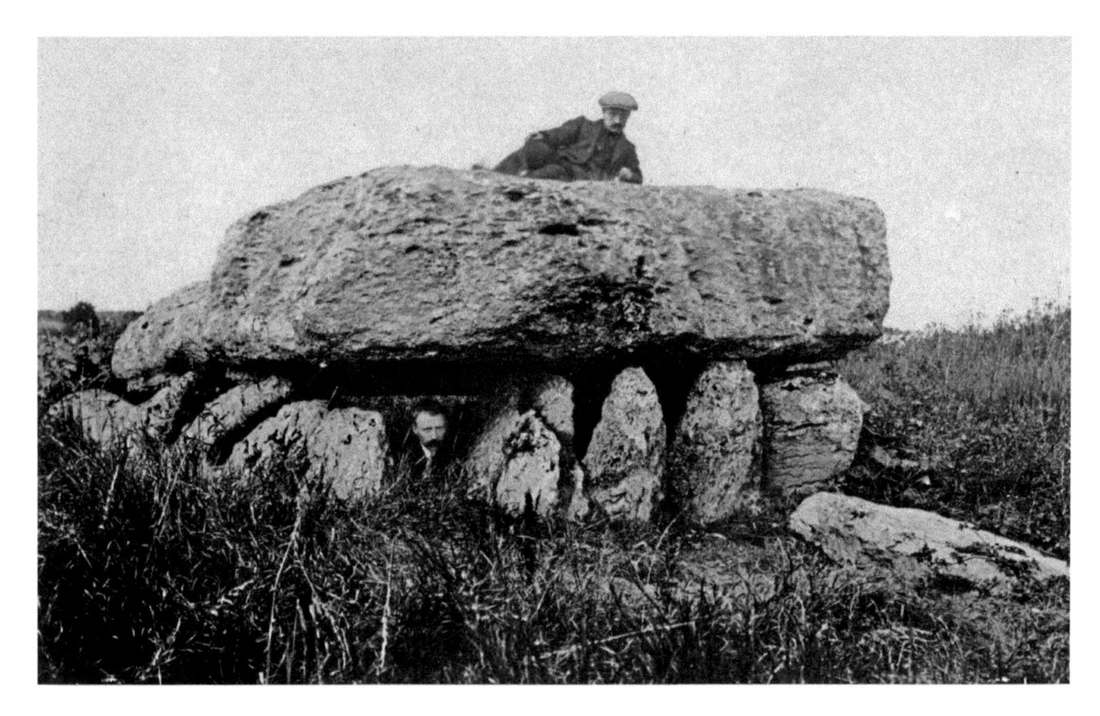

Lligwy Burial Chamber, Early Twentieth Century
Anglesey is rich in prehistoric monuments and remains. This Neolithic burial chamber, near Moelfre, dates to the third millennium BC. It originally would have been covered by a mound of earth or stone, with a passage into the central chamber where the bones of the dead would have been interred. It was excavated in 1908, when the remains of up to thirty people were found alongside pottery shards. The unusually large capstone weighs about 25 tons. (AA WSH-3-18)

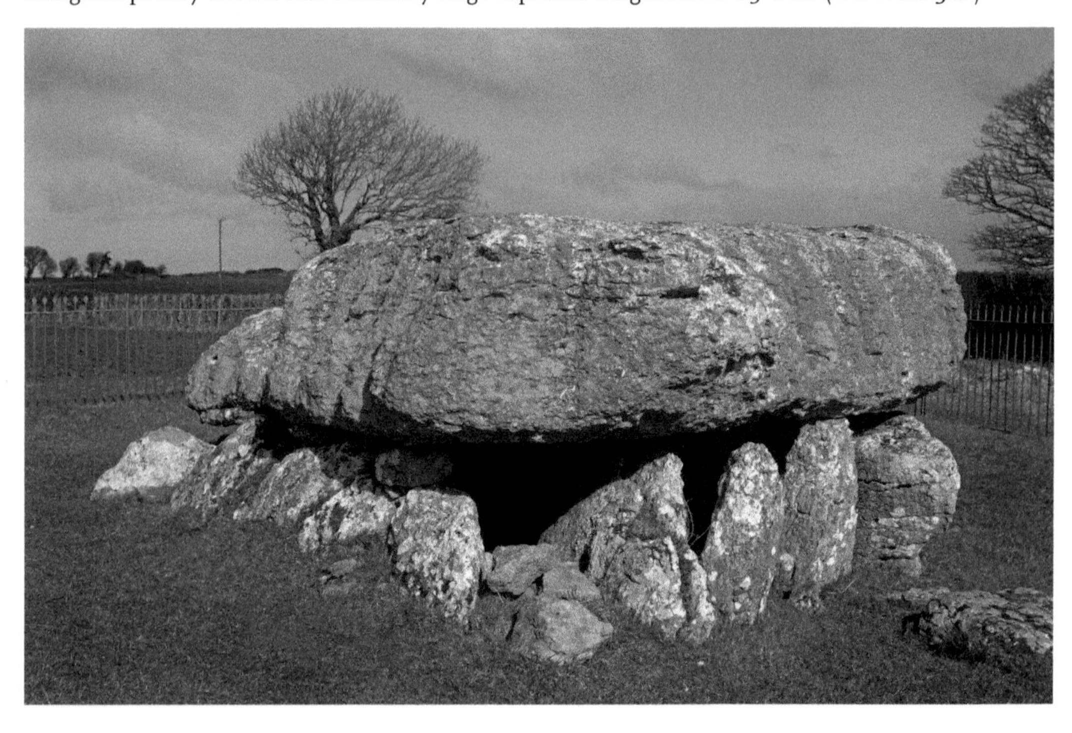

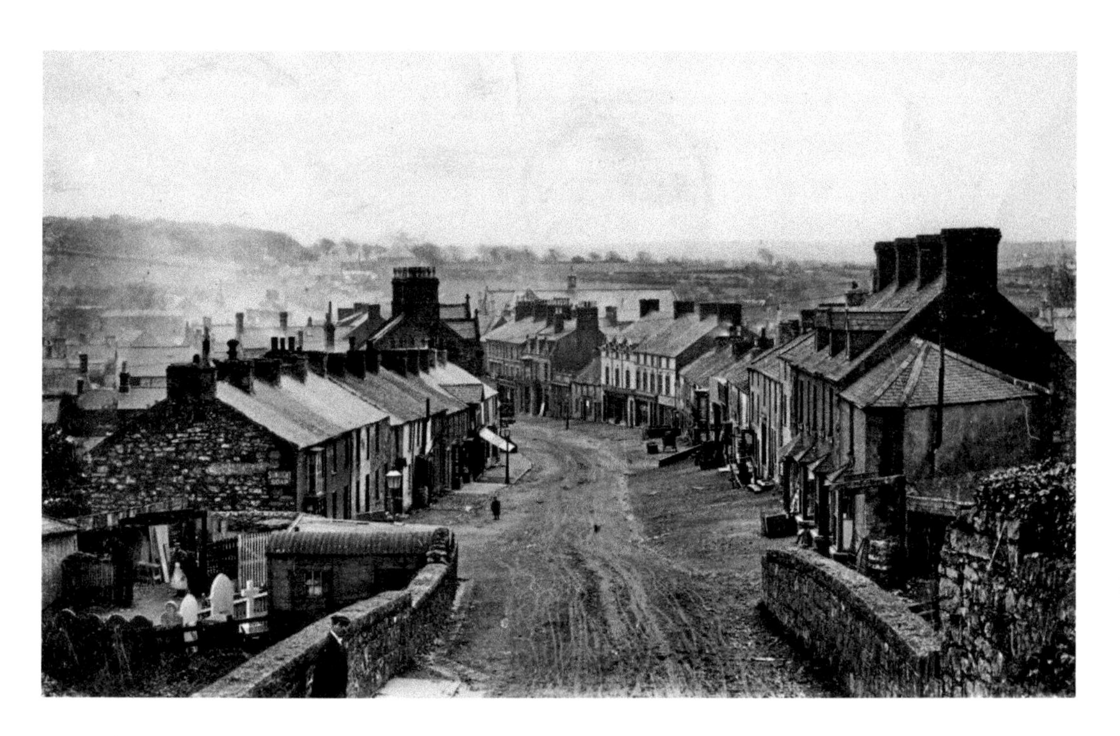

Llangefni High Street, Late 1880s

Looking down the Llangefni High Street from the railway bridge shows the town in transition in the 1880s. The roof of the recently built town hall can be seen in the distance, but the street is still unpaved. The smallest building in the middle of the picture is the old Oddfellows Arms pub. Along with the other small building next to it, a confectioner's shop, it was knocked down and rebuilt in the 1900s. (AA WSE-230)

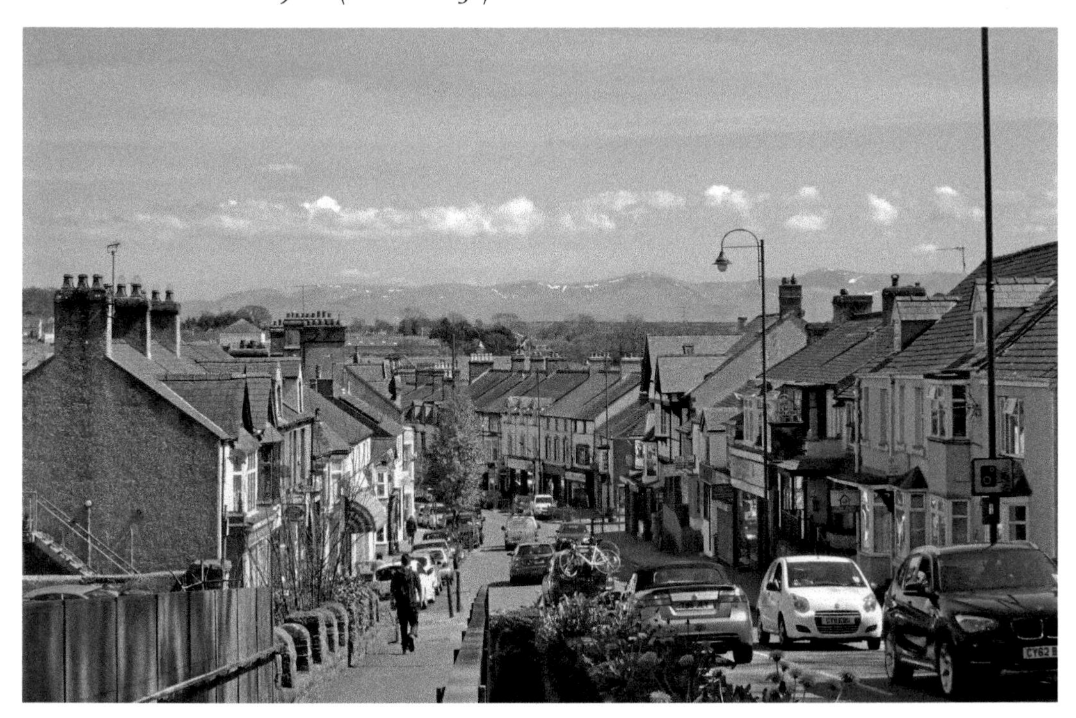

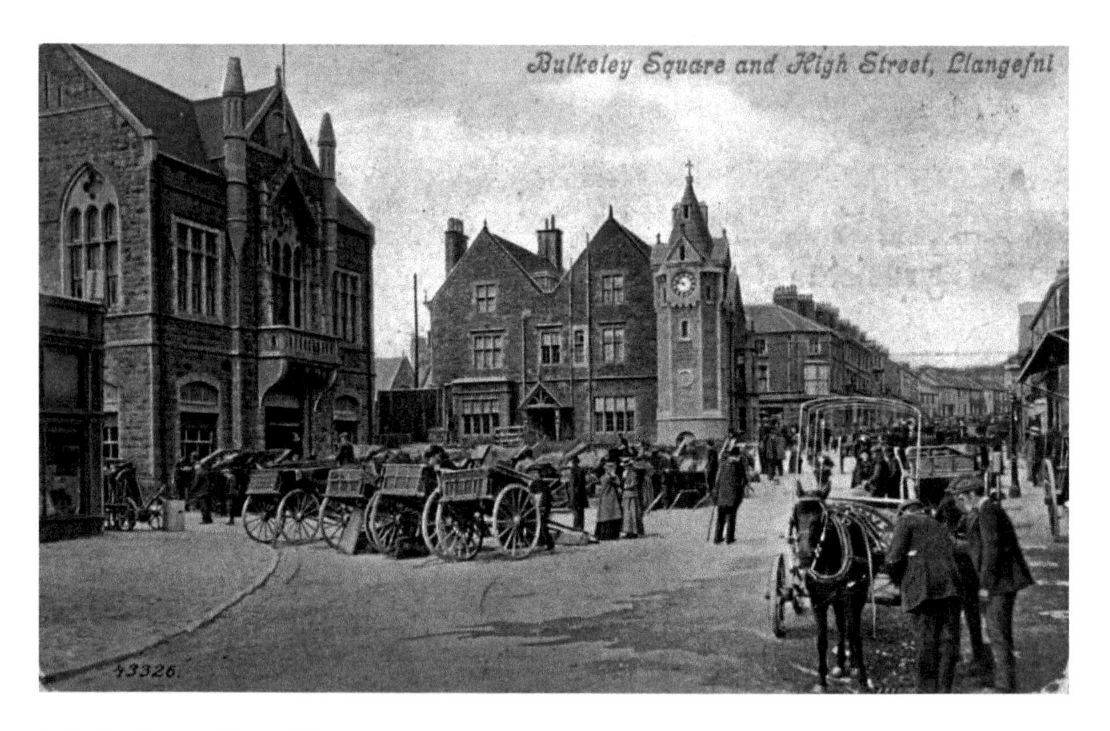

Bulkeley Square, Llangefni, 1904
By the late nineteenth century, the centrally placed Llangefni had overtaken Llanerchymedd as the main market town on Anglesey. The market is held in the shadows of the Bull Hotel (built in 1856), the town hall (1884) and the memorial clock (1902). In the above picture, traders have arranged their wagons for customers to browse their goods. The market, once considered one of the best in North Wales, originally occurred every Thursday; these days it is also held on Saturdays. (AA WSE-273)

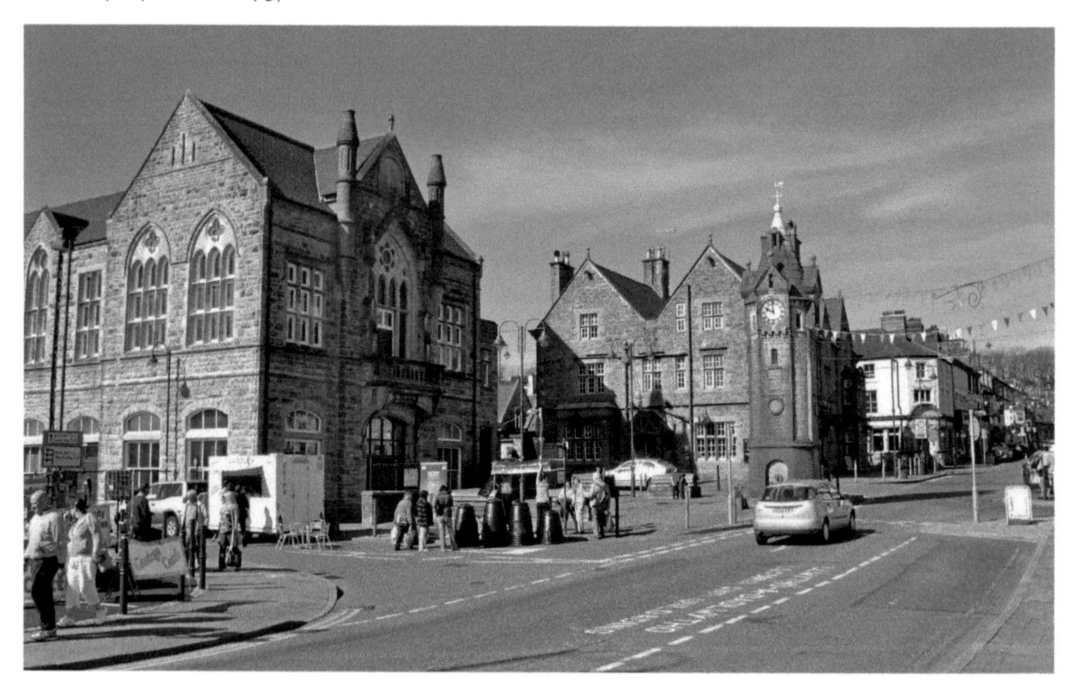

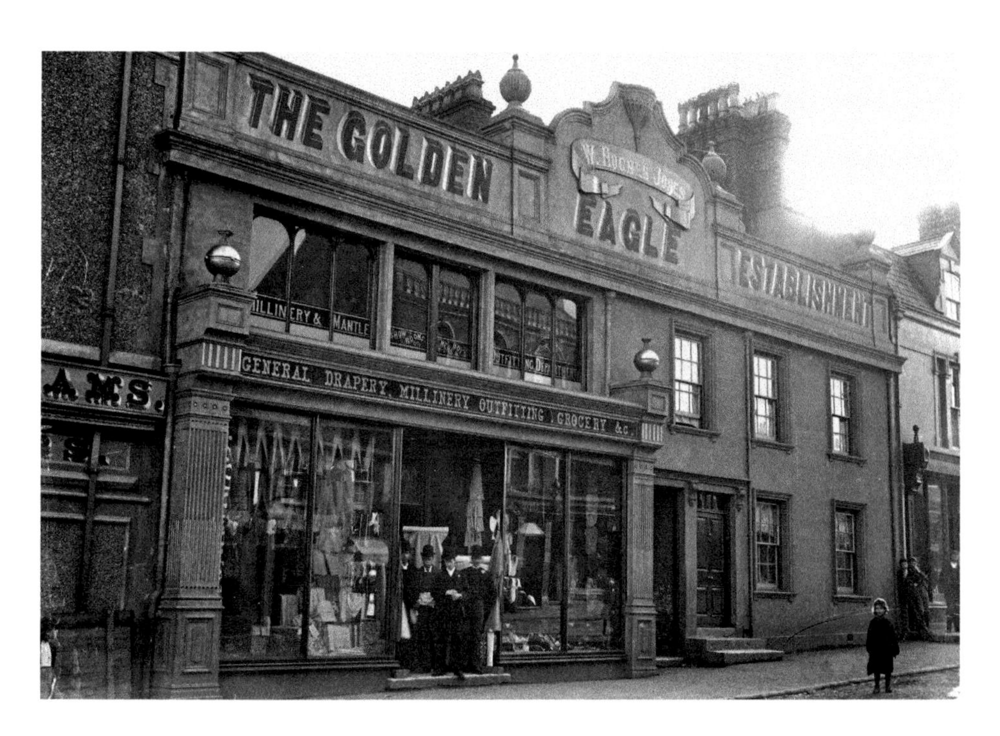

Golden Eagle, Llangefni, *c.* 1900

This rather imposing shopfront was the Golden Eagle Establishment, selling drapery, clothing, millinery and groceries. It was run from the late 1870s by William Hughes Jones, who in 1871 was an assistant to the previous owner, John Edwards. Jones turned part of the building (previously also a shopfront, visible in the picture on page 41) into a large residence that housed not only his substantial family, but also several assistants, apprentices and servants (twelve in all in 1901). (AA WSM-383-32)

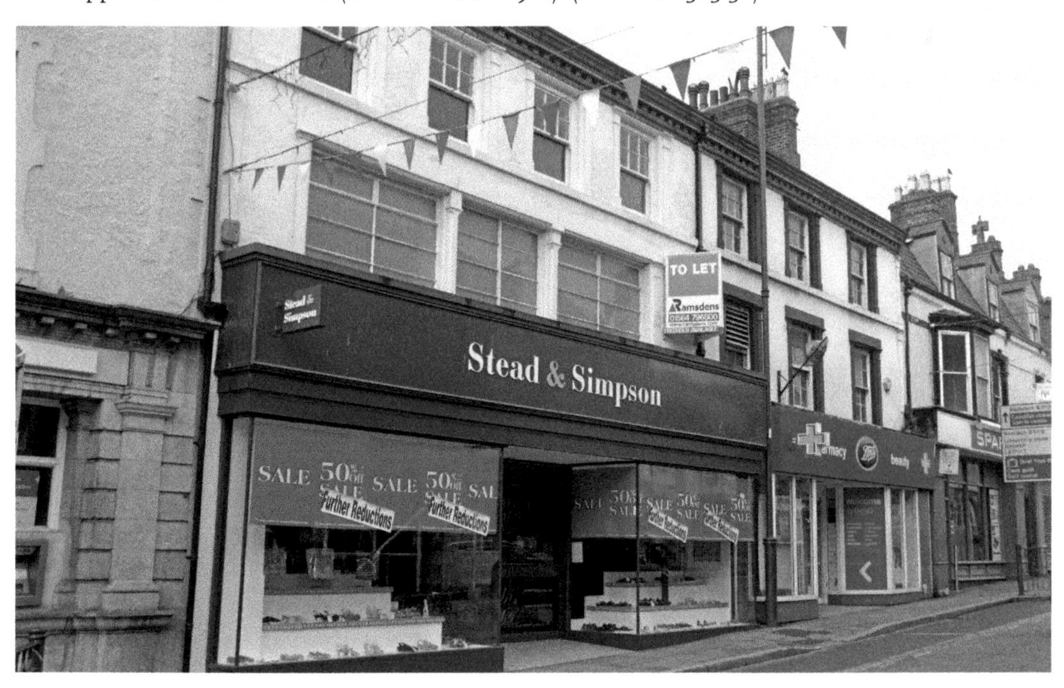

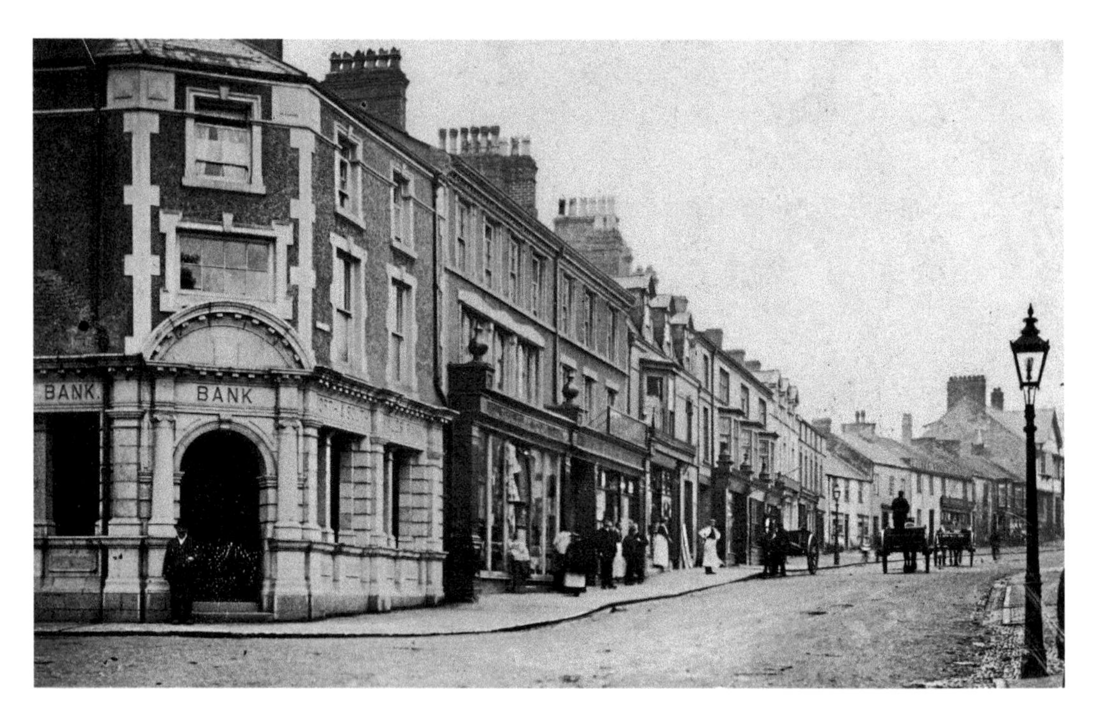

Llangefni High Street, 1909

By 1909, the large Golden Eagle Establishment sign had come down and the living accommodation turned back into a shop, housing Star Grocers. The Golden Eagle proprietor, William Hughes Jones, was living at Fron Farm with his two daughters, but still running the shop, which continued to take up all floors of the building. It was thus one of the few on the High Street that did not have accommodation upstairs. The building on the corner had previously been the Liverpool Arms, before being converted briefly to a draper's shop and then a bank in the 1900s. (AA WSE-33)

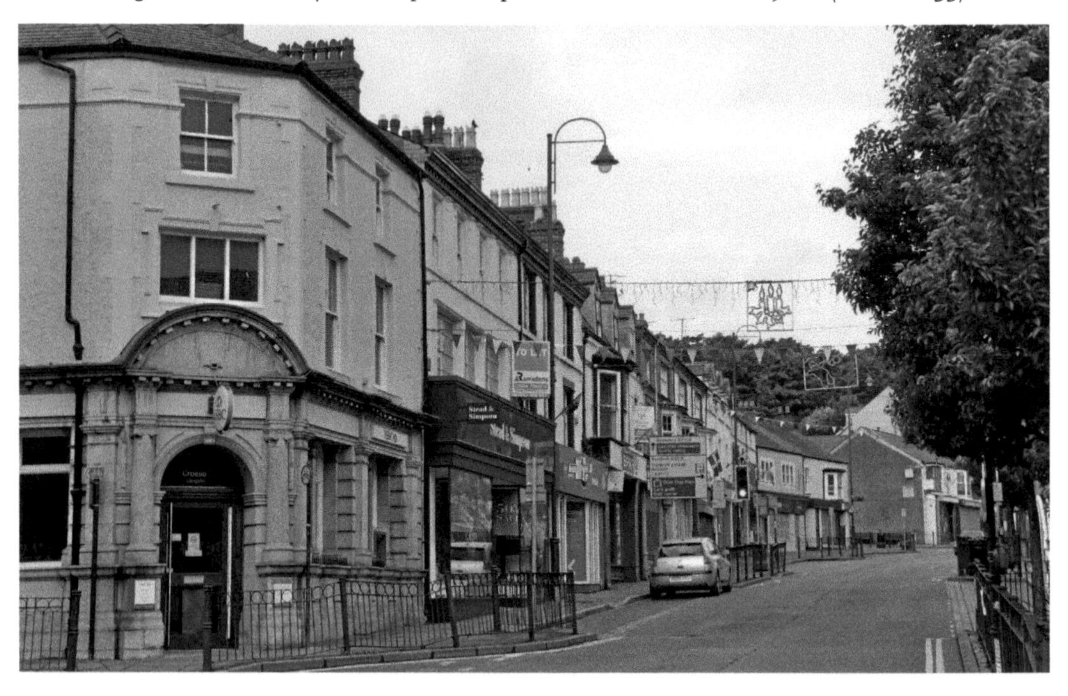

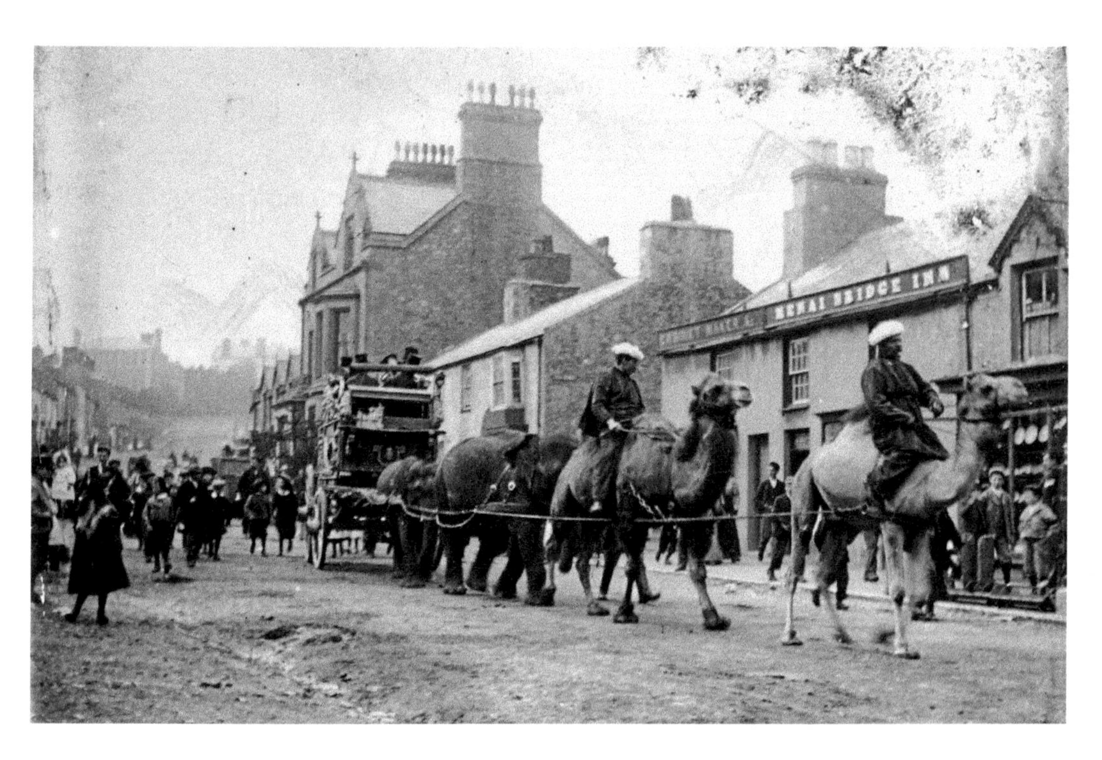

Circus in Llangefni, Early Twentieth Century
The circus is coming to town! Excited children follow a coach carrying musicians, drawn by a team of elephants and camels, down Llangefni High Street. This photograph was taken by Maurice Price, stationer, bookseller and professional photographer, from outside his shop on the High Street (most recently Guests newsagent). Camels and elephants are rarely seen on the streets of Llangefni these days. (AA WSM-383-33)

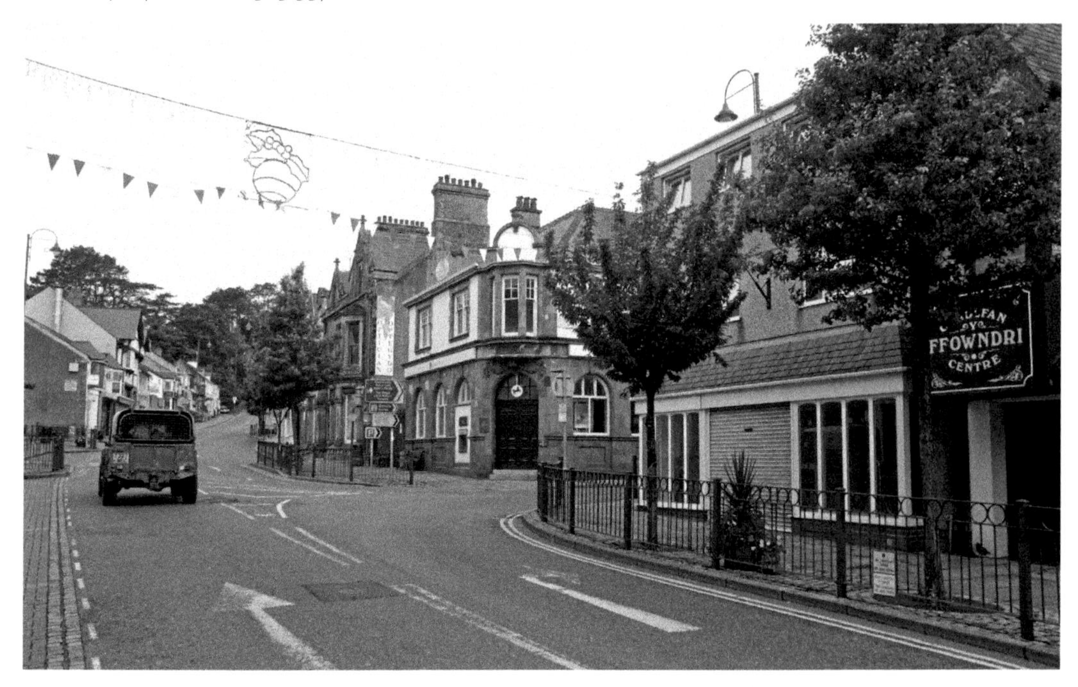

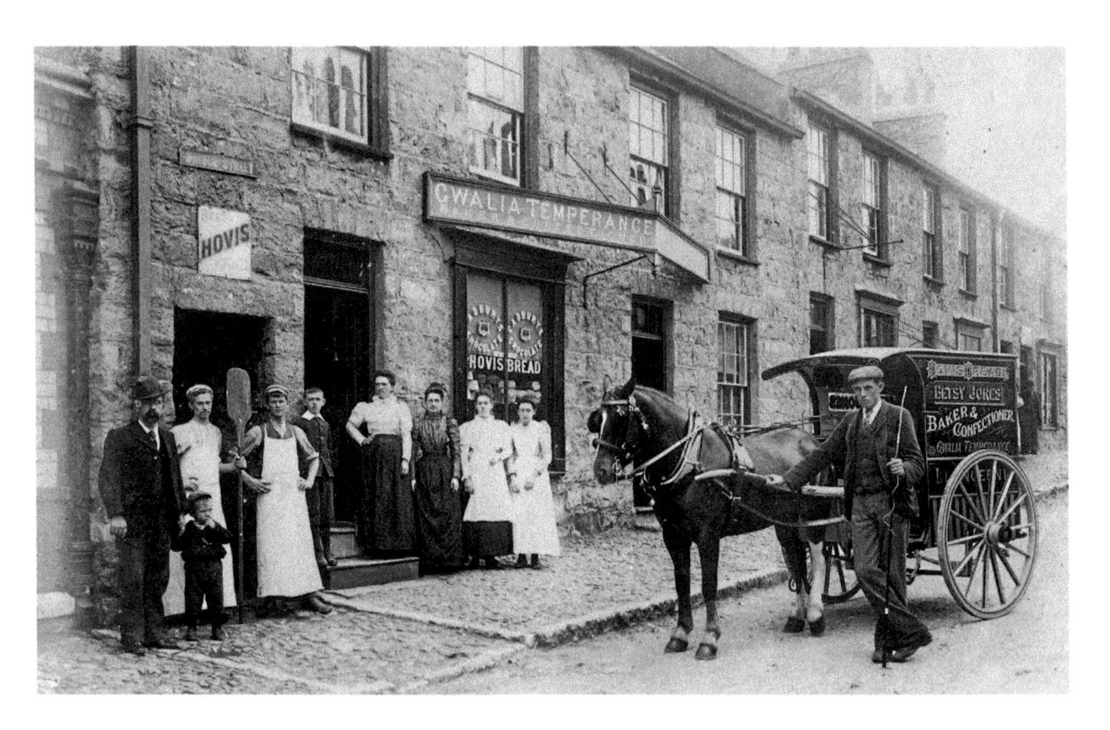

Gwalia Bakery, Llangefni, *c.* 1910

Little could the owner of the Gwalia Temperance Bakery, Betsy Jones, and her workers, posed outside the shop above, imagine the changes that would occur through the twentieth century. However, they would be proud that the bakery has survived to this day, still occupying the same building. In 2011, Gwalia Bakery was threatened with closure and thousands signed a successful petition to save it. It has even moved into the twenty-first century with a Facebook page. (AA WSE-155)

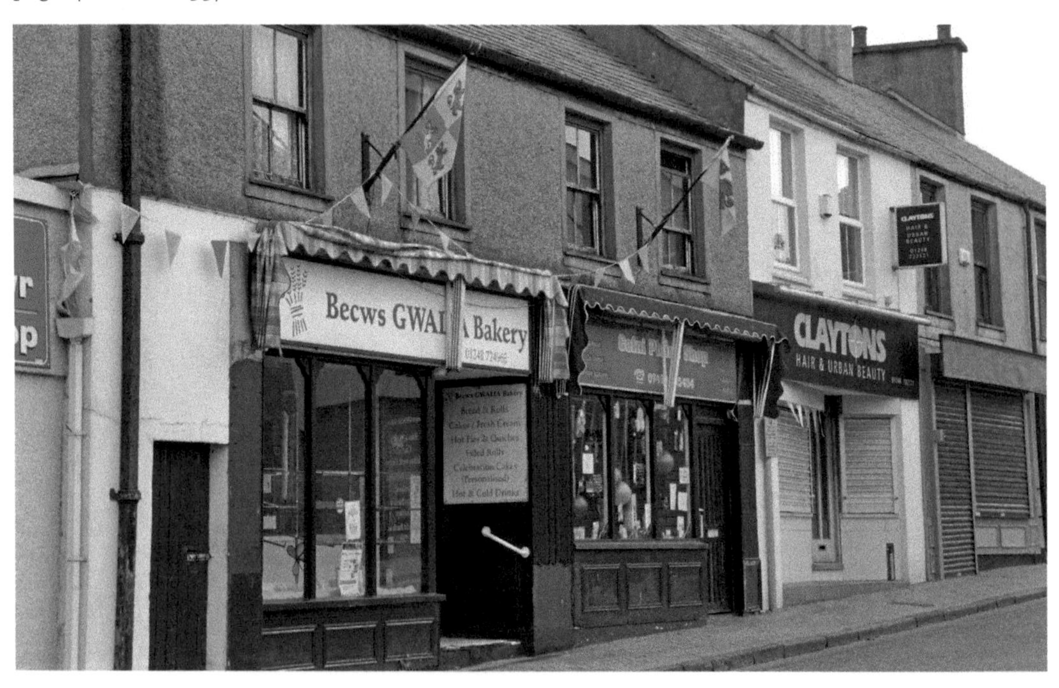

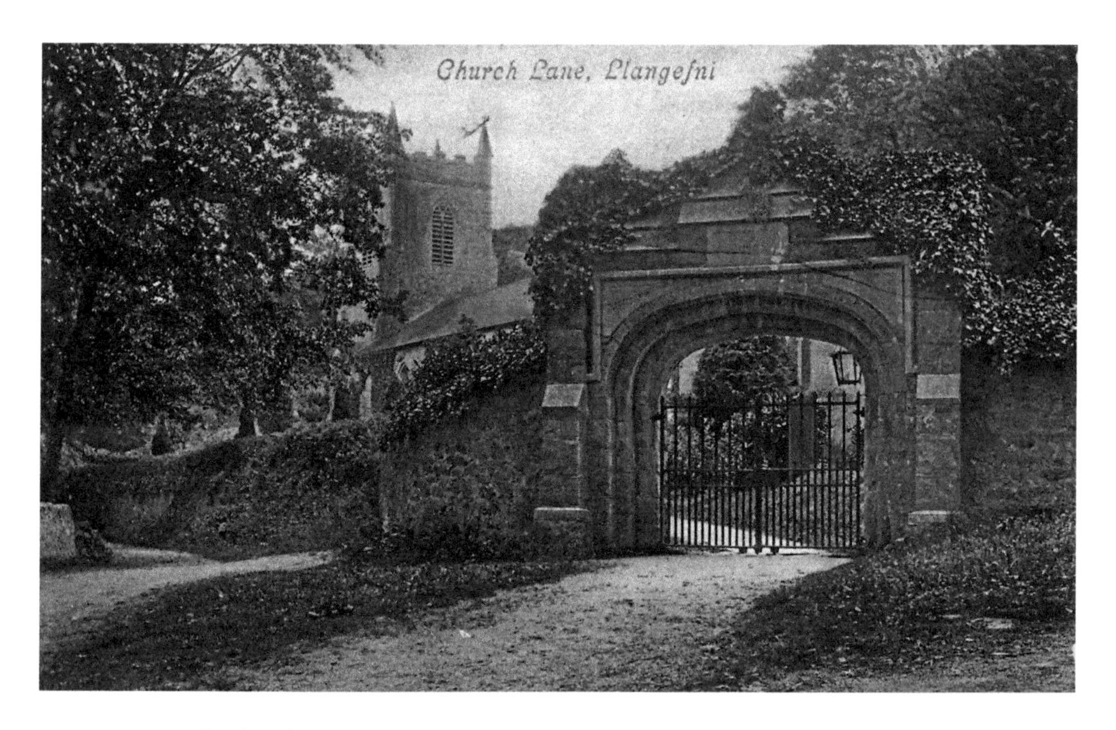

St Cyngar's Church, Llangefni, 1904
This image of St Cyngar's church proudly displays the relatively new gateway added to the churchyard in 1890. The church itself was built in 1824 and houses the font, one doorway arch and a few memorials rescued from the previously demolished medieval building. The lane alongside the churchyard wall led to the Cefni River, where St Cyngar's well is located, but today is part of one of the town's main car parks.

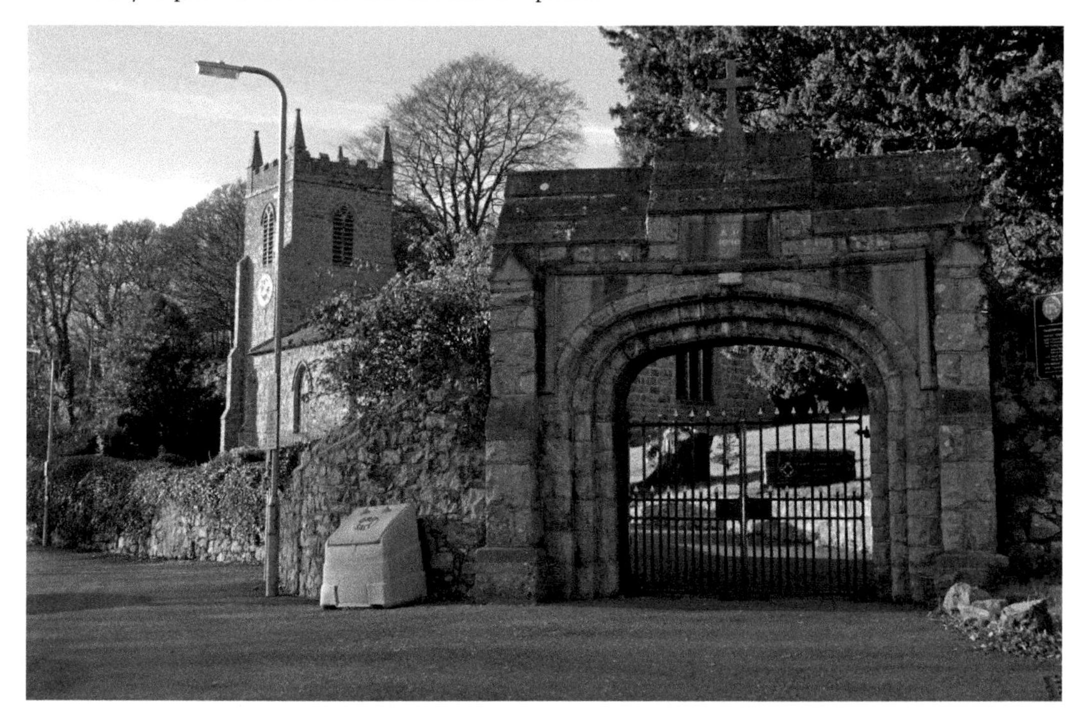

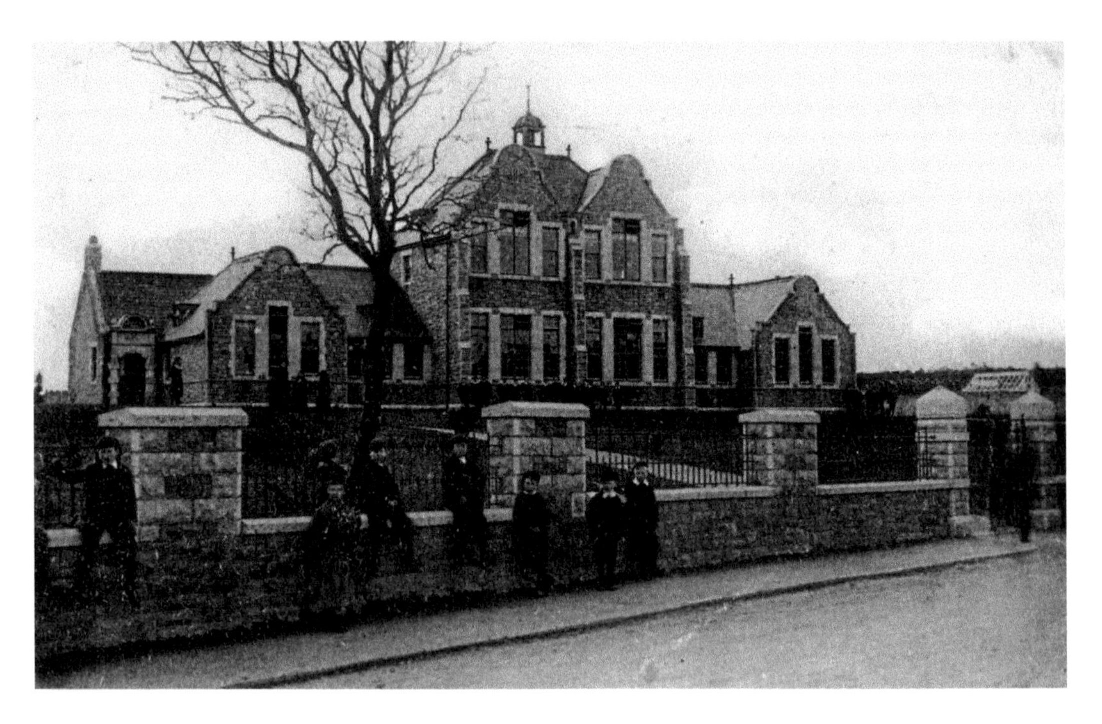

County School, Llangefni, 1905

State-sponsored secondary schools began appearing in Wales in the late nineteenth century. Anglesey's first was founded in Llangefni in 1897 when seventy-one students met in the cramped loft in the town hall. By 1900, they had moved into this purpose-built school on the edge of town. This later became a campus of Coleg Menai after the new secondary school, Ysgol Gyfun, was built nearby in 1953. (AA WSE-38)

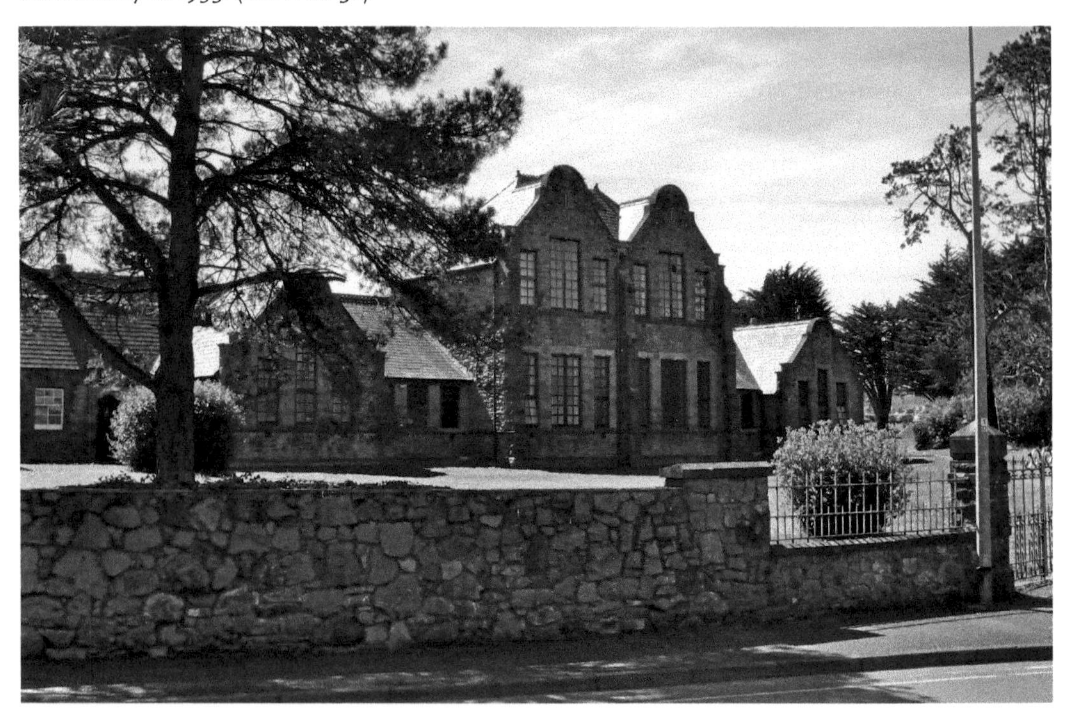

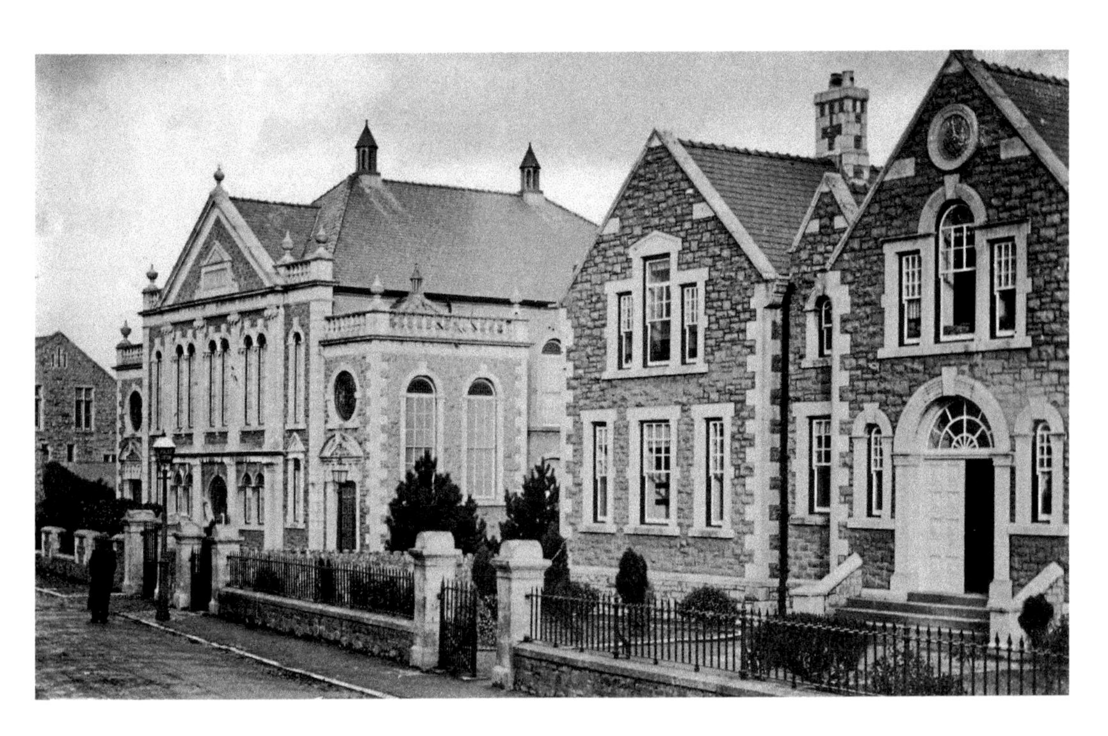

Capel Moreia and Shire Hall, Llangefni, *c.* 1900

The last years of the nineteenth century saw two impressive new buildings erected on Glanhwfa Road. Moreia Calvinistic Methodist chapel was built between 1896 and 1898 to replace an earlier chapel. The older chapel's most famous preacher was John Elias, and this new one is also known as the John Elias Memorial chapel (Capel Coffa John Elias in Welsh). Next to it, the Shire Hall, housing county offices, was built in 1899 to a design by Lloyd Williams of Denbigh. It was extended southwards in 1912. (AA WSE-72)

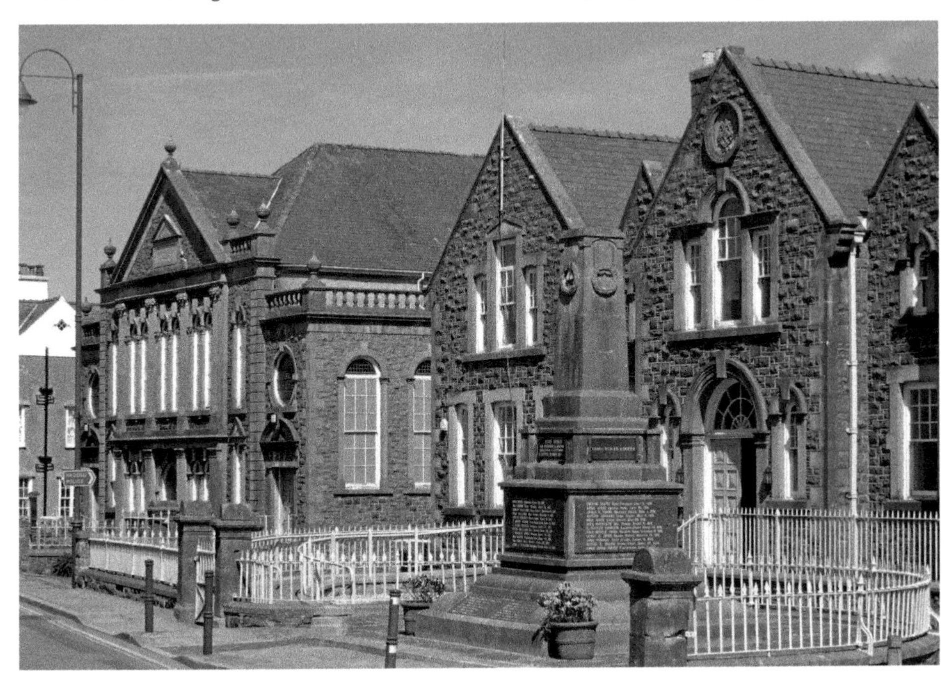

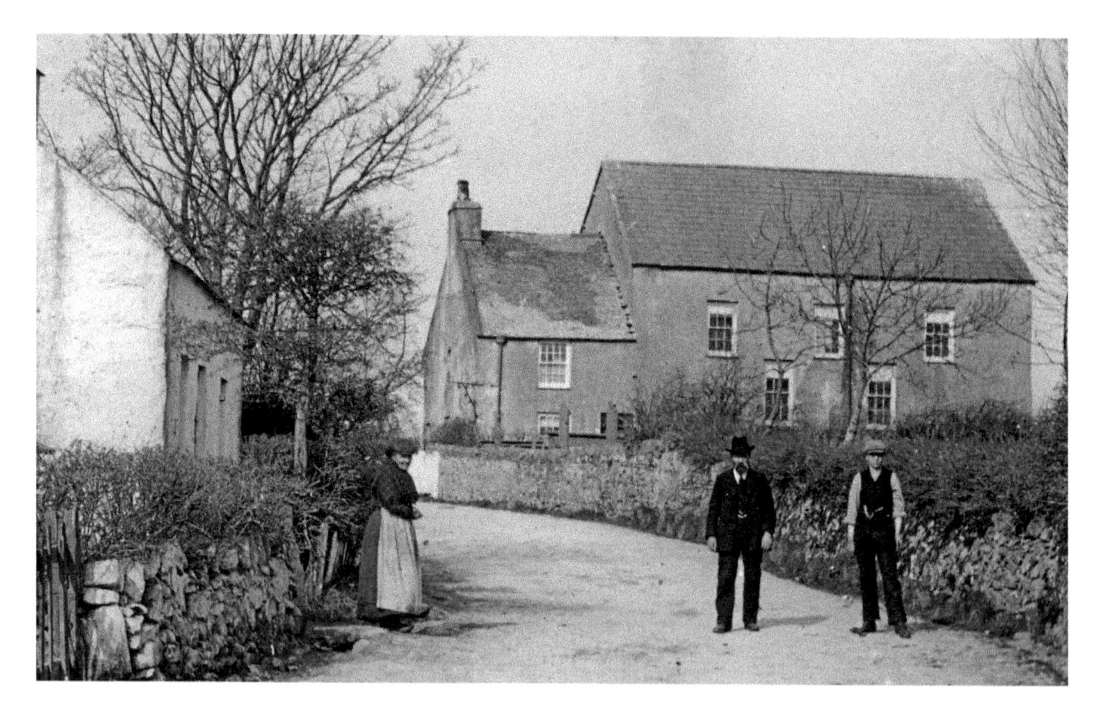

Capel Cildwrn, Llangefni, *c.* 1910

Another famous preacher associated with Llangefni was Christmas Evans. Renowned for his powerful preaching style and vivid imagination, he served at Capel Cildwrn, the first Baptist chapel on Anglesey, from when it was first built in 1791 until 1826. The chapel was rebuilt in 1878, but fell into disuse after Capel Penuel was built in 1897, closer to the town centre. It was reopened as an independent Evangelical chapel in the 1980s. The building itself has changed little, but the road is considerably wider and busier. (AA WSM-383-45)

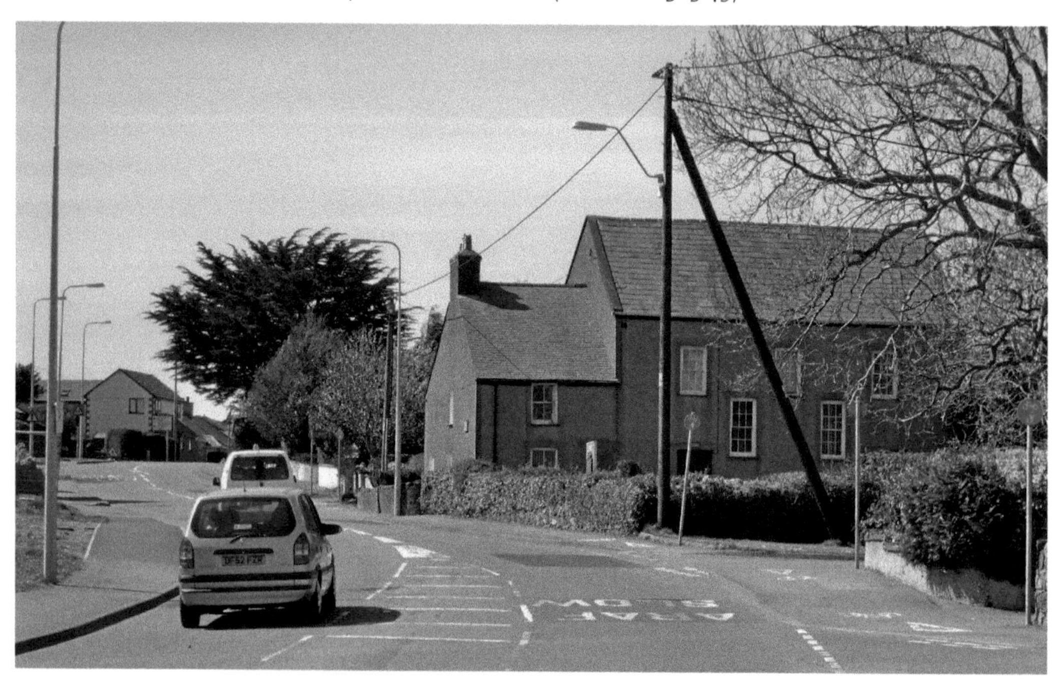

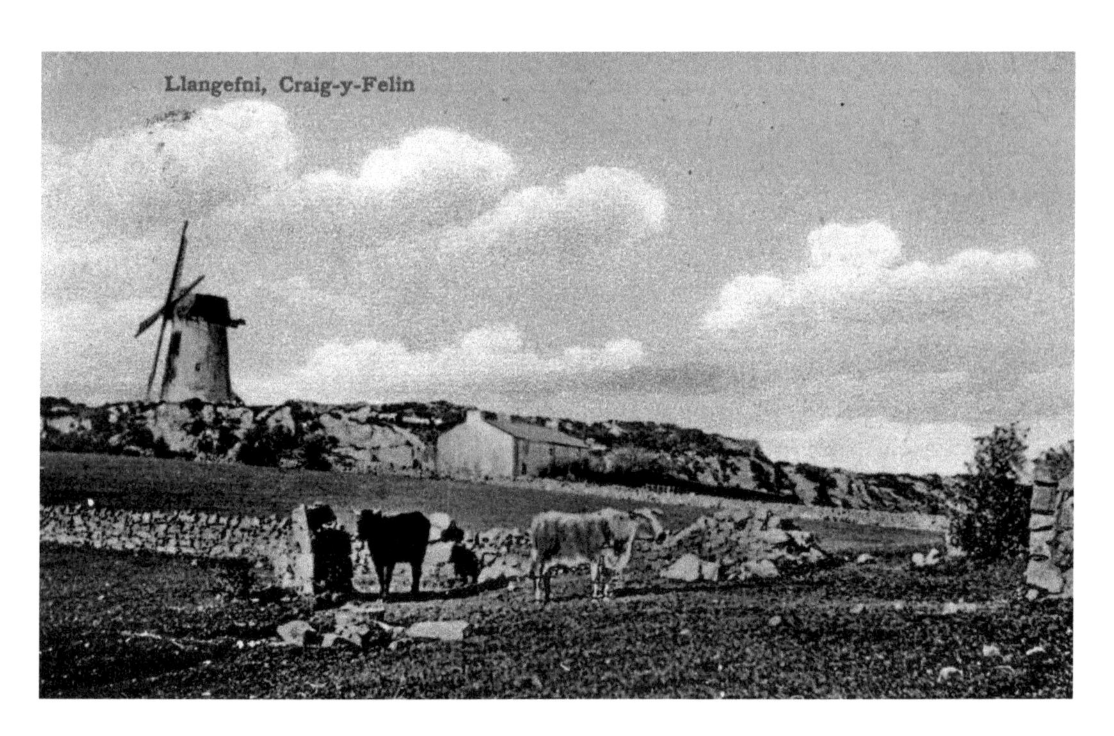

Melin Wynt-y-Craig Windmill, Llangefni, 1912
The windmill in Llangefni stands above the town on a rocky outcrop and can be seen for miles around. Built around 1830, it was in an excellent place to capture the wind, but the steep paths leading up to it were problematic for farmers bringing their grain for milling. It closed in 1893, and began to deteriorate. Its prominent position is also excellent for its second life, initiated in the late 1990s, as a mobile phone mast. (AA WSE-284)

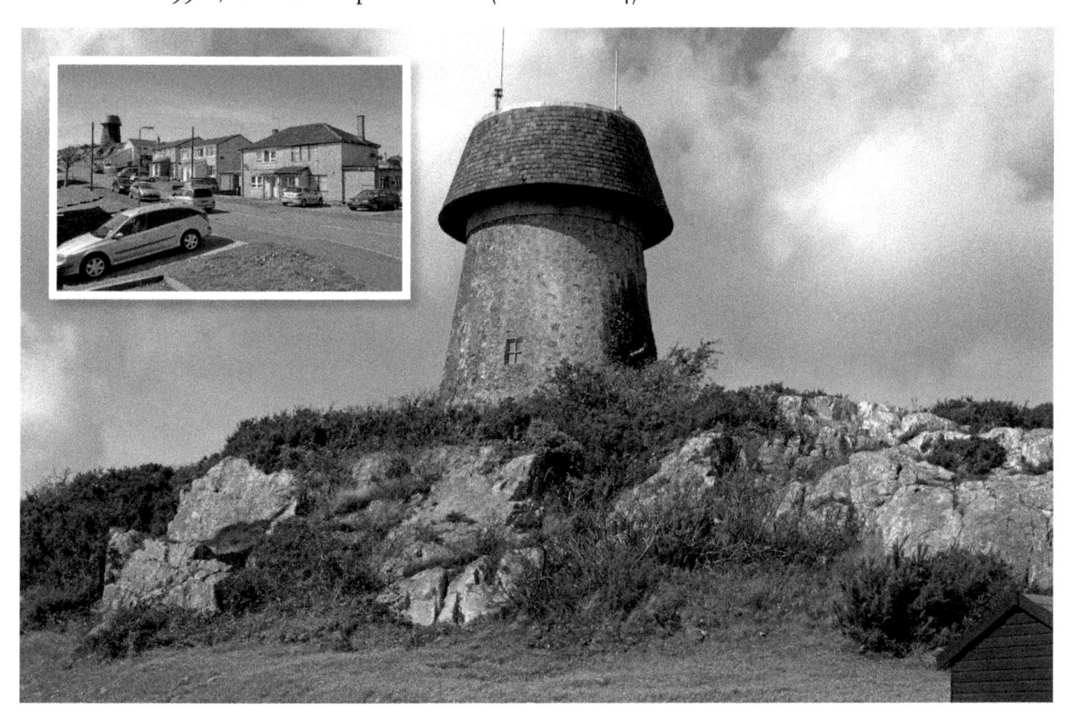

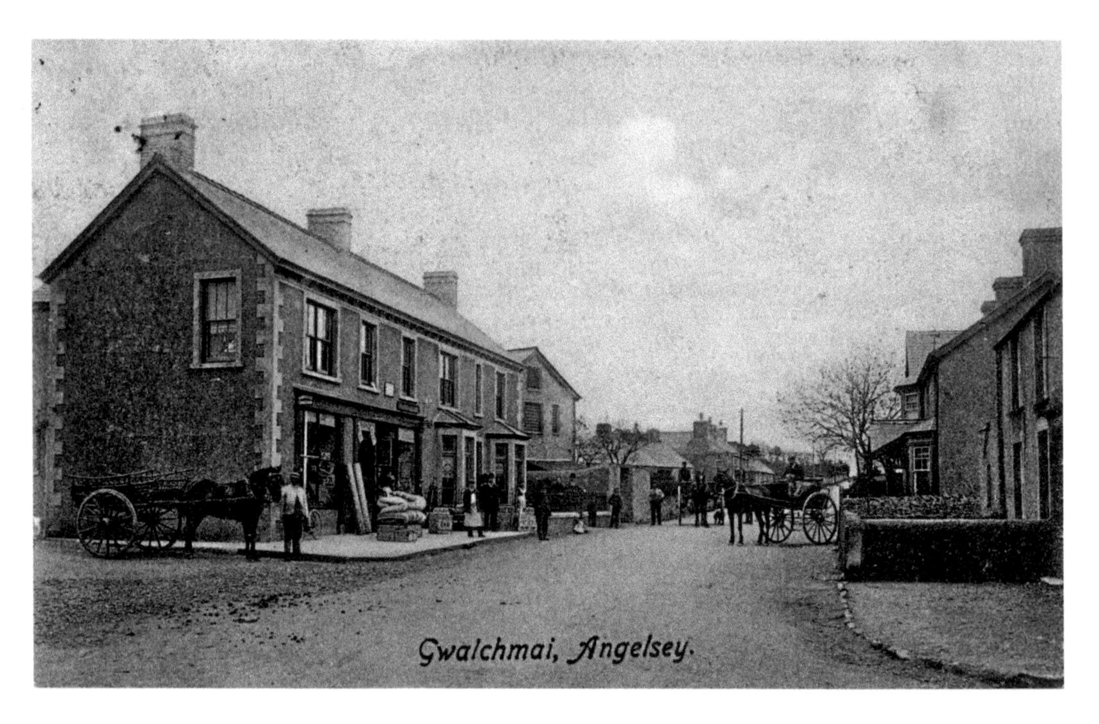

London Road, Gwalchmai, 1909
Named after the twelfth-century royal court poet Gwalchmai ap Meilyr (whose portrait appears on the local pub's sign), this substantial village lies on the old main road from the Menai Bridge to Holyhead. The post office and draper's/grocer's shop at the left was run for decades by David Robert Jones. The Gwalchmai Hotel, formerly known as the Red Horse, lies across the road. (AA WSJ-18-19)

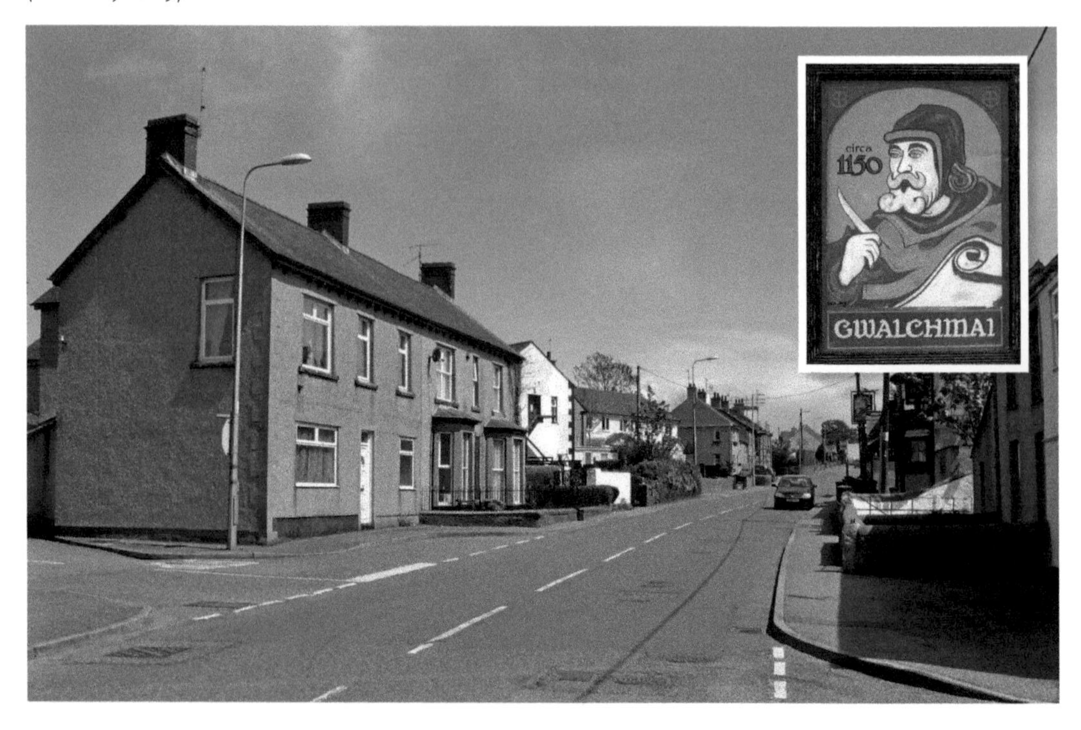

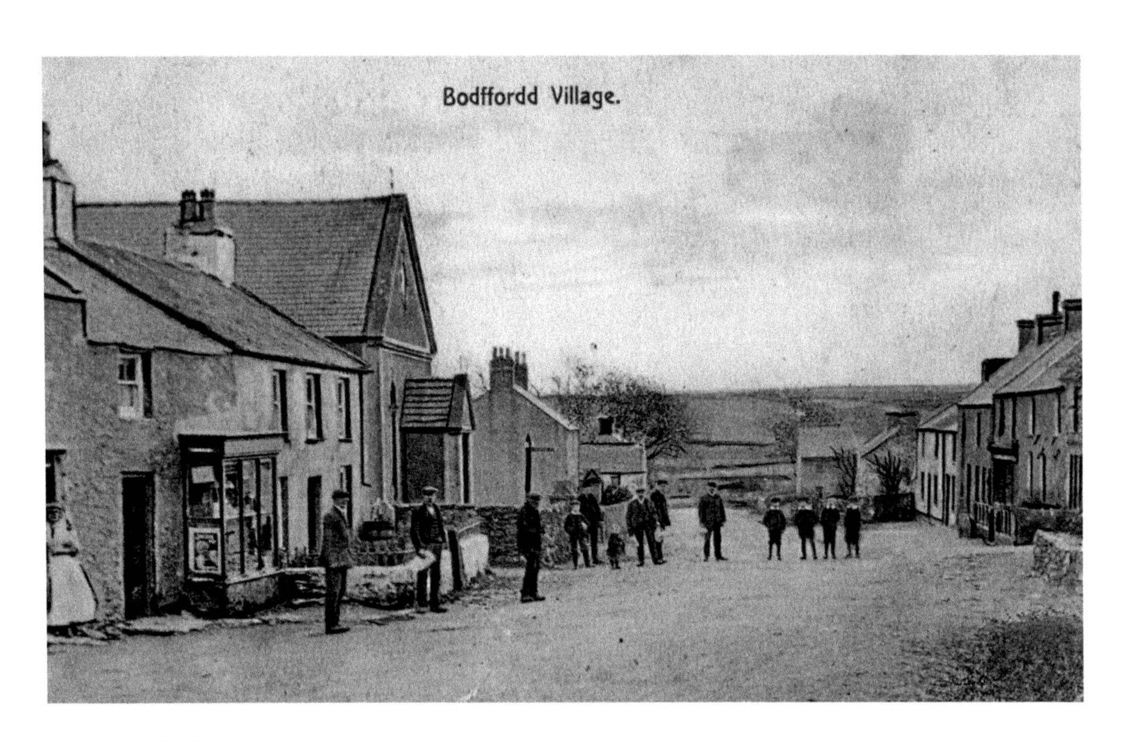

Bodffordd Village, *c.* 1910
In the nineteenth century, Bodffordd was a vibrant agricultural village, with several inns catering for drovers taking cattle to Llangefni market, and farmers taking grain to the nearby Frogwy wind- and watermills. By the time this picture was taken, all the inns had been converted to houses or shops. At the left, next to the post office, is the Baptist chapel, Capel Sardis. The current building was erected in 1895 to replace an older nearby chapel, built in 1814 and rebuilt in 1865. (AA WSJ-5-18)

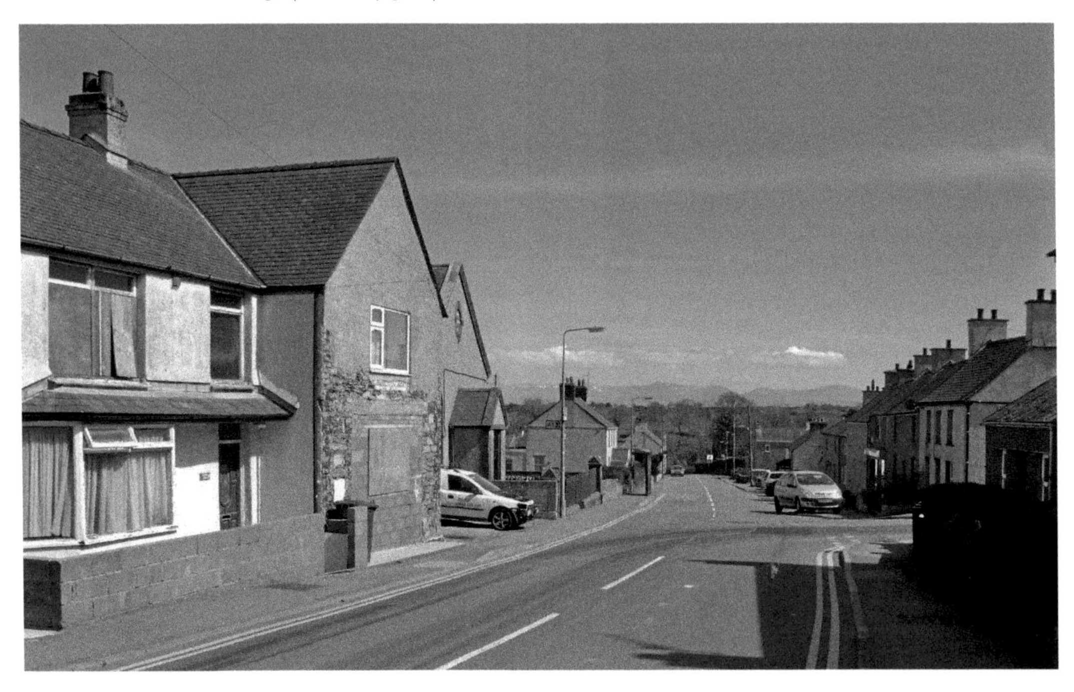

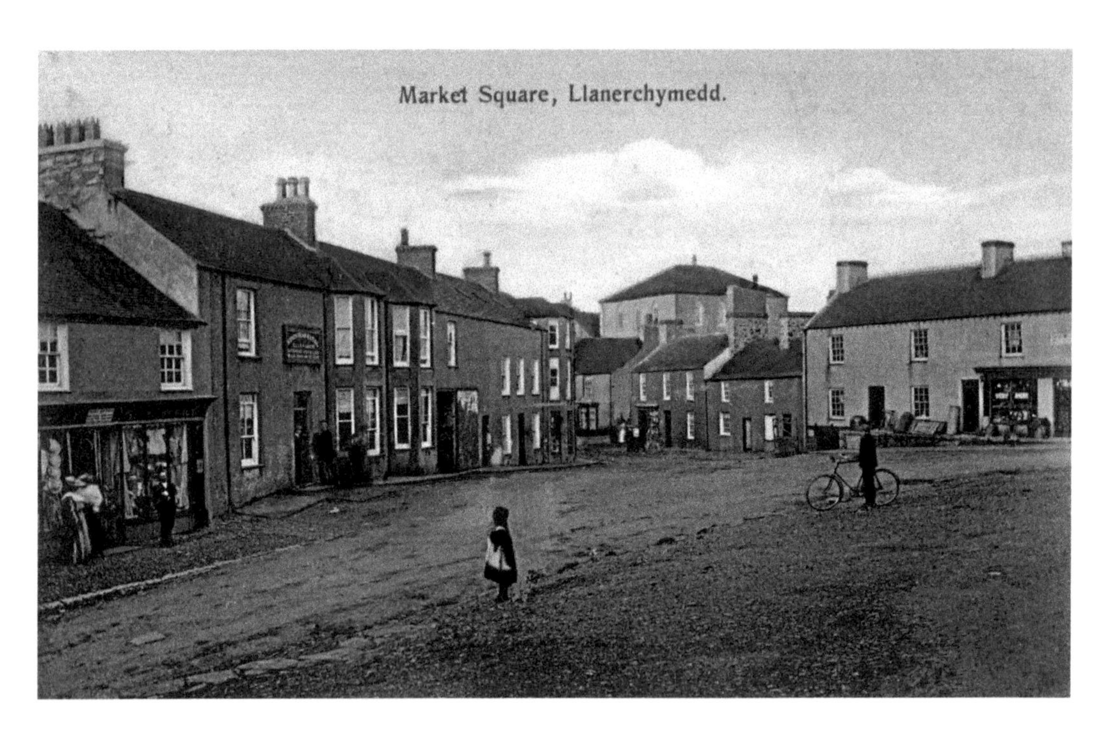

Market Square, Llanerchymedd, Early Twentieth Century

Llanerchymedd was the main market town of Anglesey, and traders plied their wares here in the market square every Wednesday. The right to hold a market was granted by Oliver Cromwell in 1657, adding to the fairs that were held several times a year since medieval days. In the eighteenth century, a market was established in Llangefni, which gradually took prominence, to the detriment of the Llanerchymedd market. The old post office and Kings Head Hotel can be seen to the left above. (AA WSH-9 -32)

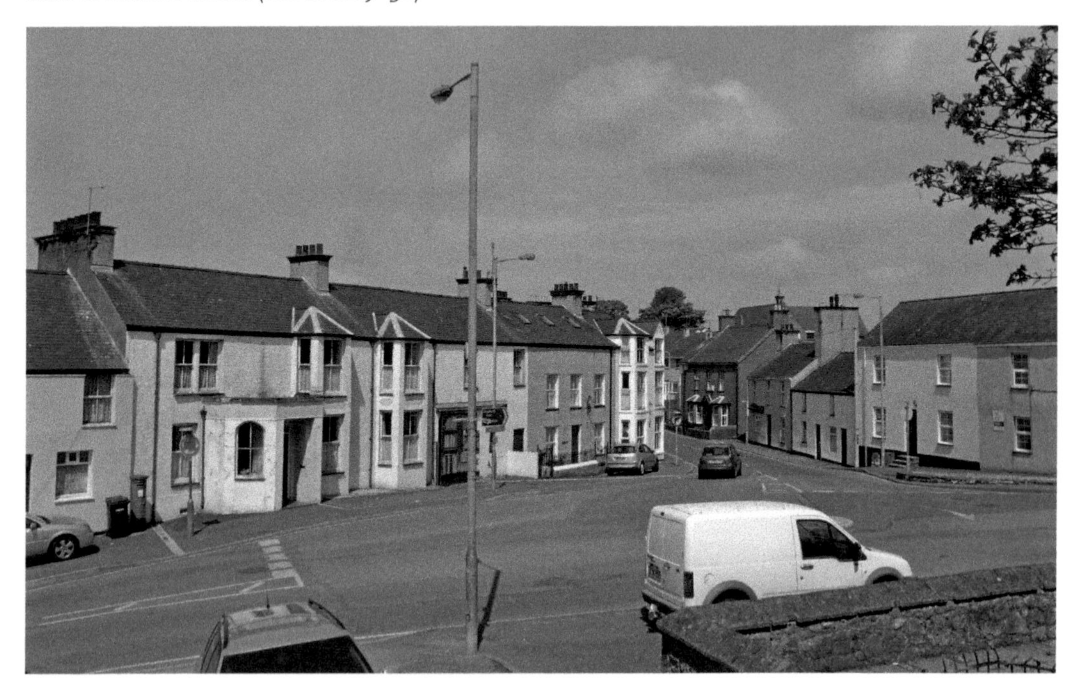

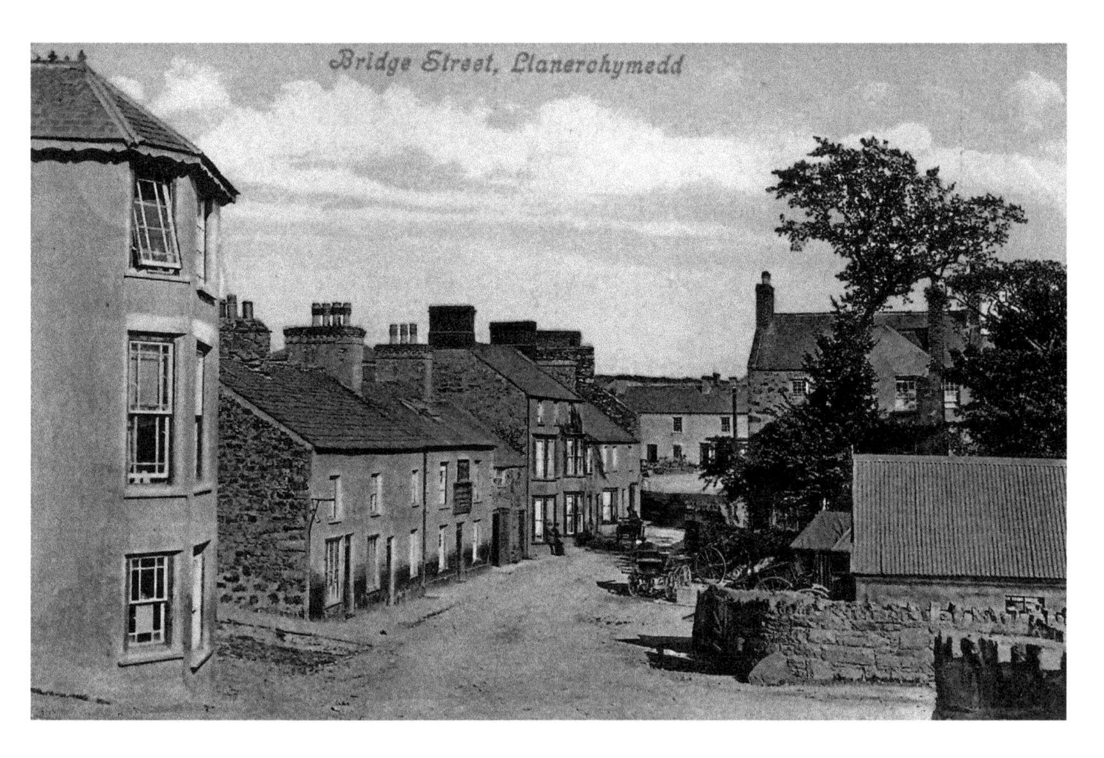

Bridge Street, Llanerchymedd, 1905
Viewed from the entrance to the railway station, Bridge Street was dominated on the left by the now demolished Anglesey Central Hotel. Further up the street was the Menai Bridge Inn (with the sign). The taller building beyond that, Alaw House, was occupied by the Williams sisters, Mary and Kate, who had recently turned their brother's butcher shop into a Temperance café. It closed in 1920.

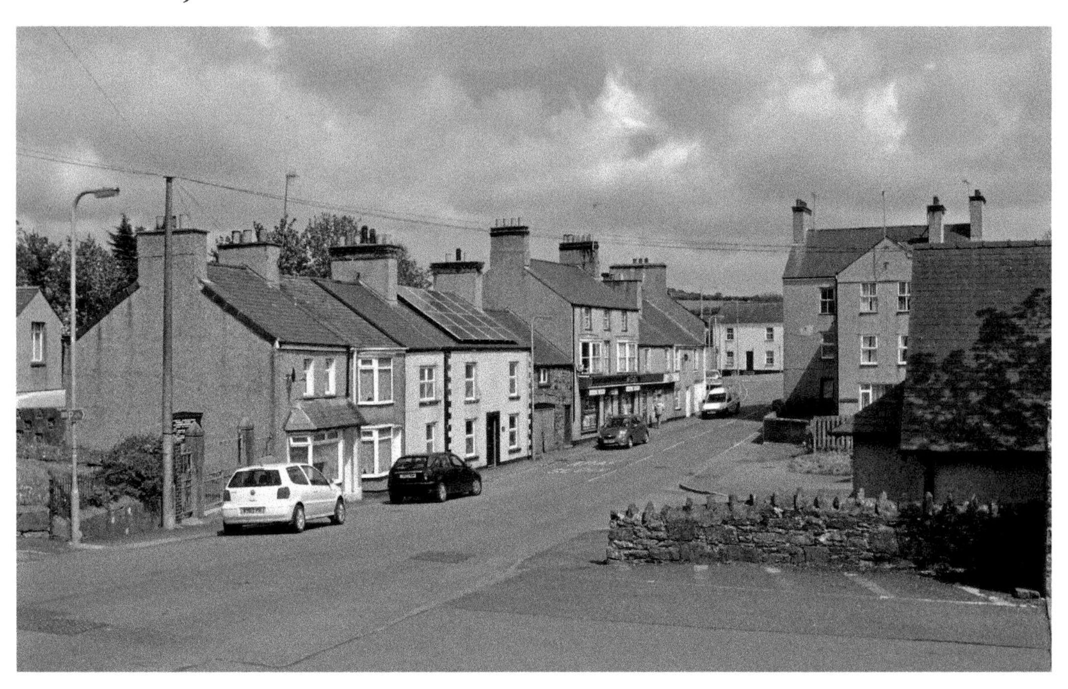

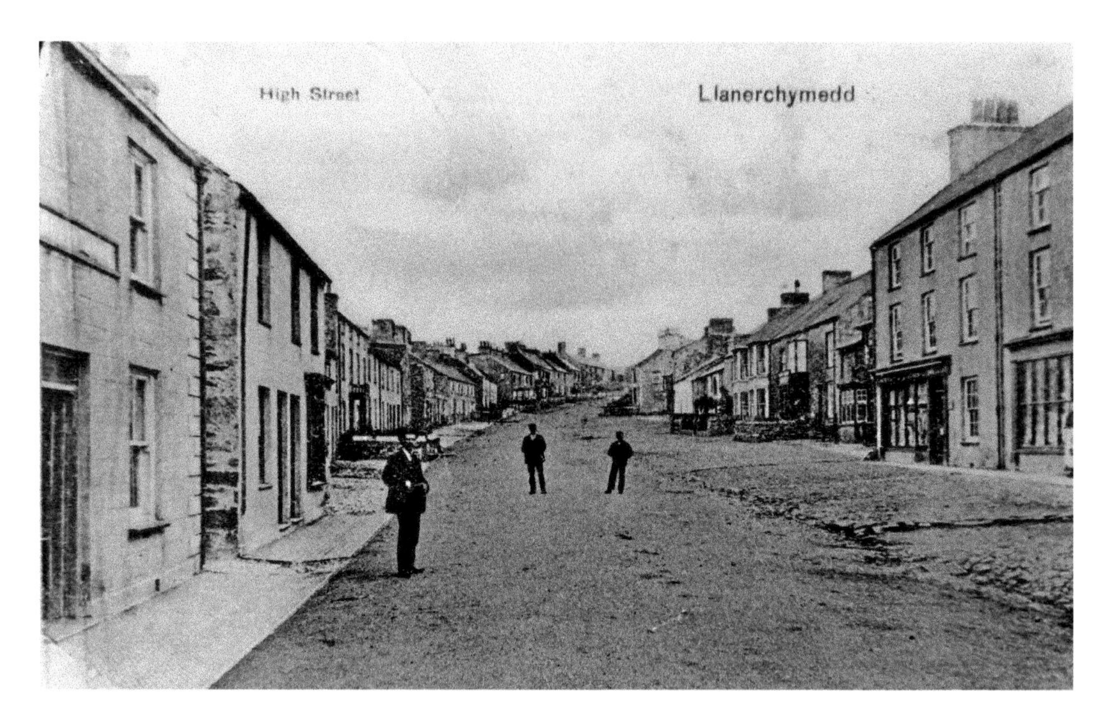

High Street, Llanerchymedd, Early Twentieth Century
In the mid-nineteenth century, Llanerchymedd had more than 250 shoemakers, many of them living on High Street, shown above. Their main trade was supplying shoes to miners at Parys Mountain. However, by the beginning of the twentieth century, the easy import of factory-made shoes from England meant only a few were left. This end of the High Street contained many of the town's pubs and inns, including the Druid Arms on the left and the Bull Hotel on the right. (AA WSH-9-23)

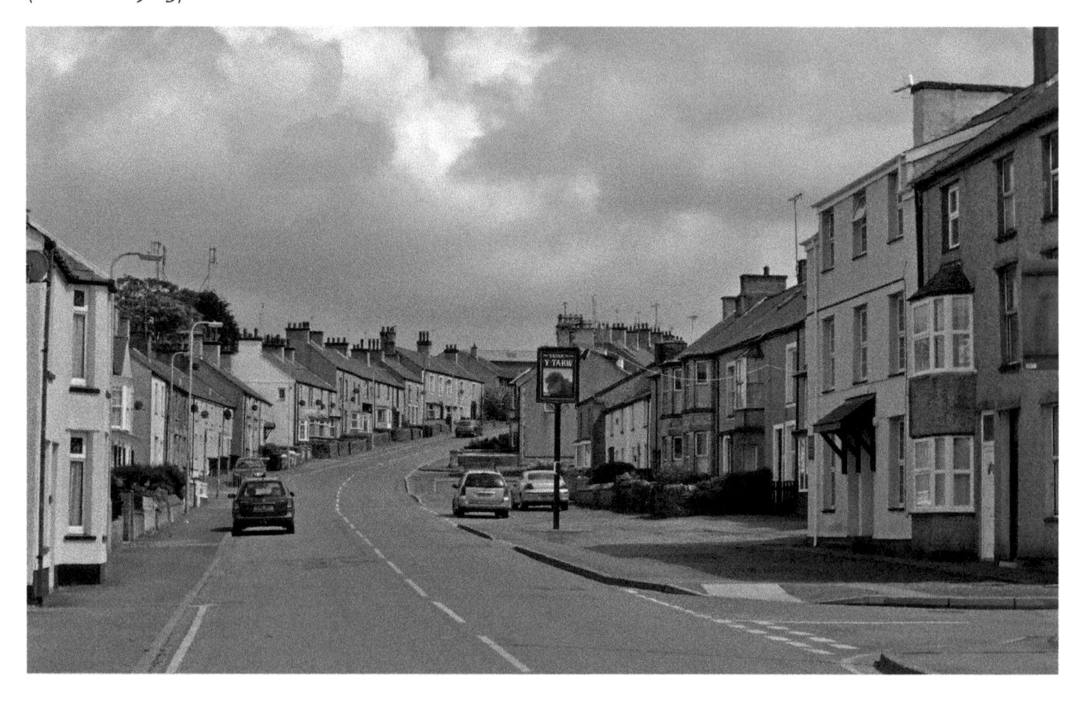

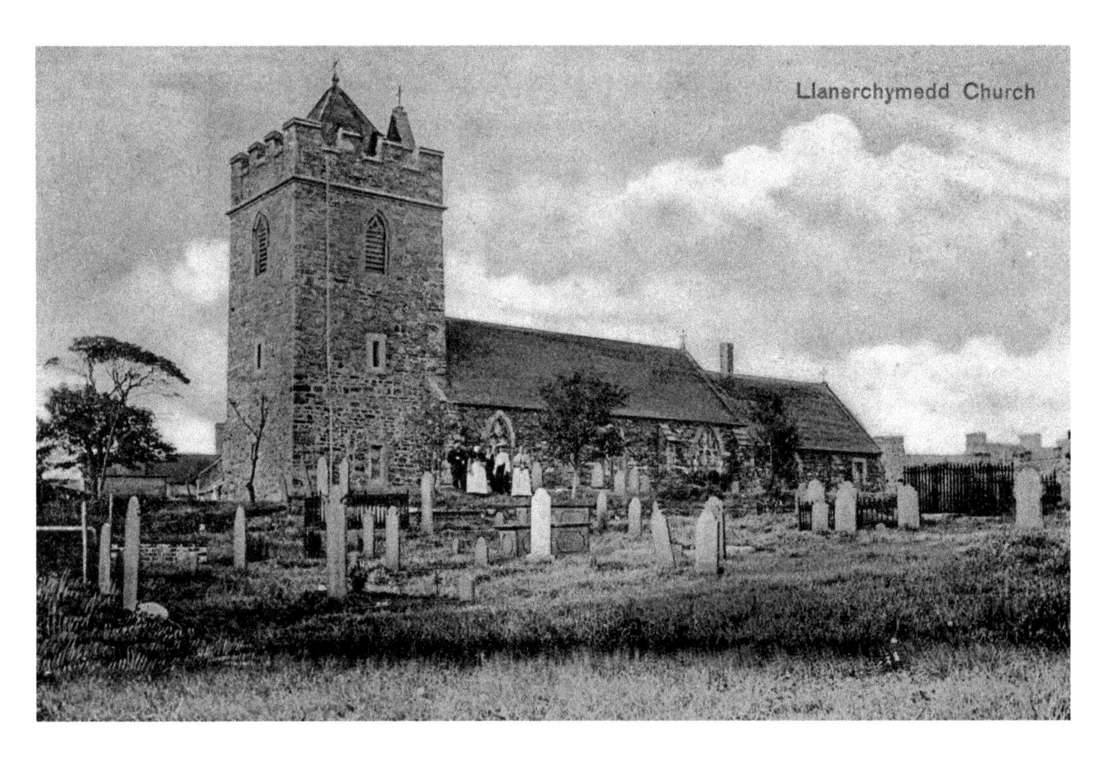

St Mary's Church, Llanerchymedd, 1908
A church has stood on this site since medieval days, described in early nineteenth century directories as 'neat and ancient'. However, the present building dates to the 1840s, with just the base of the tower, the doorway and the nave surviving from the old building. The church was rebuilt with money provided by public subscription, which raised £1,000 (about £700,000 in today's money). (AA WSH-9-2)

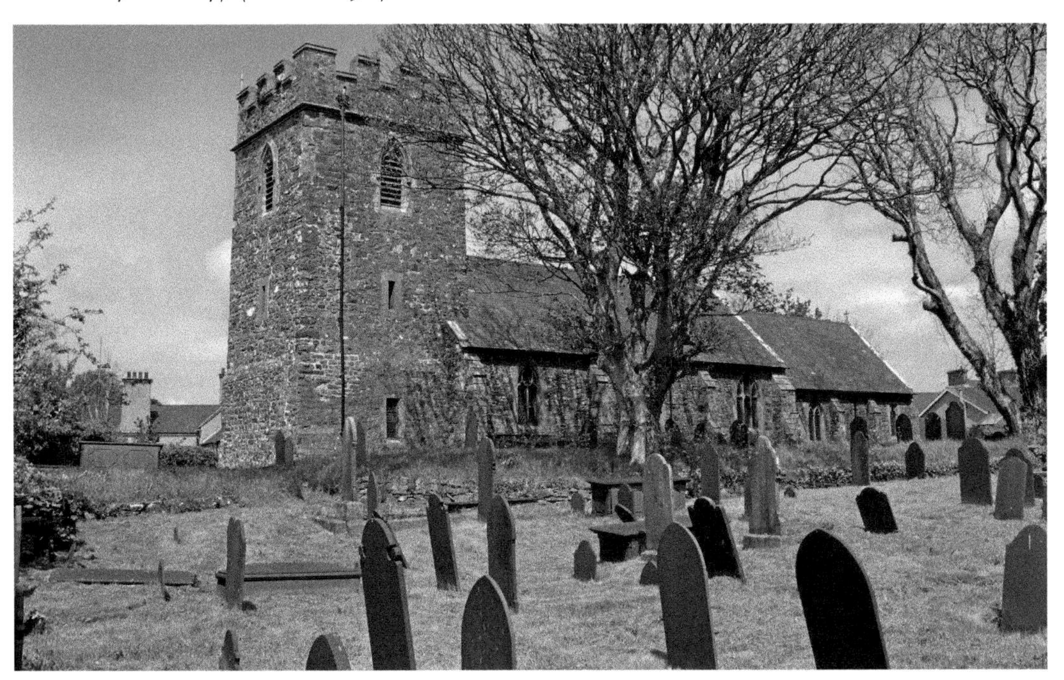

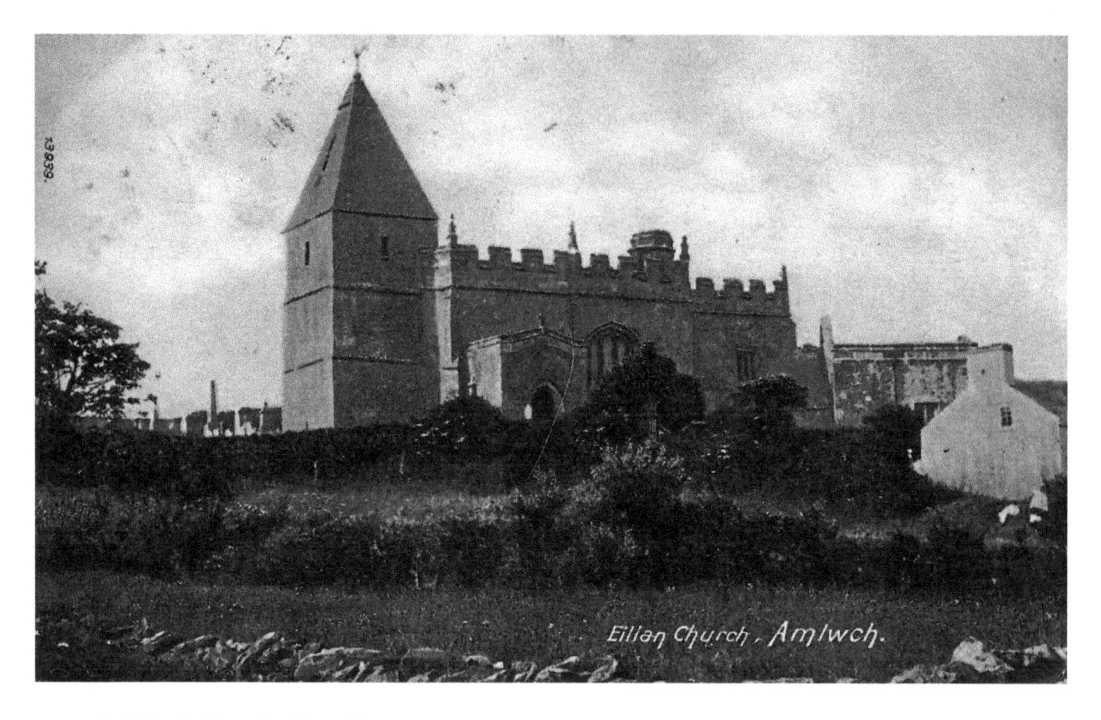

St Eilian's Church, Llaneilian, *c.* 1909

Even though it is in a fairly out-of-the-way place, St Eilian's church is well-known on Anglesey for its unusual pyramidal spire and the wooden carvings and paintings inside. The tower dates to the twelfth century, while the nave and chancel were rebuilt in the fifteenth century. Inside, the rood screen separating the nave and the chancel is exquisitely carved and bears a painting of a skeleton with a scythe and the inscription 'Colyn Angau yw Pechod' ('Sin is the sting of death').

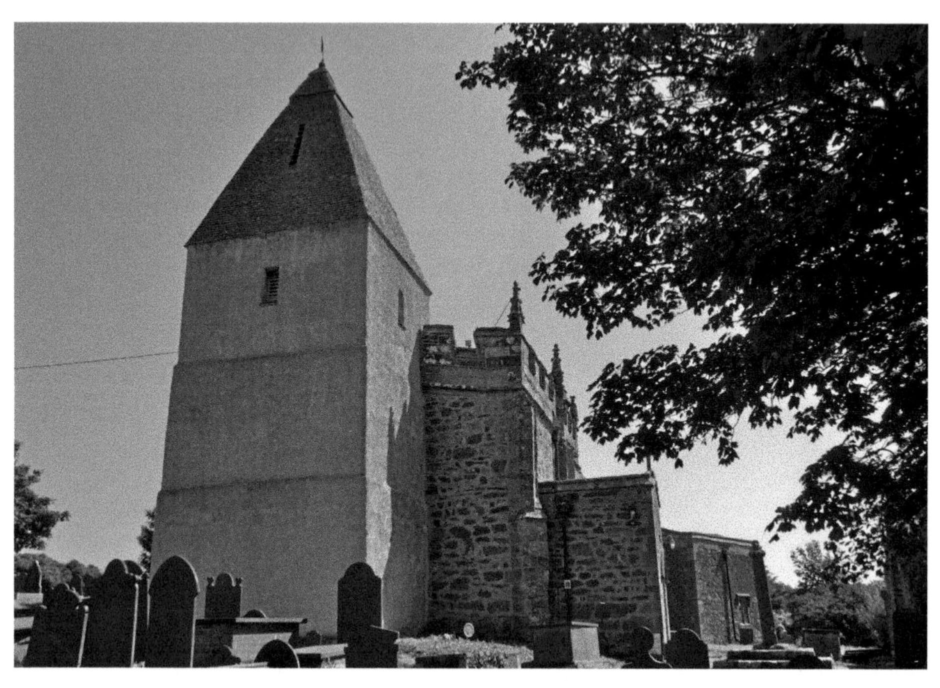

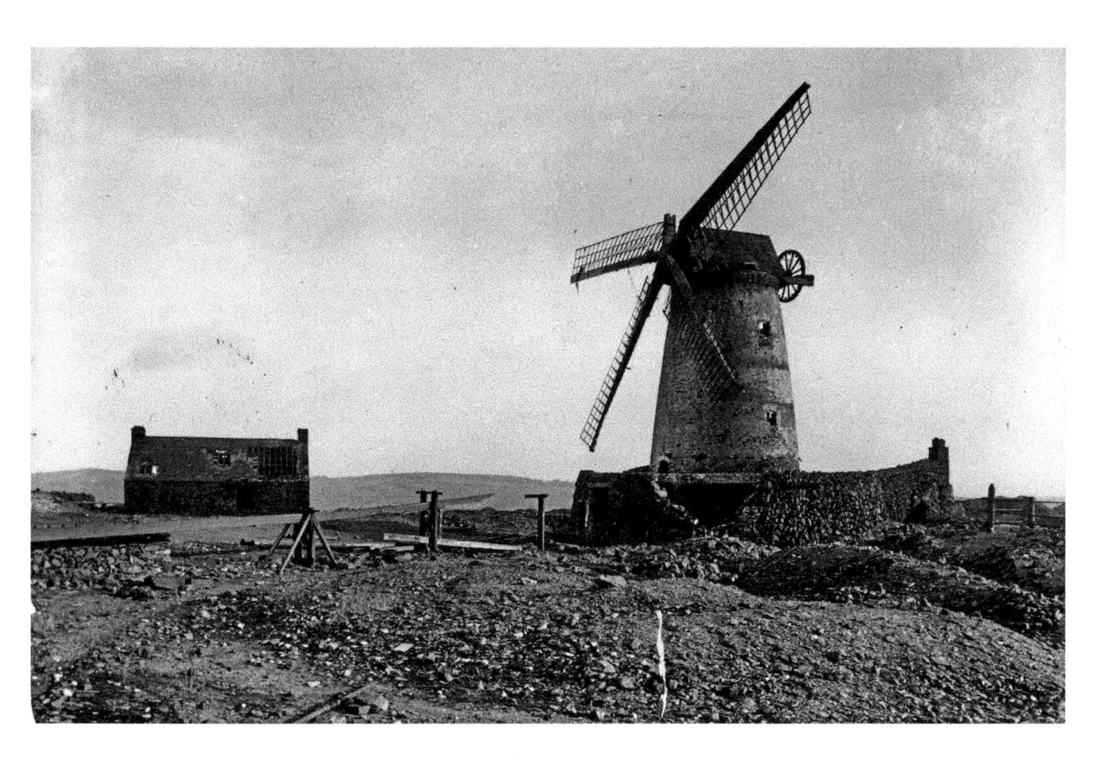

Parys Mountain Windmill, Late 1900s
Standing atop Parys Mountain, once the site of the world's largest copper mine, this windmill was built in 1878 to assist in pumping water out from the mines. Initially, this was to prevent flooding so miners could access the deep shafts. Later, it fed copper-rich water from the old shafts into precipitation ponds, where the copper could be recovered. The mine closed in 1904, and the windmill and buildings soon became dilapidated. (AA WSB-31)

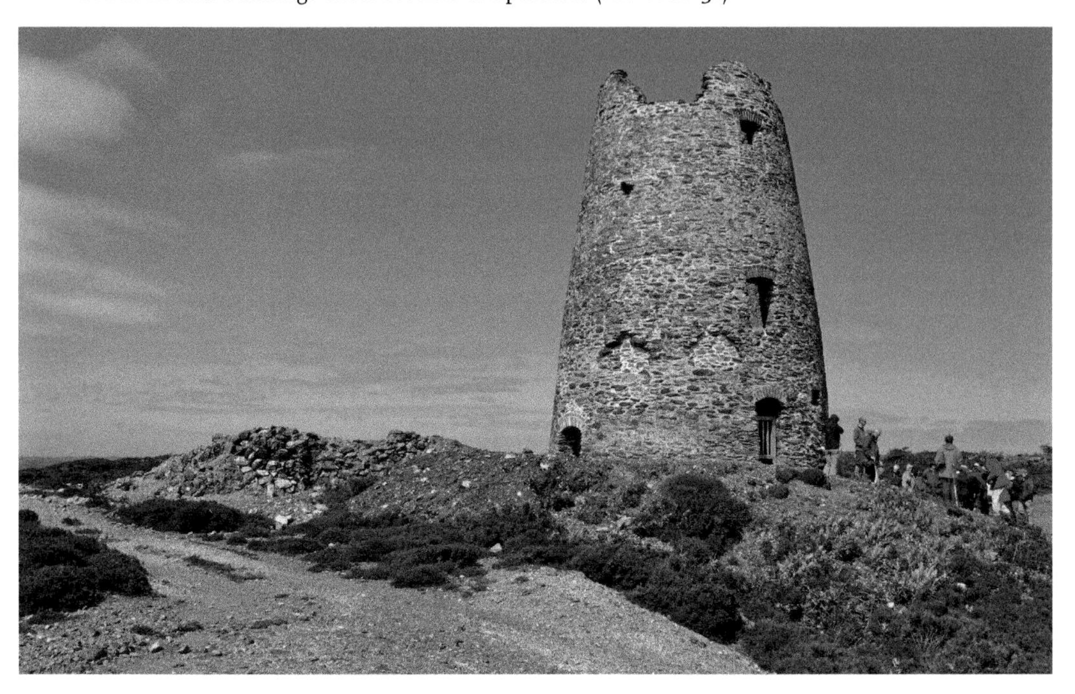

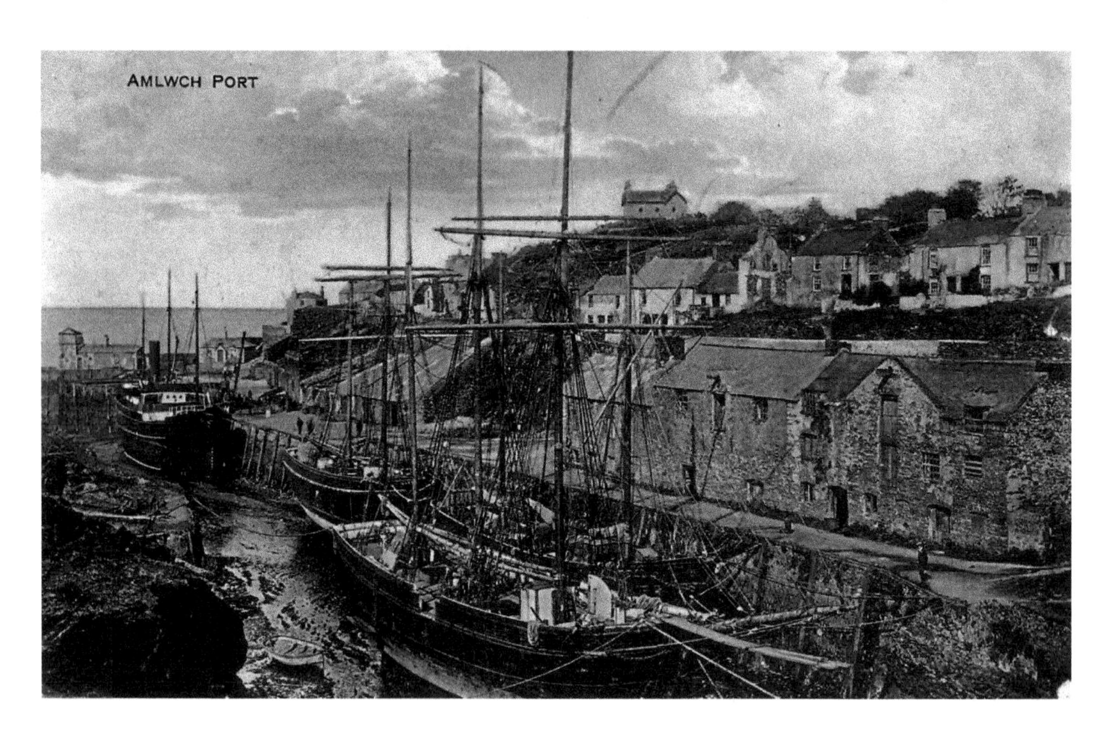

Amlwch Harbour, *c.* 1915

In the early eighteenth century, the harbour at Amlwch was just a little-used cove between two steep rocks. However, the discovery of a rich vein of copper at nearby Parys Mountain in 1768 transformed it into the main port for shipping the ore. The harbour was improved in 1793, allowing it to accommodate up to thirty ships. Activity at the port declined in the second half of the nineteenth century, along with the mine output, although some shipbuilding continued. The port was revived in the 1970s and 1980s with ships to Shell's offshore oil terminal.

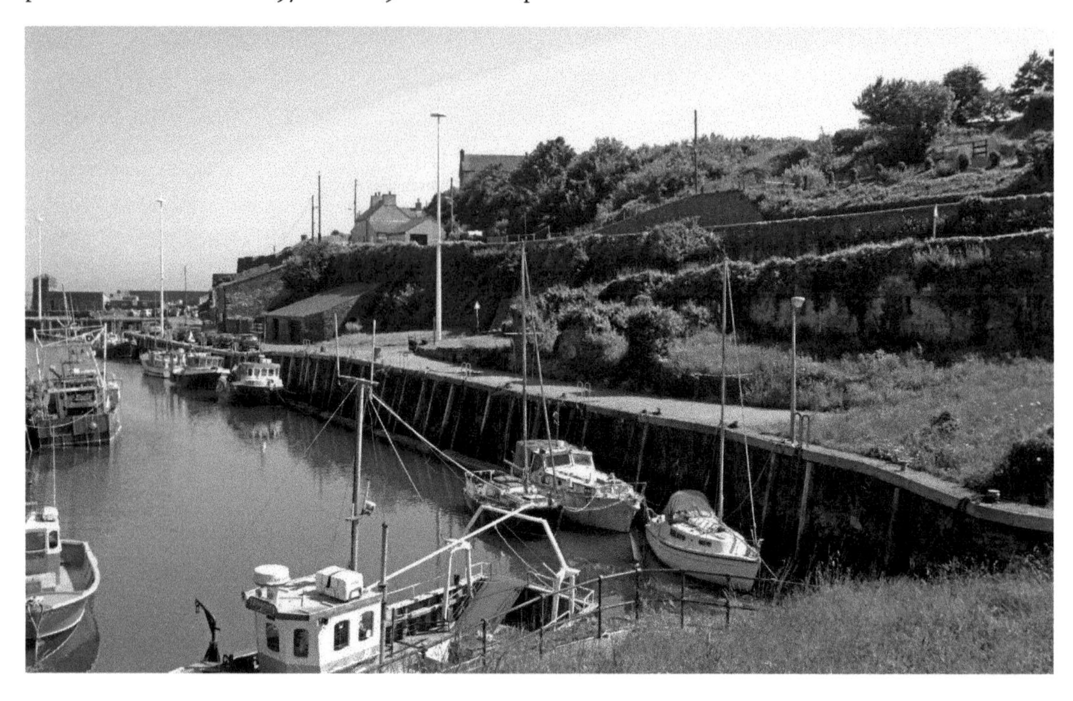

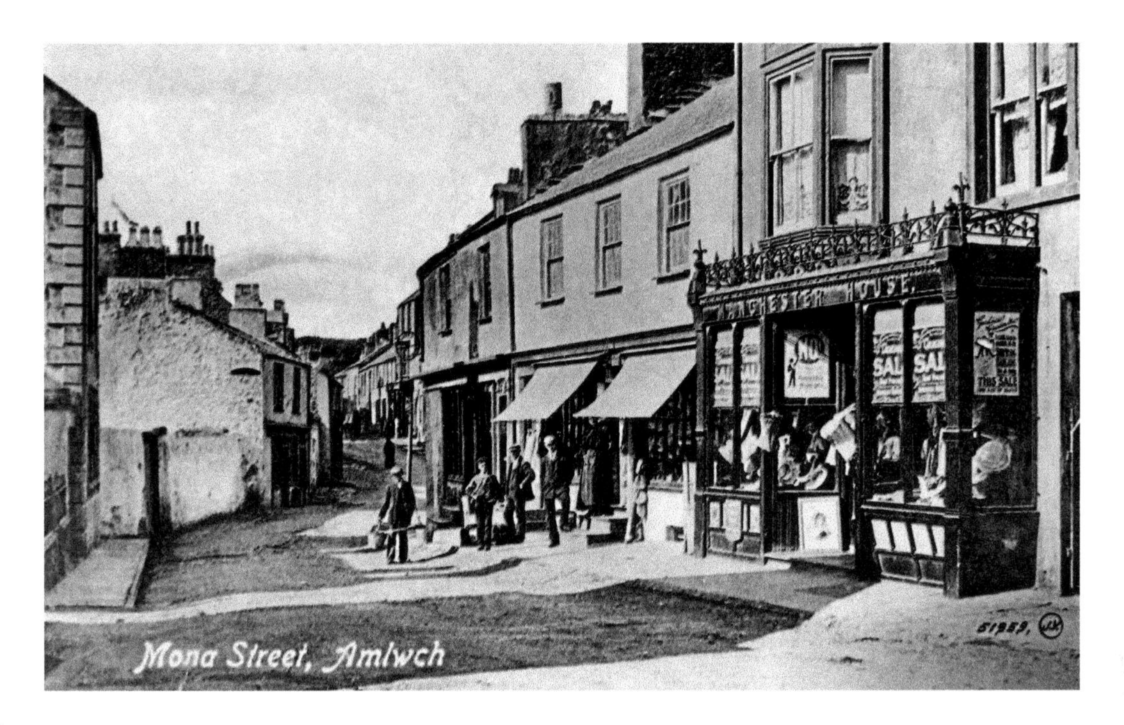

Mona Street and Manchester House, Amlwch, 1905

The decorative shopfront of Manchester House highlights the wares of the draper and dressmaker Edward Jones Evans. He was the son of a wheelwright from Merionethshire, who learned the drapery trade and moved to Amlwch to set up his own shop. He also ran the grocery shop next door. It was later managed by his son, Gwilym Rees Evans, and grandson, Derek Edward Evans. It closed sometime after 1991, and is now an optician's and a kebab shop. (AA WSB-248)

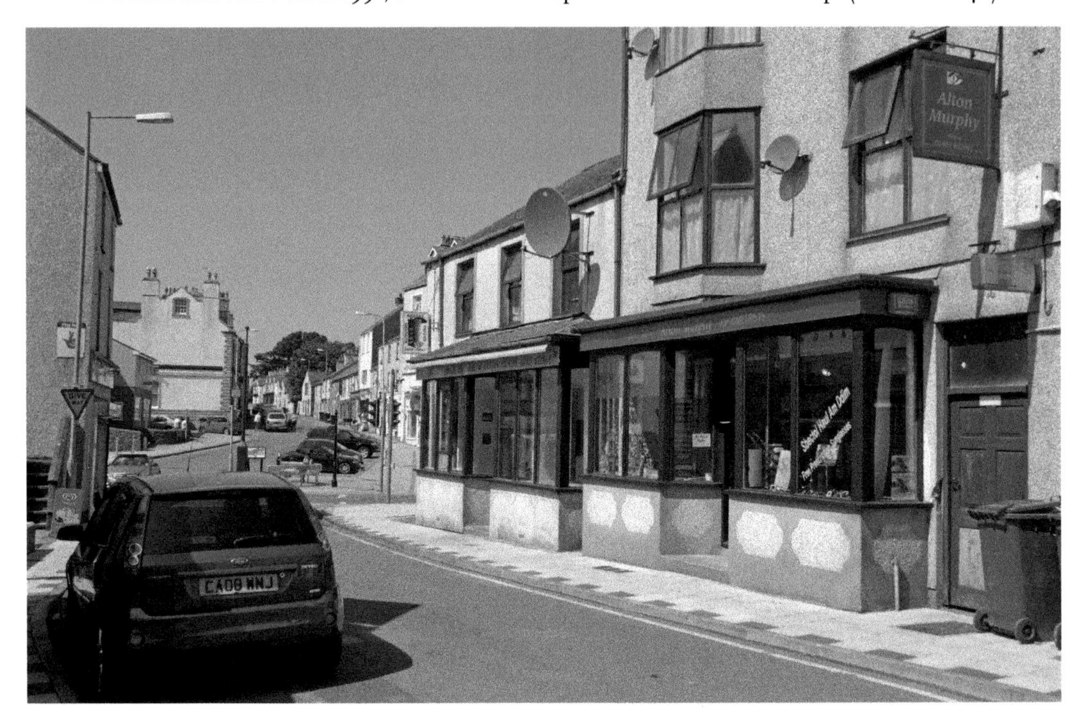

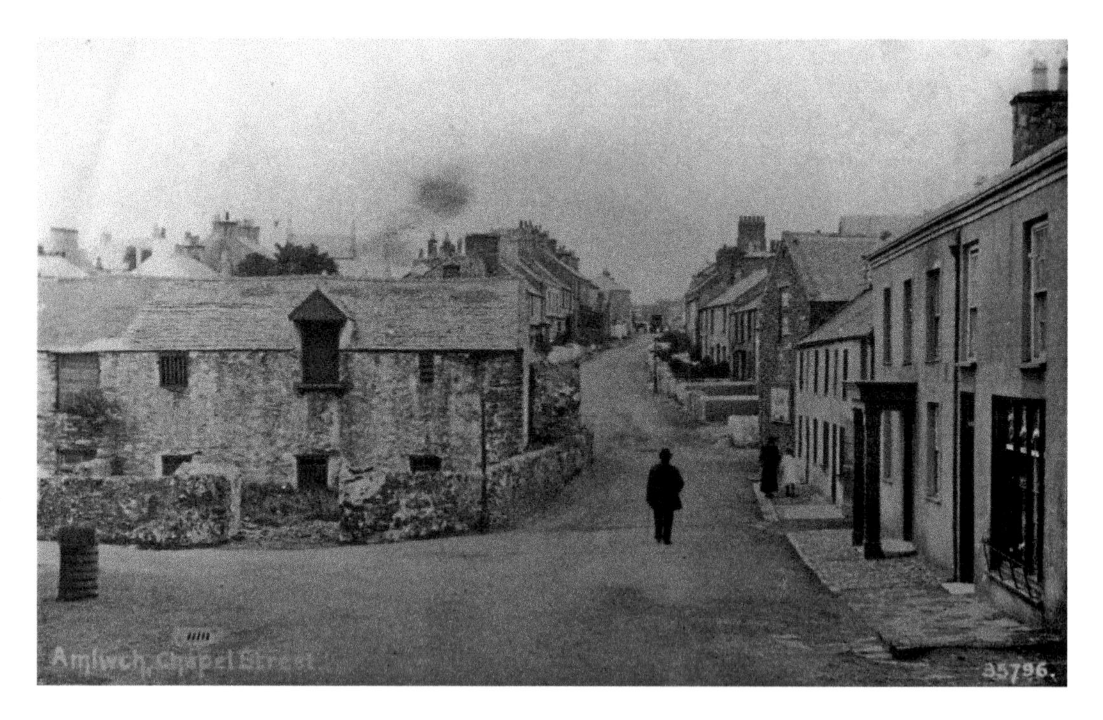

Chapel Street, Amlwch, Early Twentieth Century

The corner of Chapel and Quay Streets, near the port, was the site of the Amlwch Brewery, the largest in town. It was built around 1780 and took its water from the nearby St Elaeth's well (which reputedly had curative powers). The brewery covered a large area, with sections of the building for different tasks. The part visible above was the storehouse for the malted grain, awaiting milling. The company ceased brewing in May 1904, and the buildings had disappeared by 1924. (AA WSB-120)

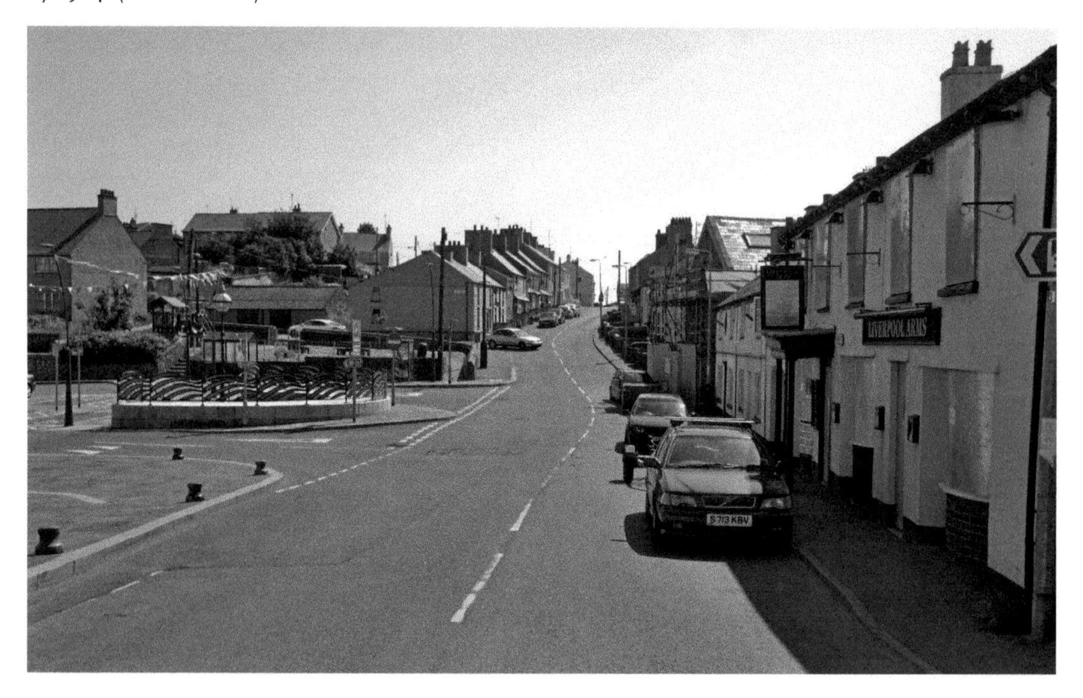

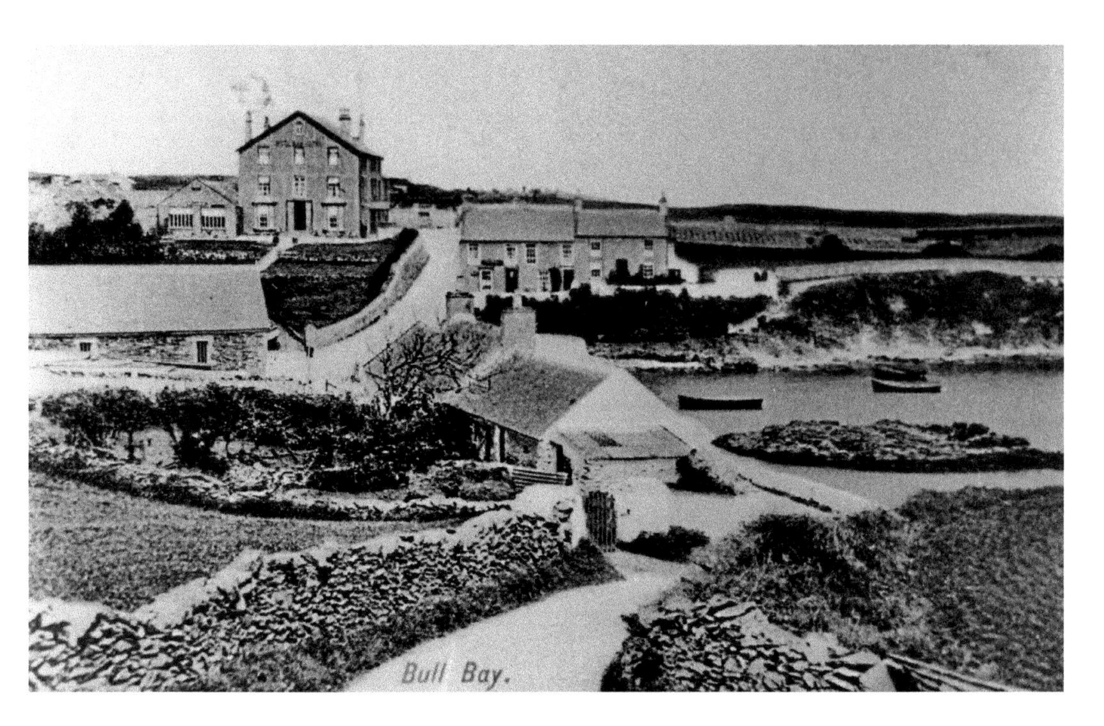

Bull Bay, Early Twentieth Century

Known as Porth Llechog in Welsh ('sheltered bay'), the English name of this bay is derived from the name of a small pool in the bay, Pwll y Tarw ('the bull's pool'). The above photograph shows the original lifeboat station on the left. Opened in 1868, it housed several different lifeboats until 1904, when a new lifeboat house was built on the far side of the bay to accommodate a larger boat. That station closed in 1924 and the newer building was demolished, although the old one survives. (AA WSB-17)

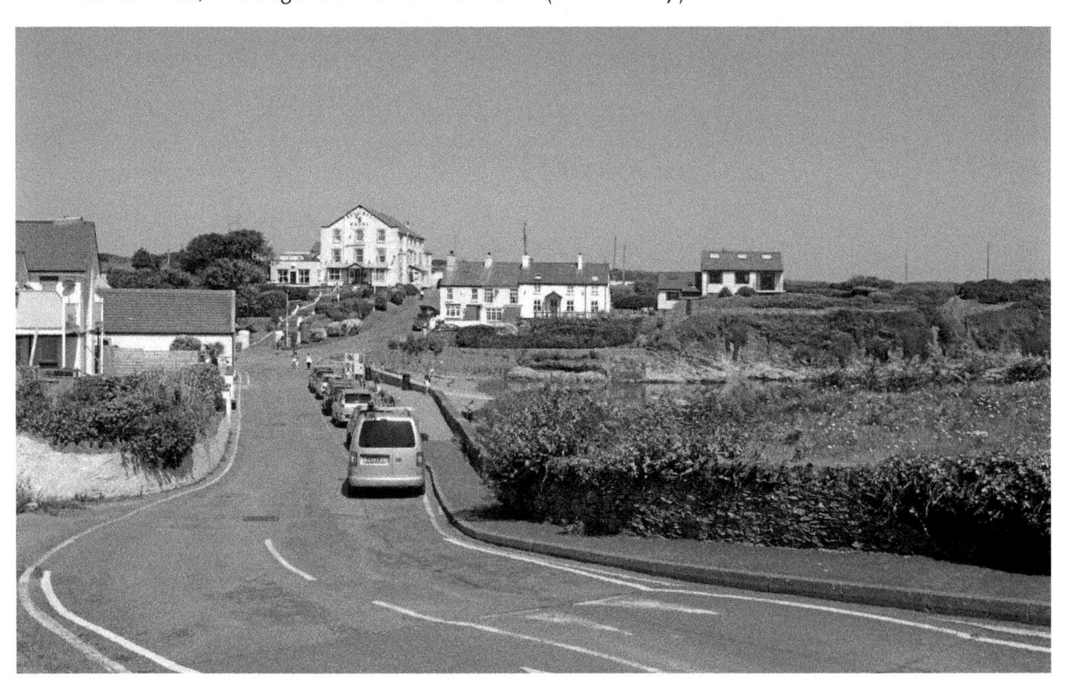

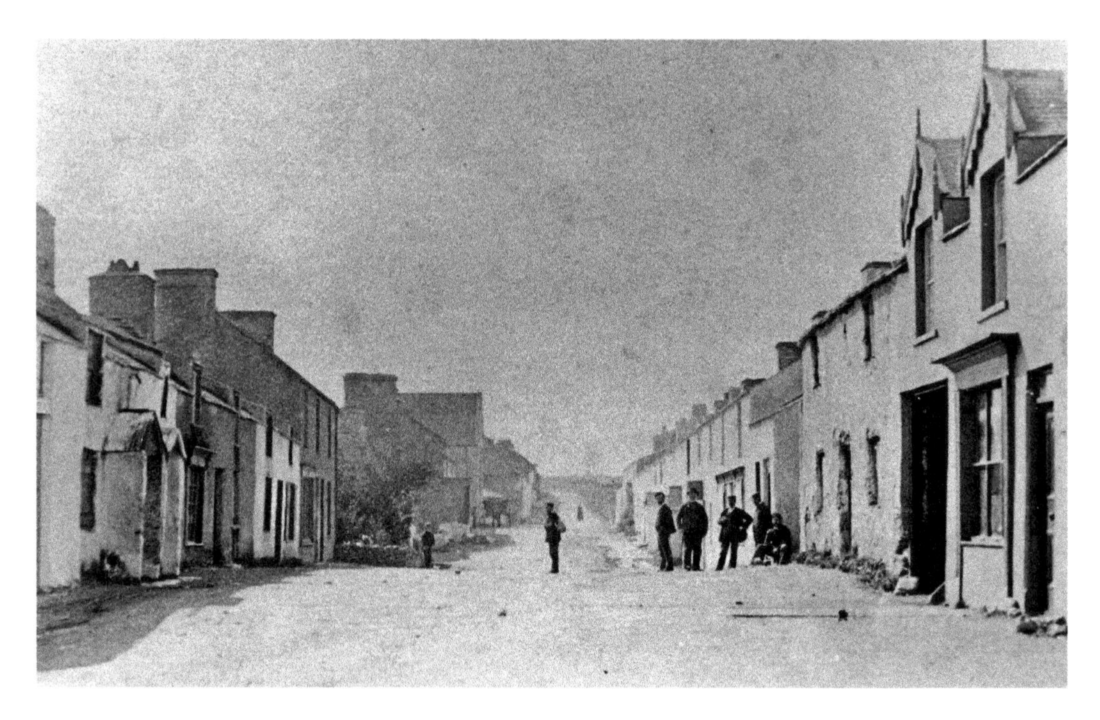

High Street, Cemaes, Late Nineteenth Century
The most northerly village in Wales, it was originally called Cemais, which in Welsh means 'river bend' and presumably refers to the meanders in the nearby River Wygyr. This part of the High Street has previously been called Bethel Street, Chapel Street and Post Office Square. The old post office was the shop on the left just before the trees, and the Bethel Independent chapel can be seen further down the road. This picture was taken before the village hall (the tower on the right below) was built in 1889. (AA WSH-5-83-20)

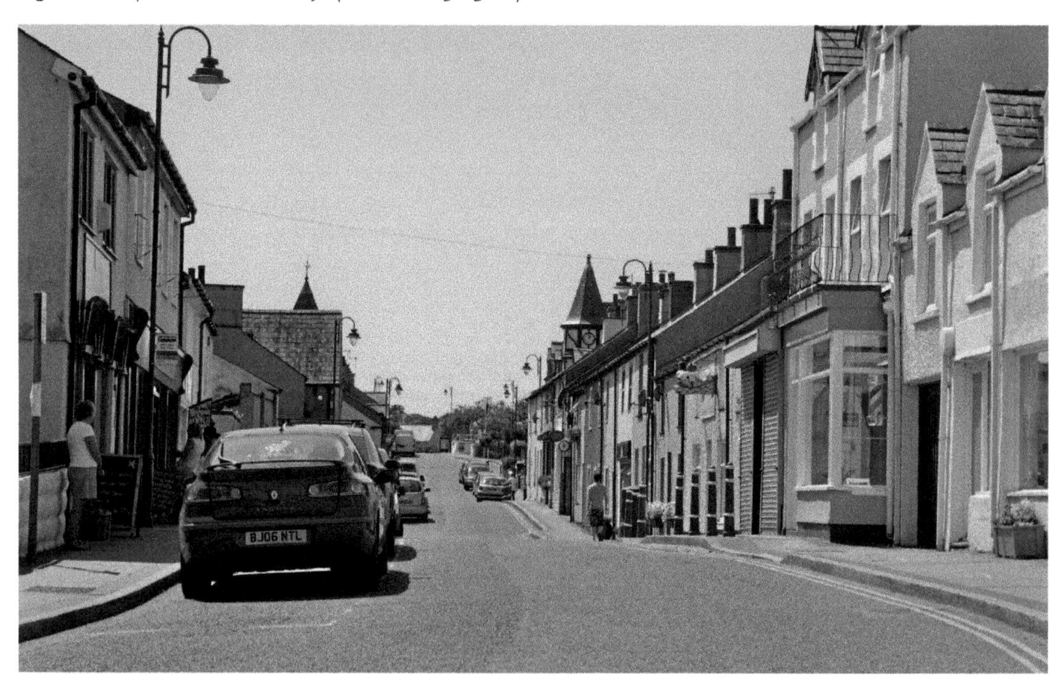

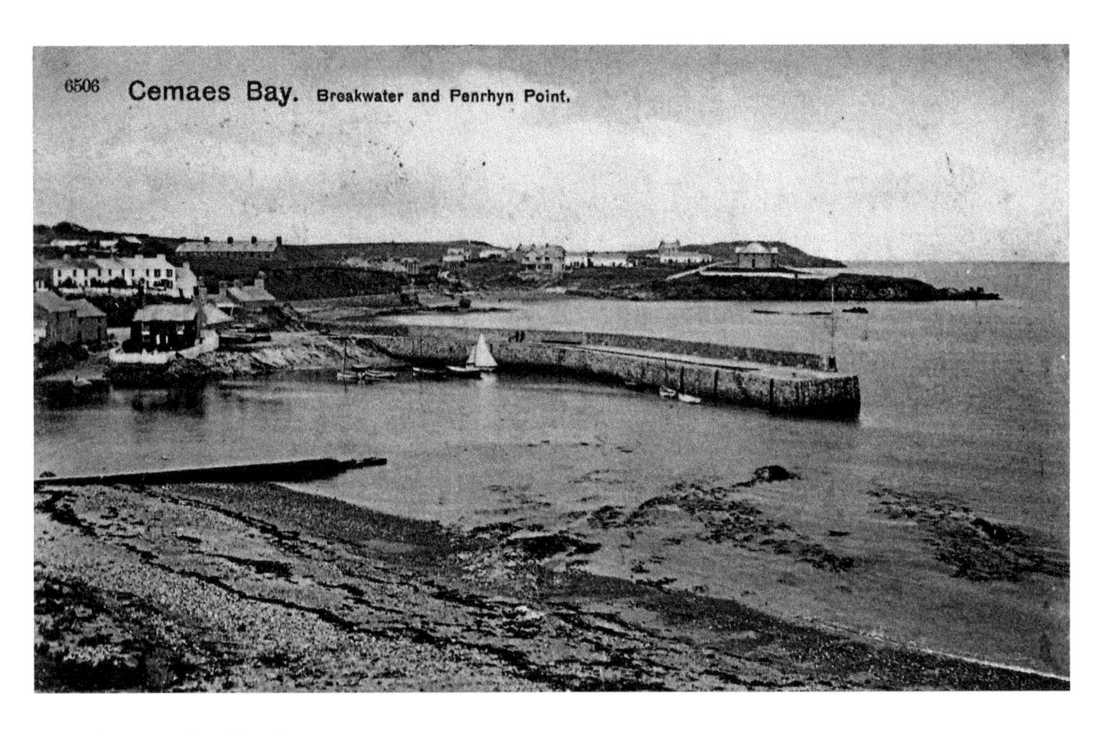

Cemaes Bay Breakwater, *c.* 1900

Cemaes was founded as a fishing village, and a small stone pier was built for the fishing boats. However, this was destroyed by a storm in 1828. After several years of attempted fundraising, it was rebuilt in 1835 and then was used not only by fishermen, but also for exporting locally quarried limestone and marble and later bricks. Another storm in 1889 swept away the end of the pier. The above photograph shows it shortly after again being repaired and extended in 1900.

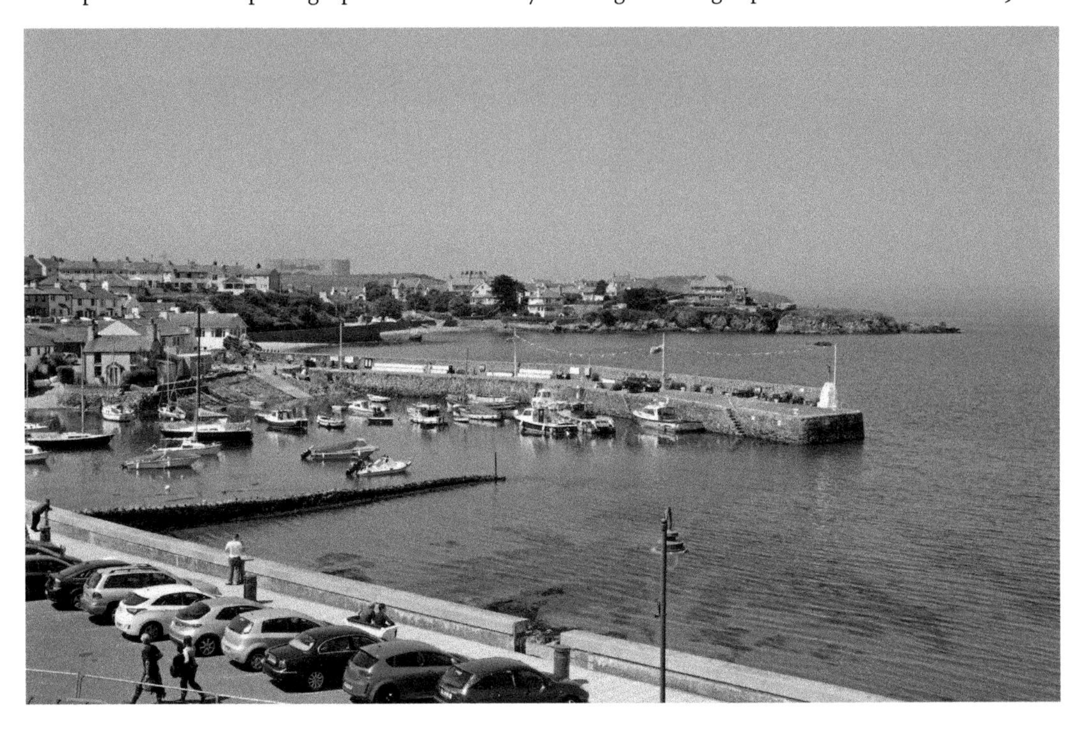

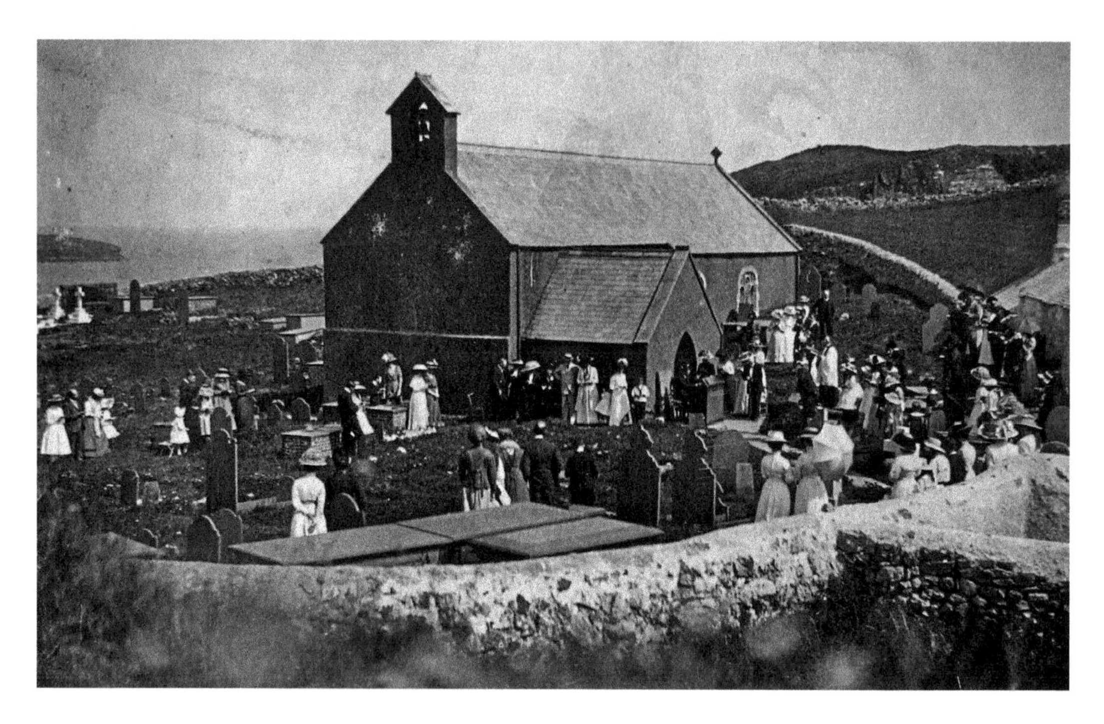

Llanbadrig Church, Early Twentieth Century

According to legend, the patron saint of Ireland, St Patrick, was shipwrecked on the island of Ynys Badrig (Middle Mouse), seen on the left above. He made it to shore and founded a church here to give thanks for his survival. The current building is probably the oldest church on Anglesey, built in the fourteenth century to replace the older wooden one. Its restoration in 1884 was funded by Lord Stanley of Alderley, a Muslim convert, who had Islamic designs incorporated into the stained-glass windows and tiles. (AA WSB-208)

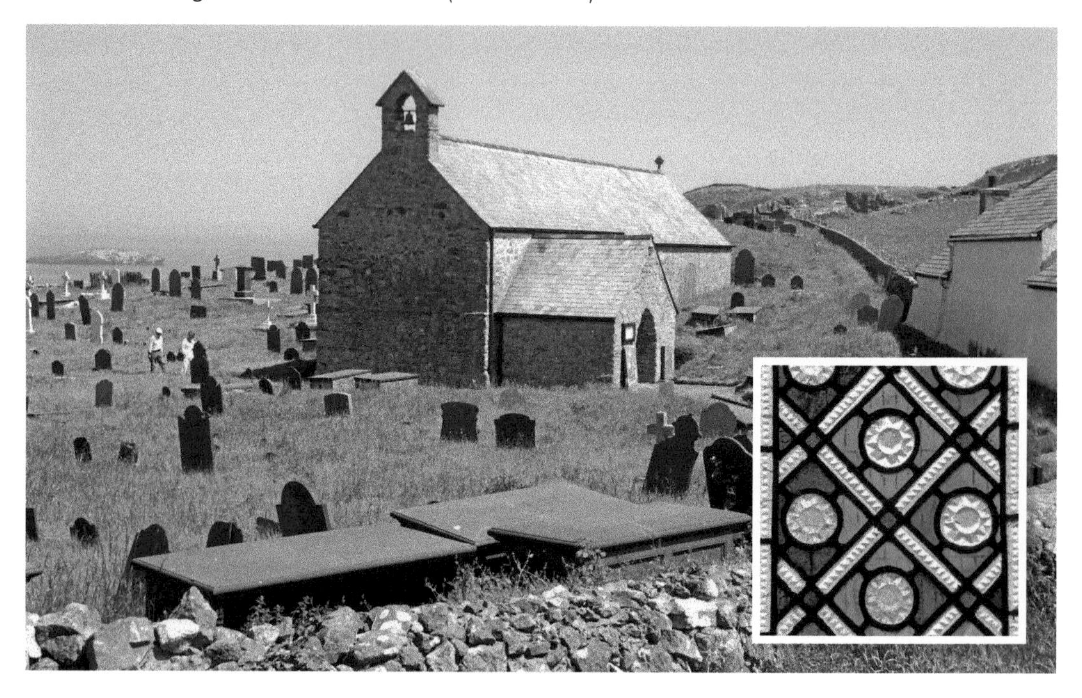

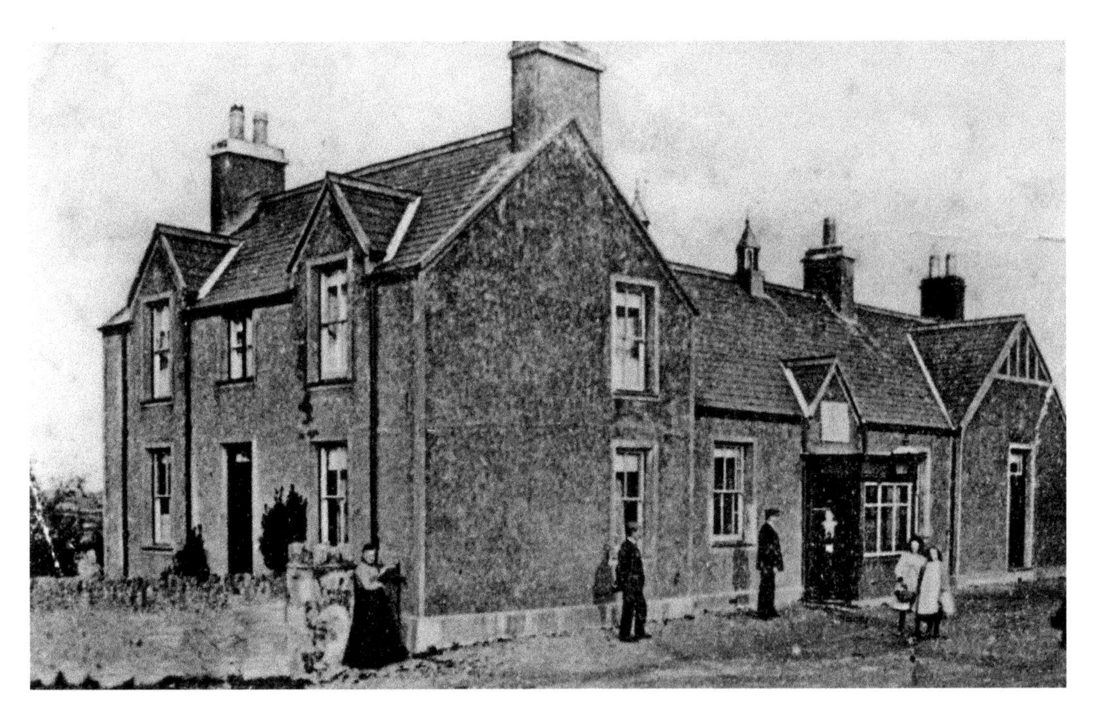

Griffith Reade Coffee House, Llanfaethlu, Early Twentieth Century
The heiress of the local Carreglwyd estate, Maria Emma Elizabeth Conway Griffiths, Lady Reade, became a Temperance campaigner after the death of her husband, Sir Chandos Reade. In 1892, she built the Griffith Reade Coffee House to act as an alternative meeting place to the local public houses. The coffee shop is still open and the building also acts as a village hall, post office, shop and Lifelong Learning Centre. (AA WSJ-10-9)

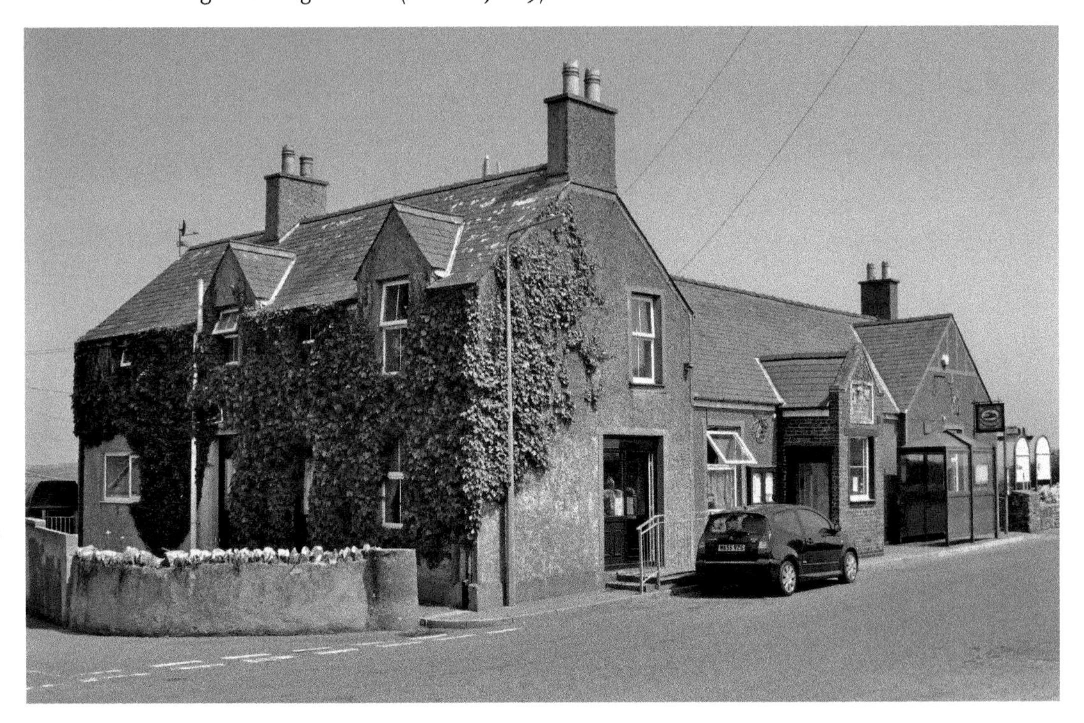

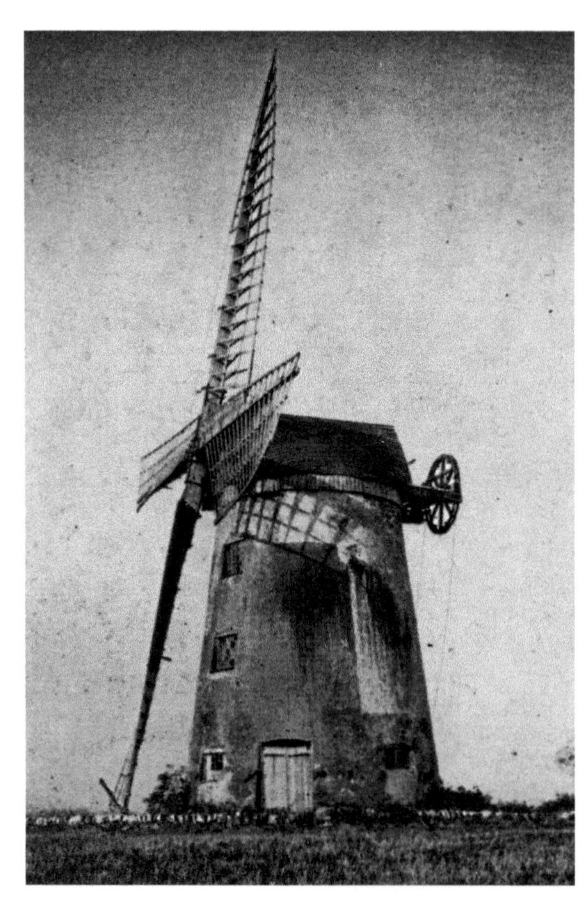

Melin Llynnon Windmill, Llanddeusant, *c.* 1936

Built in 1775, this is now one of Anglesey's most popular tourist attractions. It ground grain for almost a century and a half, most of the time run by the descendants of the first miller, Thomas Jones, who worked it until he died, aged ninety. A storm in 1918 damaged the cap, and it soon closed. It became increasingly dilapidated until 1978, when Anglesey Council bought and restored it. It is now the only working windmill in Wales, producing flour for sale in the adjacent shop.

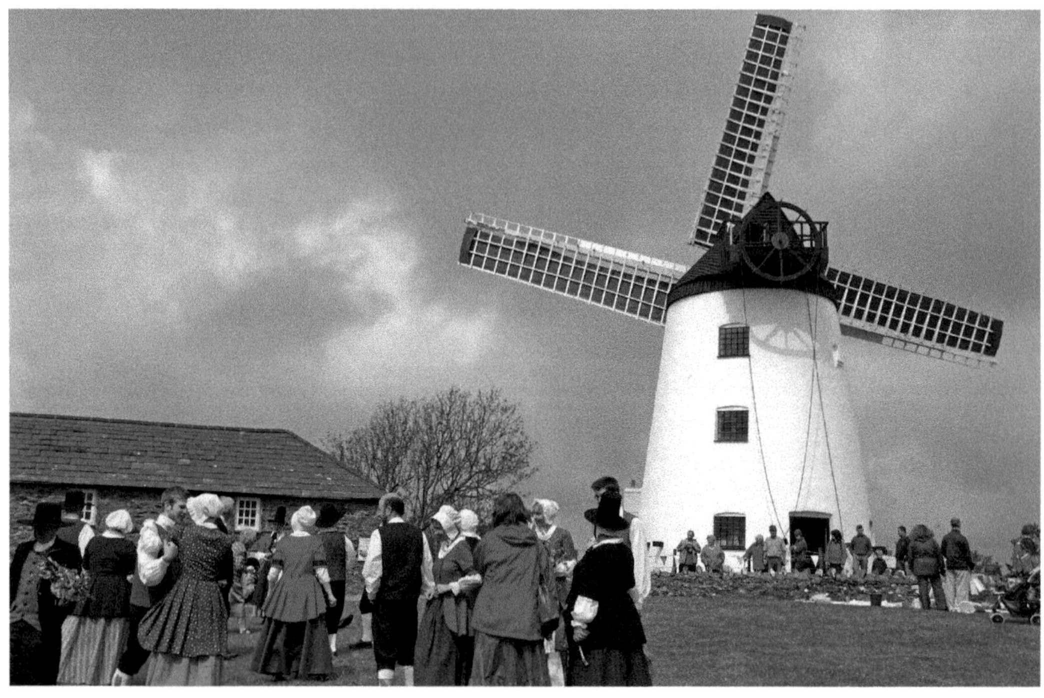

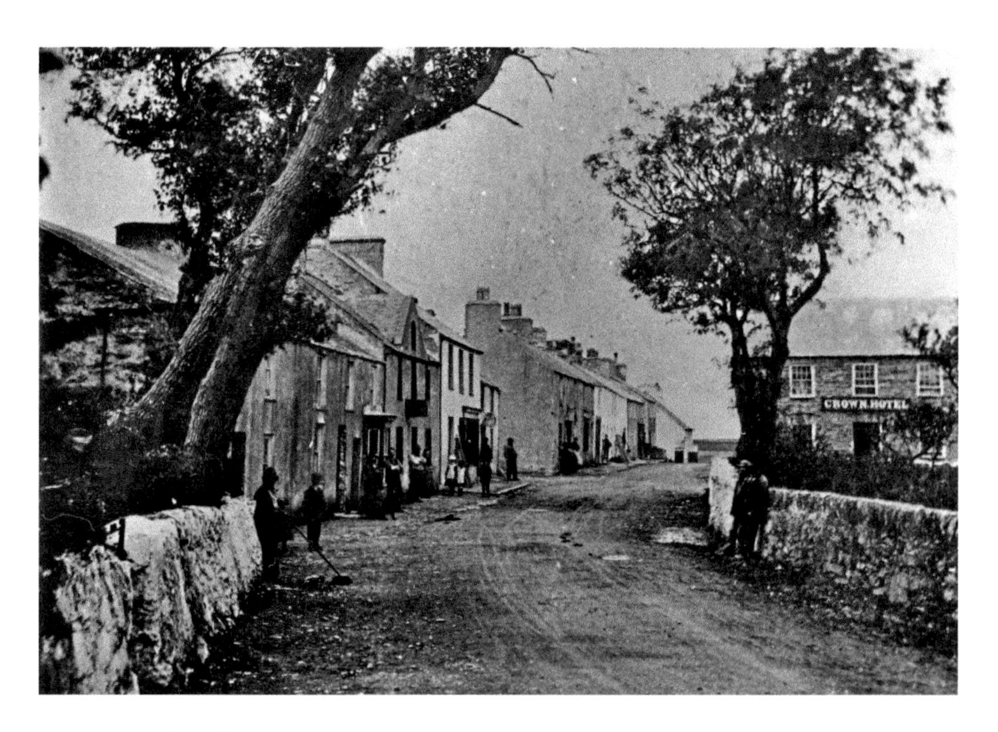

Crown Hotel, Bodedern, *c.* 1875

Sitting astride the old post road across the island to Holyhead, Bodedern had several hotels and inns. Most prominent in the picture above is the Crown Hotel, still serving the community today. Across the road was the Lamia Inn (the building on the left side with the dormer). It operated through the nineteenth century but closed before 1915, when it was converted to a butcher's shop by Evan Thomas Jones. Today it is run by his great-grandchildren and has won many national awards for its produce. (AA WSJ-2-1)

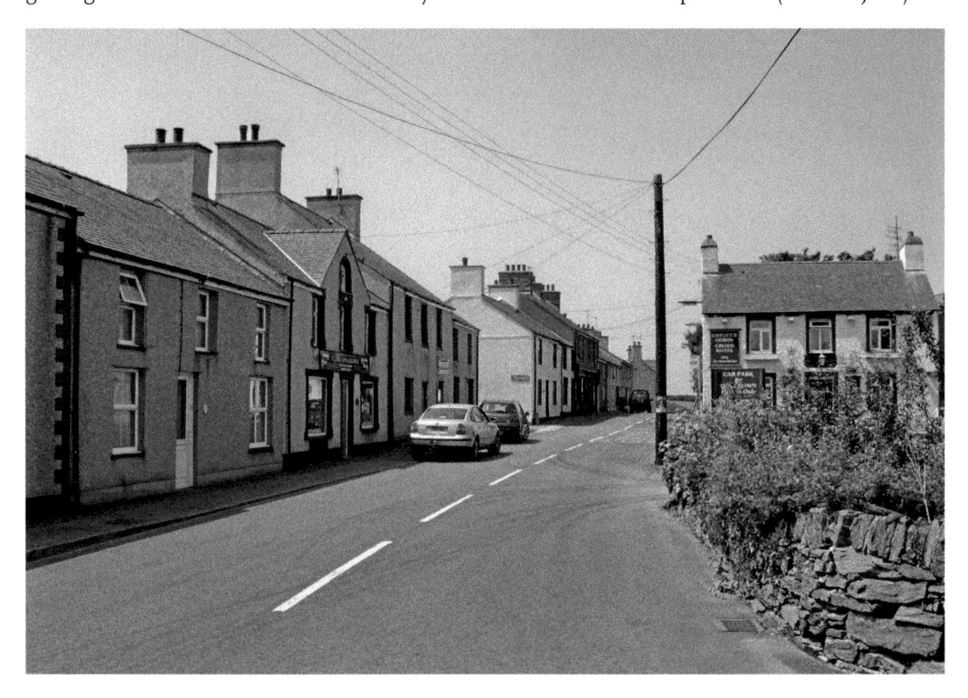

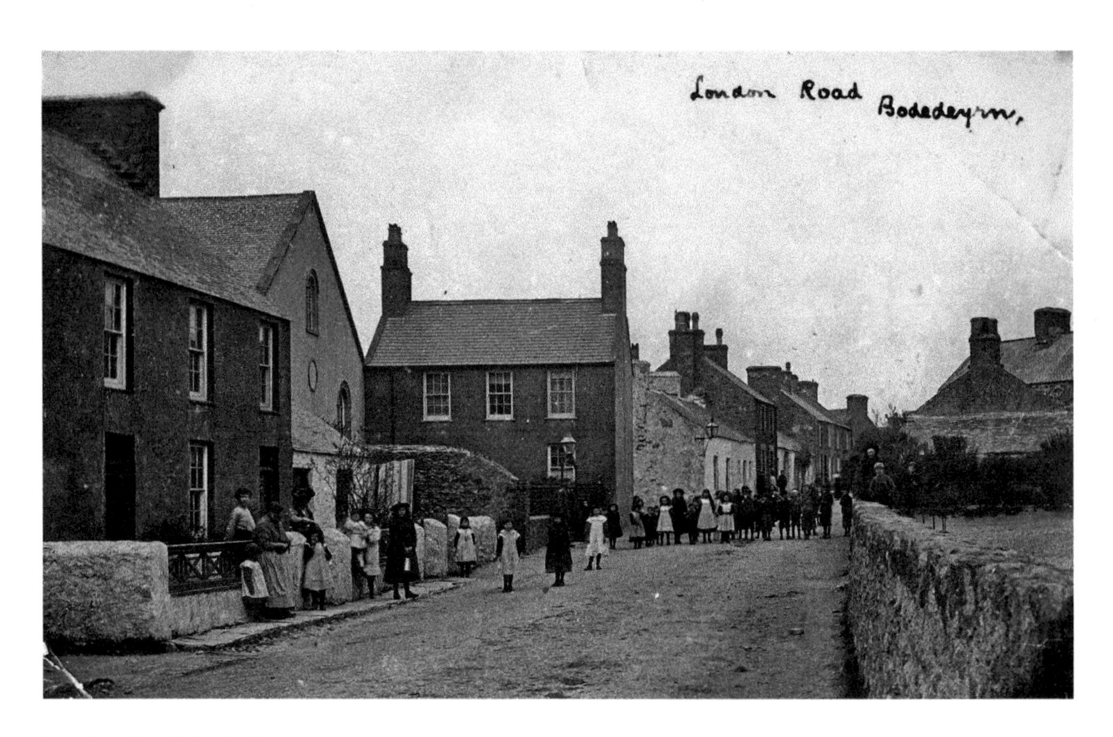

London Road, Bodedern, *c.* 1900

The main London Road running through the village was flanked by a chapel on the left and the school across the road. The Gilgal Calvinist Methodist chapel was first built here in 1806, but was rebuilt and enlarged several times. The photograph above shows it before the most recent remodelling in 1911. Sadly, it was demolished just days before the photograph below was taken in July 2013. The school, whose pupils were proudly posing for the above photograph, opened in 1822. (AA WSJ-2-23)

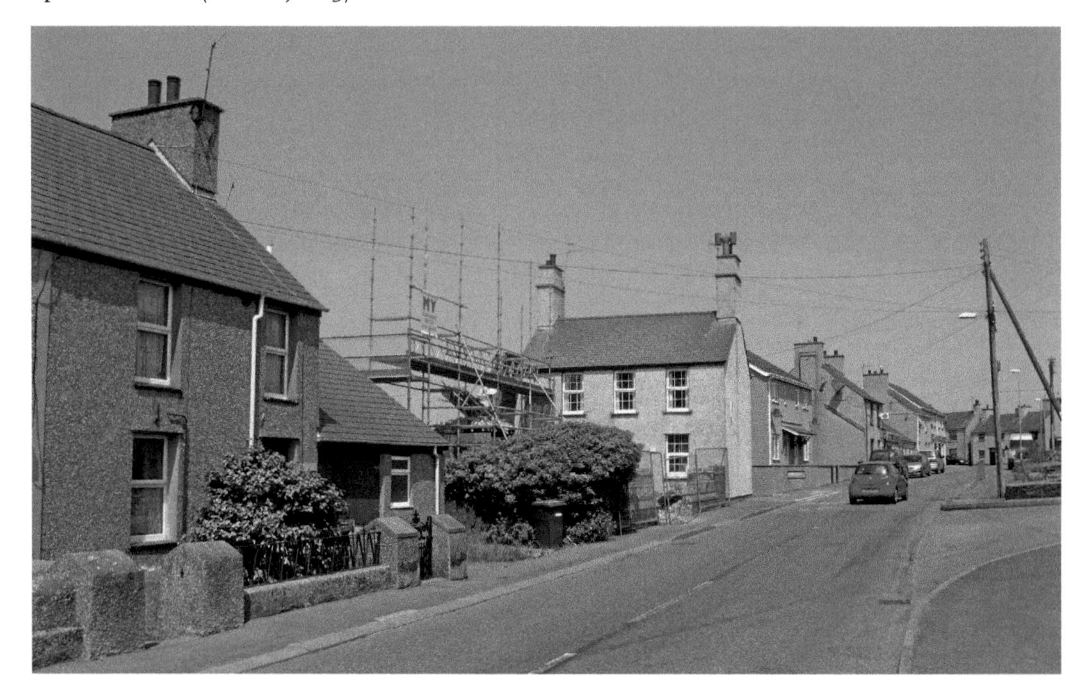

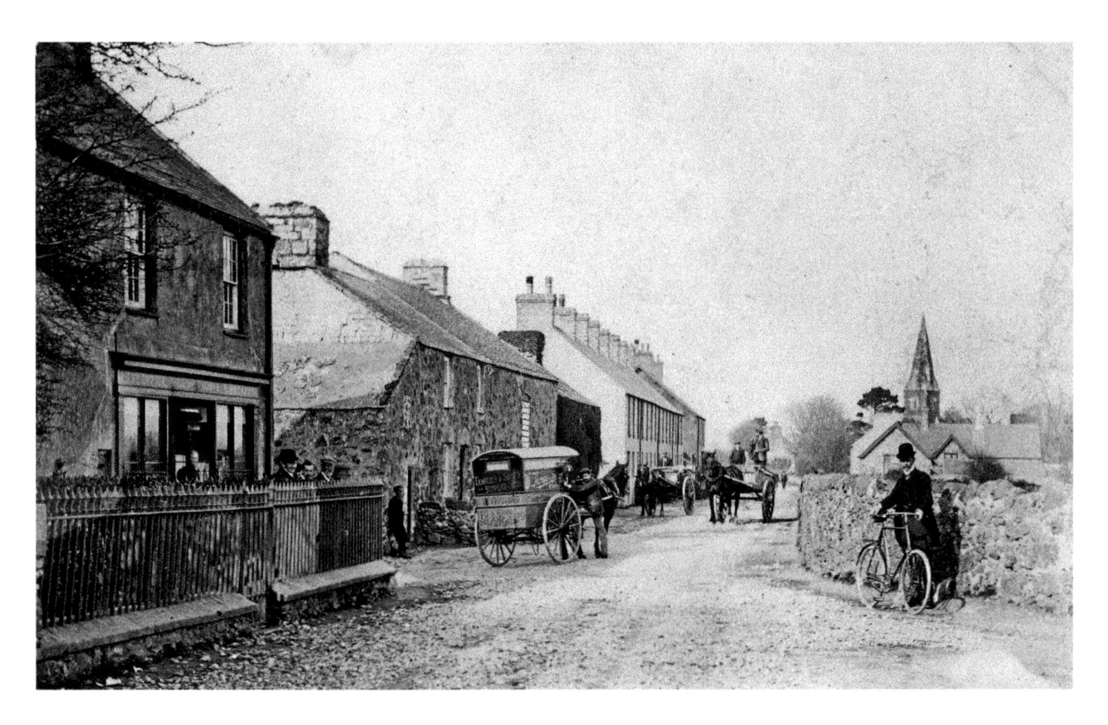

High Street, Llangaffo, *c.* 1910
Williams Thomas' post office and grocery shop occupied this corner in Llangaffo, where one of his employees poses with the shop's horse and delivery cart. The building directly behind the cart was originally a chapel, but had been converted to a joiner's shop by this time. The small vine-covered building next to it, originally the joiner's house, was shortly to be demolished and rebuilt. The post office still occupies this corner, one of the few on Anglesey to have persisted in the same building. (AA WSG-7-1)

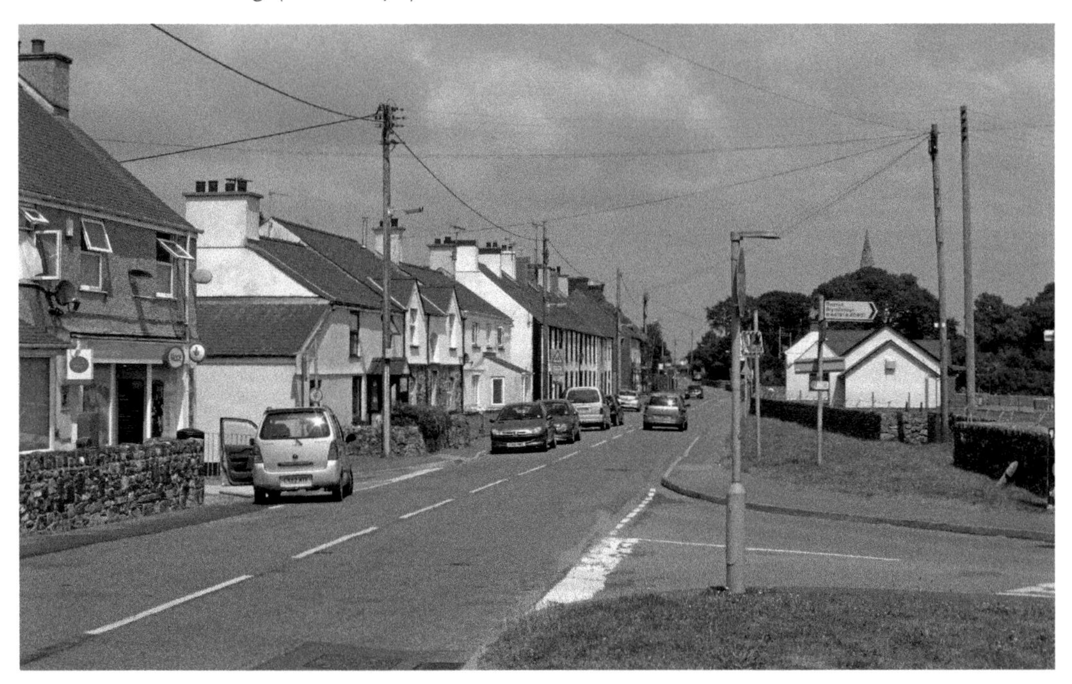

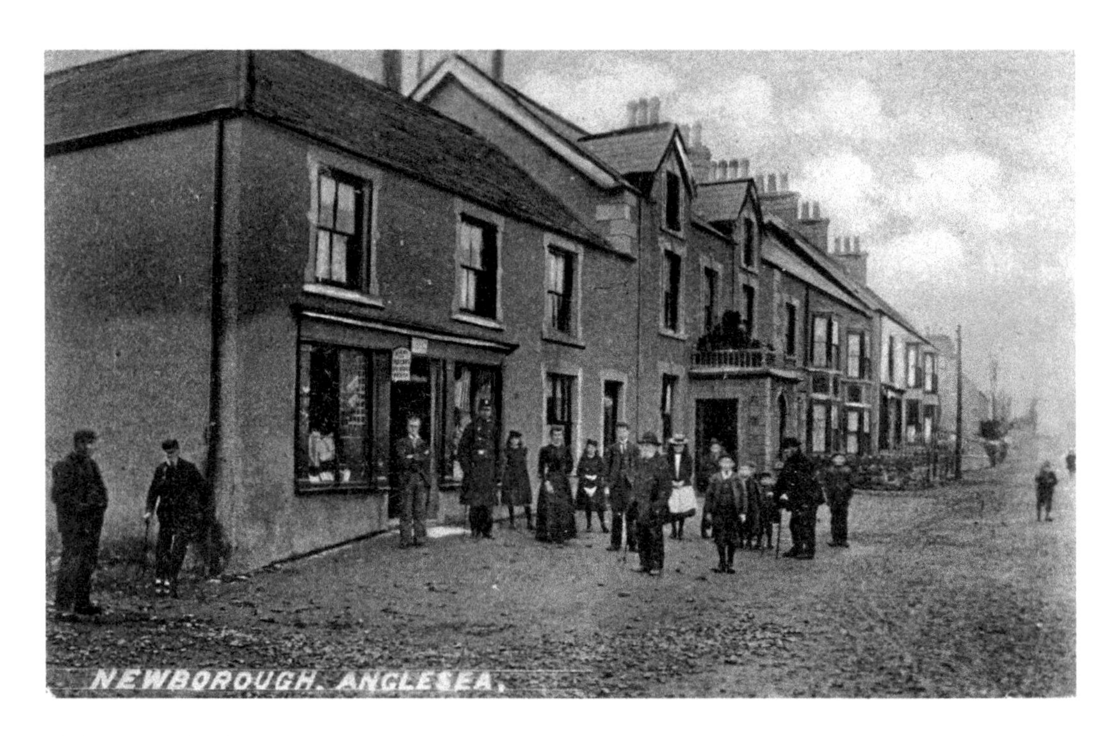

High Street, Newborough, *c.* 1910

Once the site of the Rhosyr medieval royal court (now excavated and open to visitors), the village of Newborough was founded by the people evicted from Llanfaes when Edward I built the Beaumaris castle and town nearby. The above photograph shows Robert Griffiths' drapery and general merchandise shop, Cambrian House, in the foreground, with a smartly dressed man (probably the owner) standing in the doorway. The White Lion pub is next to it, and the post office is the white building beyond that. (AA WSG-14-58)

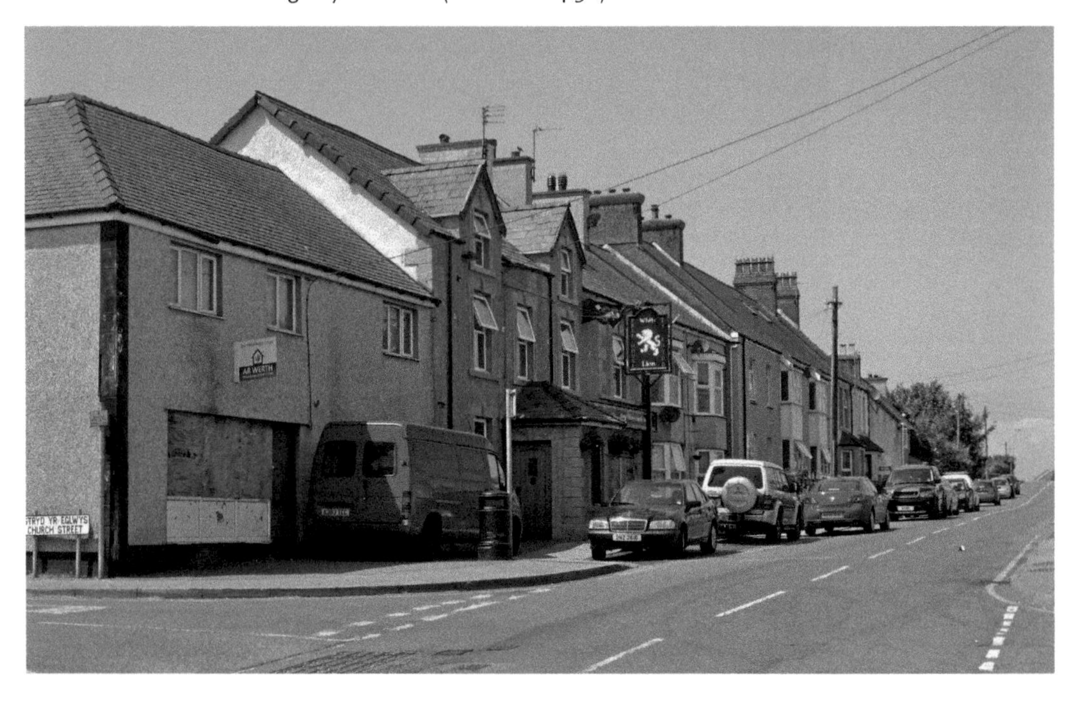

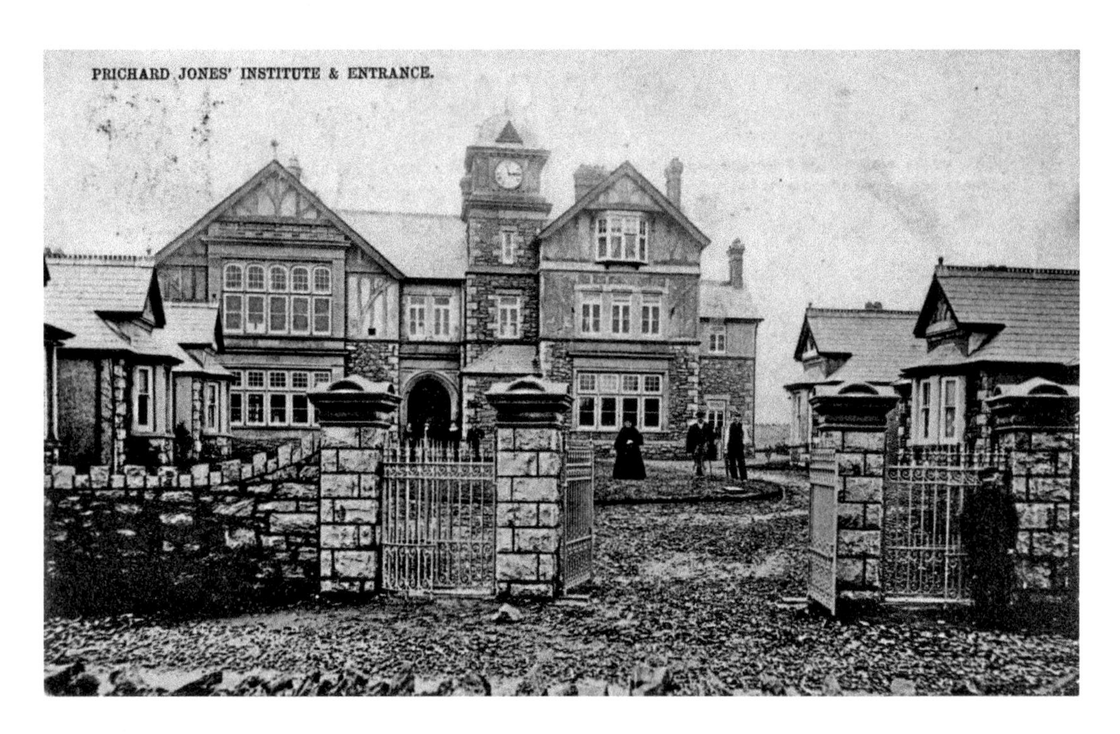

Prichard Jones Institute, Newborough, 1905

In 1872, a young draper's apprentice, John Prichard Jones from Newborough, began working for a department store on Regent Street, London. He rose to become co-owner of the store, a baronet, and fabulously wealthy. But he never forgot his home village. He funded the building of this community centre, opened in 1905, which provided a free library, meeting, reading and recreation rooms, as well as cottages and pensions for local elderly people in need. It has recently been restored and still serves the local community. (AA WSG-14-57)

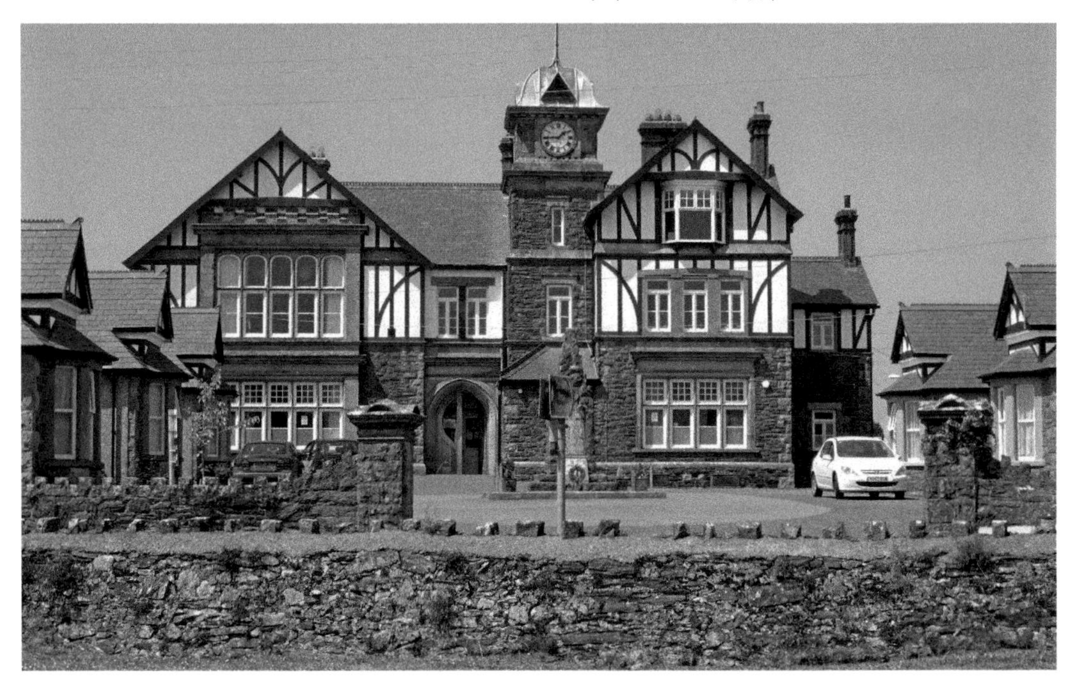

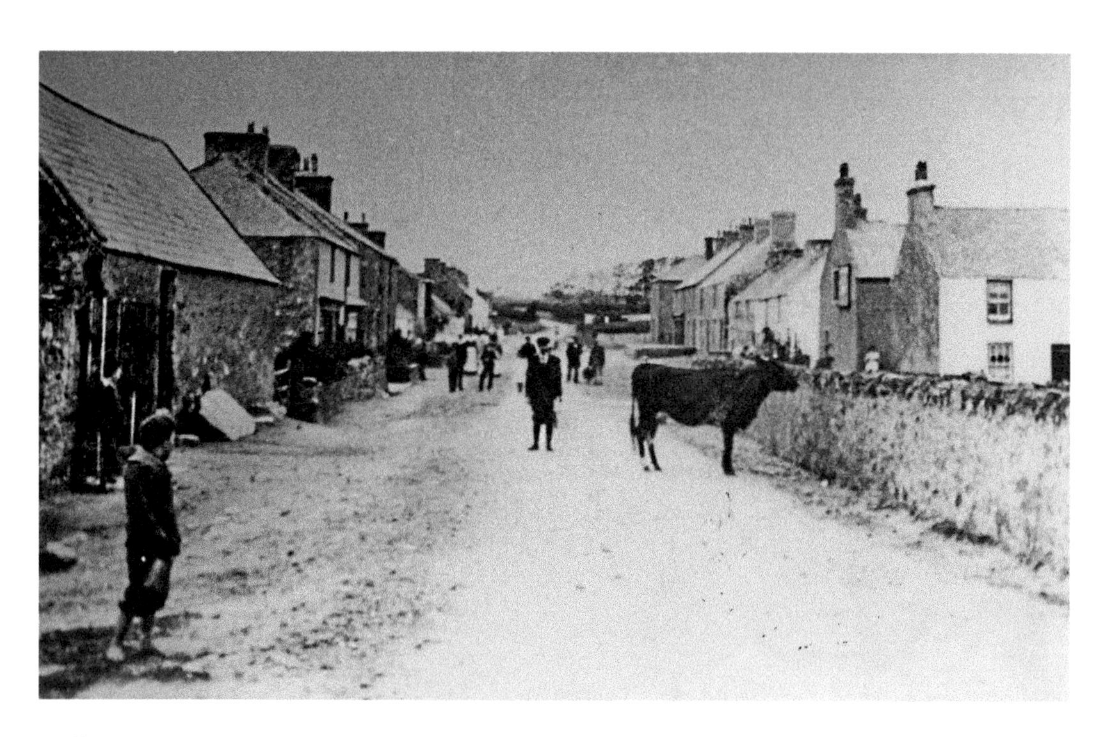

Malltraeth Village, 1871

Originally called Yard, and later Malltraeth Yard, this village grew with the influx of workers building the Cob. This dyke was built across the Malltraeth estuary to drain the marshes that extended far into the Anglesey heartland. Work began in 1790, but it was soon damaged by an unusually high tide and work stopped. It was finished in 1812. In the photograph above, the Joiner's Arms pub can be seen behind the now demolished building on the right. (AA WSG-17-4)

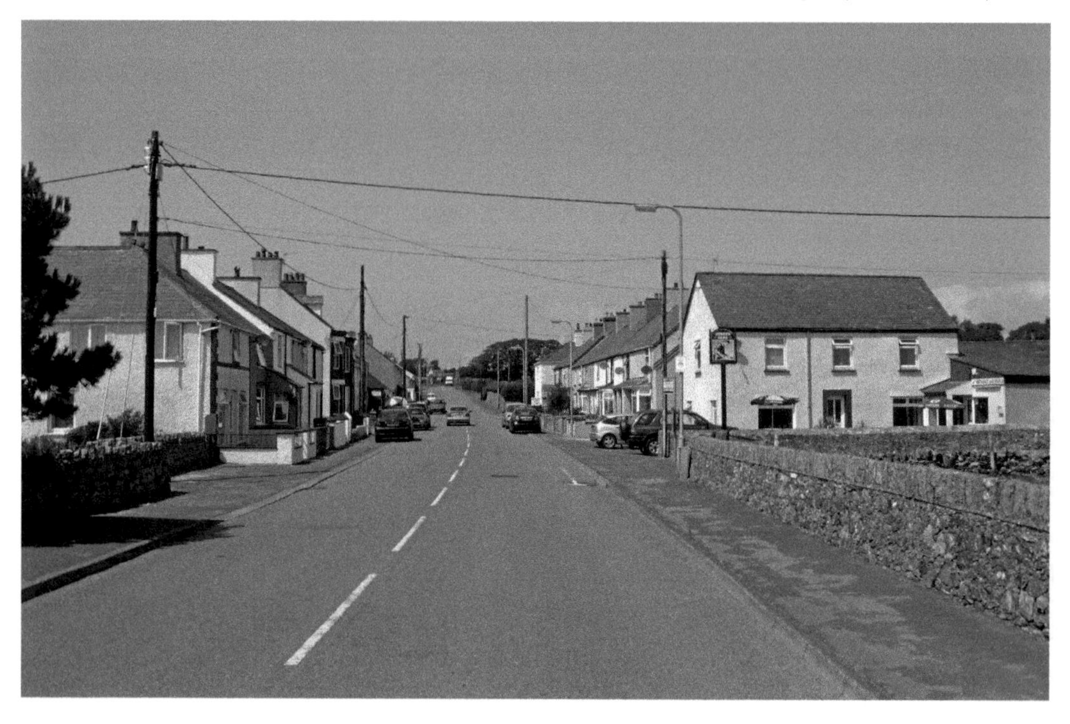

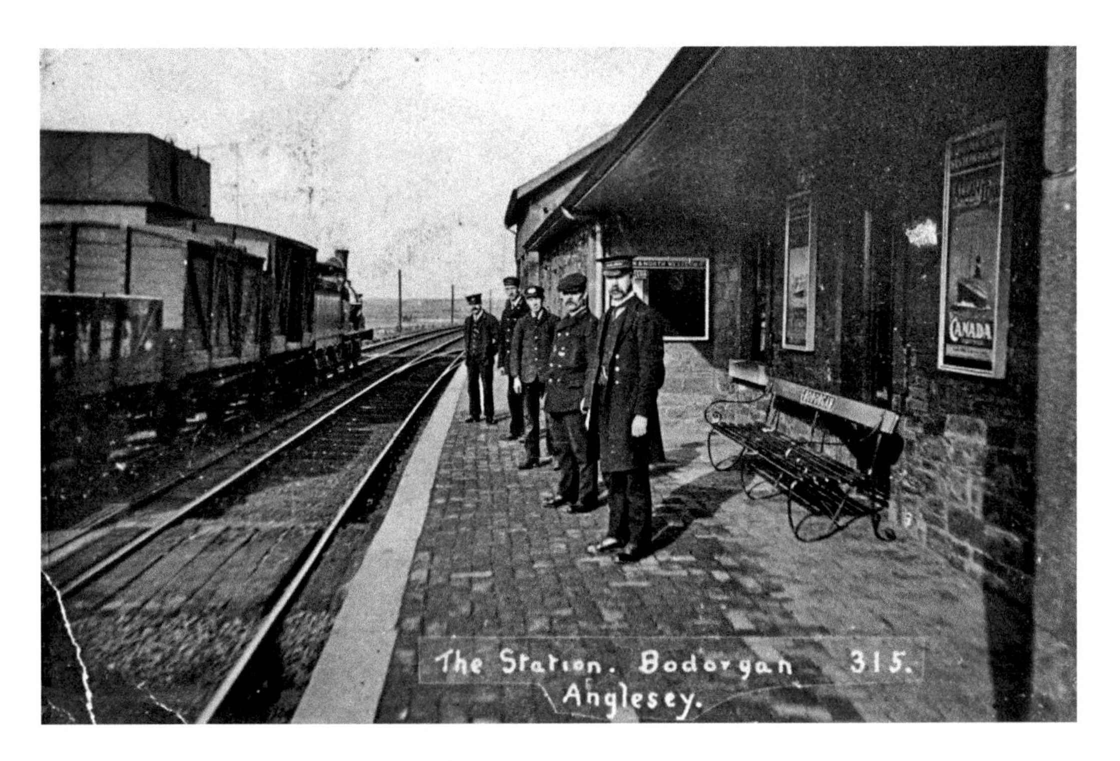

Bodorgan Railway Station, Bethel, *c.* 1920

The stationmaster and his staff pose proudly outside Bodorgan station in the above photograph. Opened in 1849, it included not only the station building but also a goods yard, water tower and signal box, all now gone. Today the station is considerably quieter, as it is unmanned and is a request-only stop on the Holyhead line. (AA WSG-6-13)

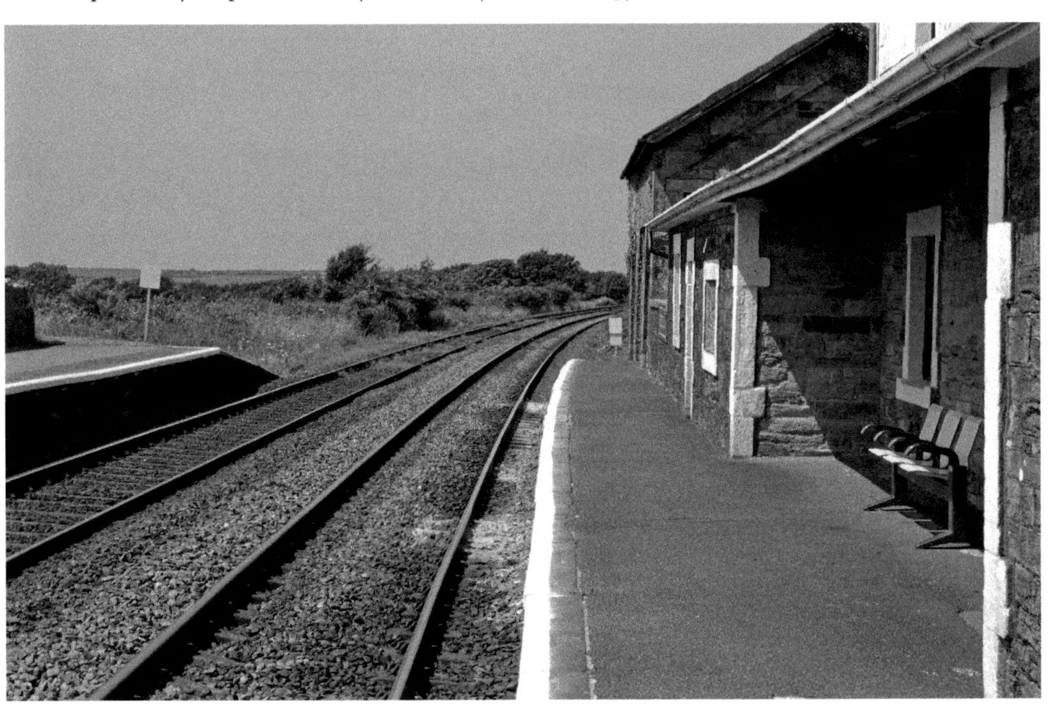

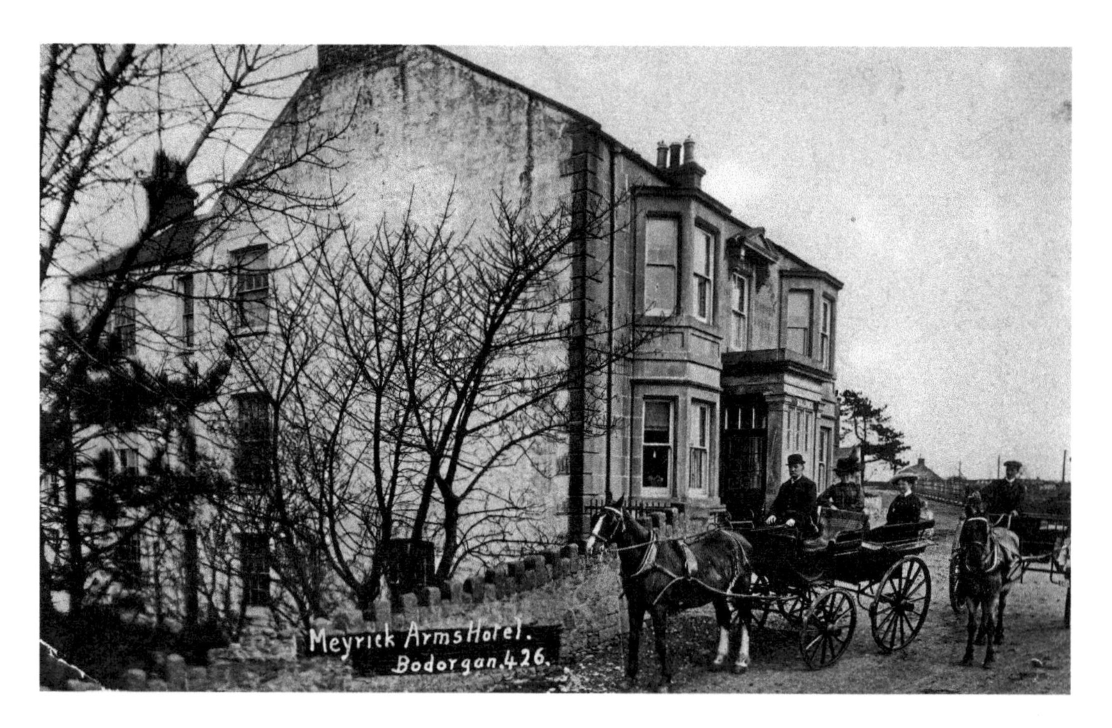

Meyrick Arms Hotel, Bethel, *c.* 1920

Although the area around Bodorgan station is now quiet, it was once the site of two hotels. The Meyrick Arms, shown here, stands directly opposite the station, and the Bodorgan Arms is just up the road. They were next to a cattle market, which took advantage of the adjacent station to transport cattle and agricultural equipment and supplies for sale. Both hotels have now been turned into private homes. (AA WSG-6-24)

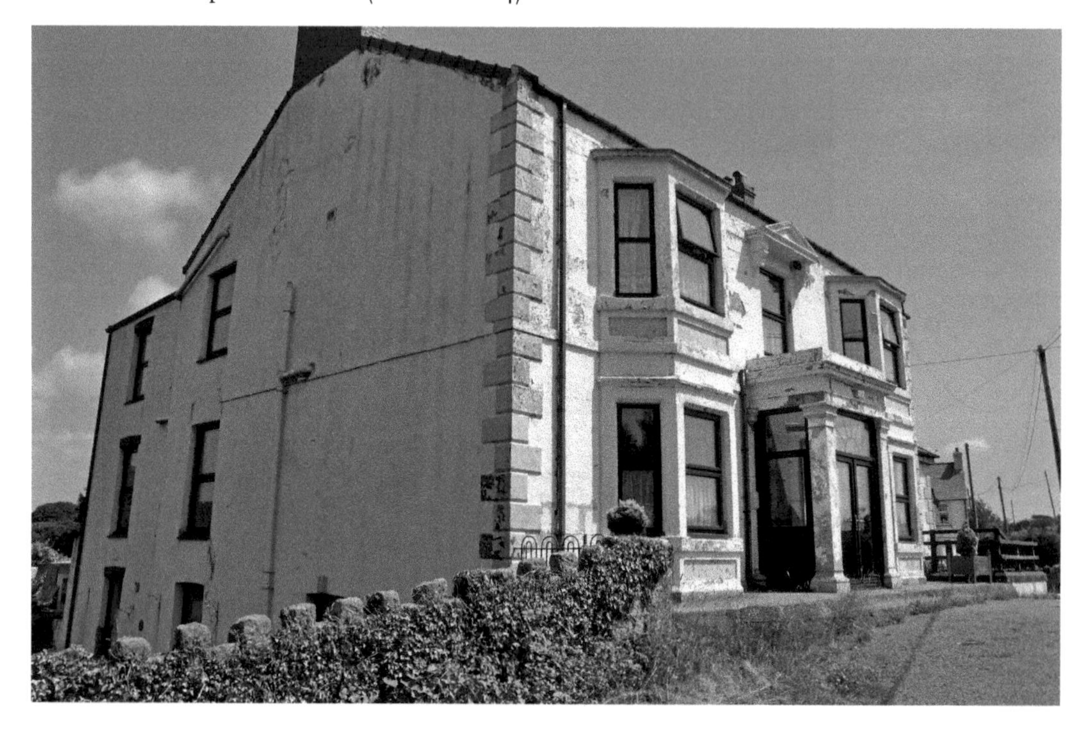

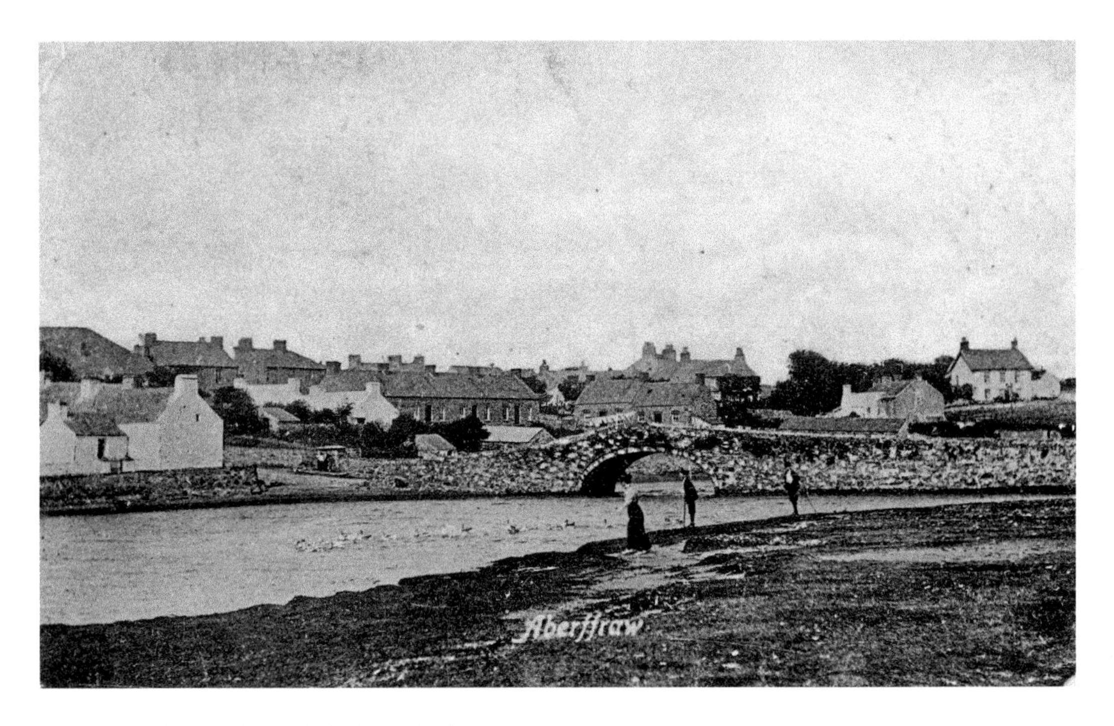

Aberffraw Bridge, Early Twentieth Century

This picturesque bridge over the Afon Ffraw was built in 1731 by Sir Arthur Owen of the nearby Bodowen estate, who owned much of the village at the time. Sir Arthur also funded the conversion of a ruined church into a school for teaching poor children of the village in Welsh. That building later became the Eagles Inn, and is now a private house on Church Street. The bridge is now bypassed by a more modern one and is open only to pedestrian traffic. (AA WSJ-1-13)

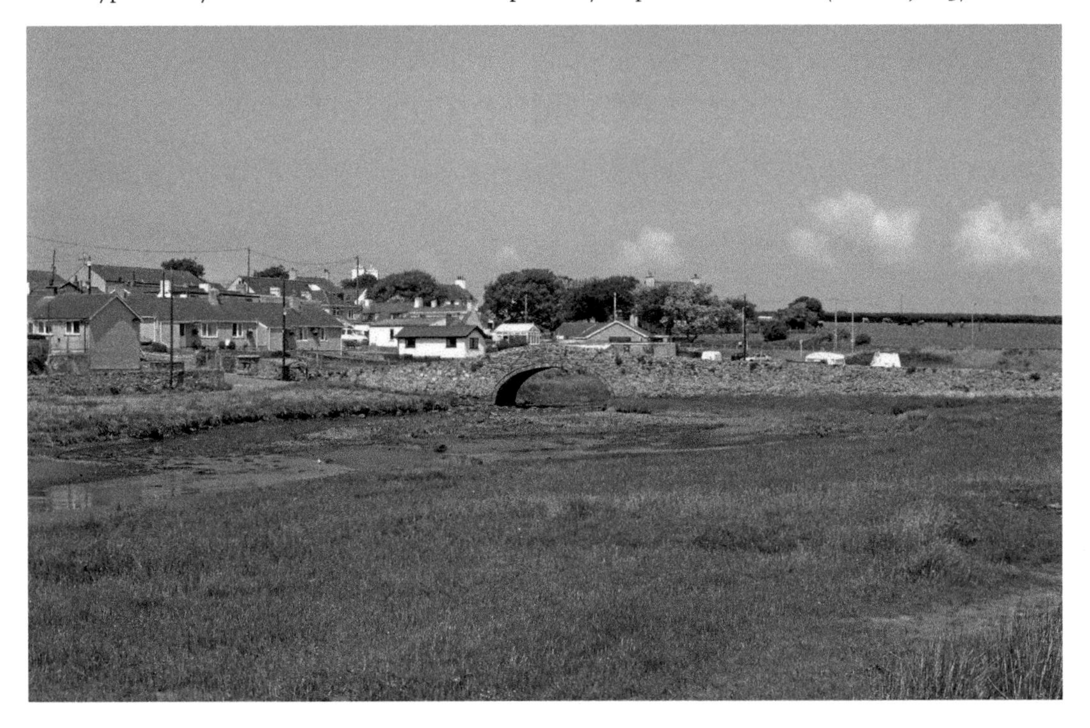

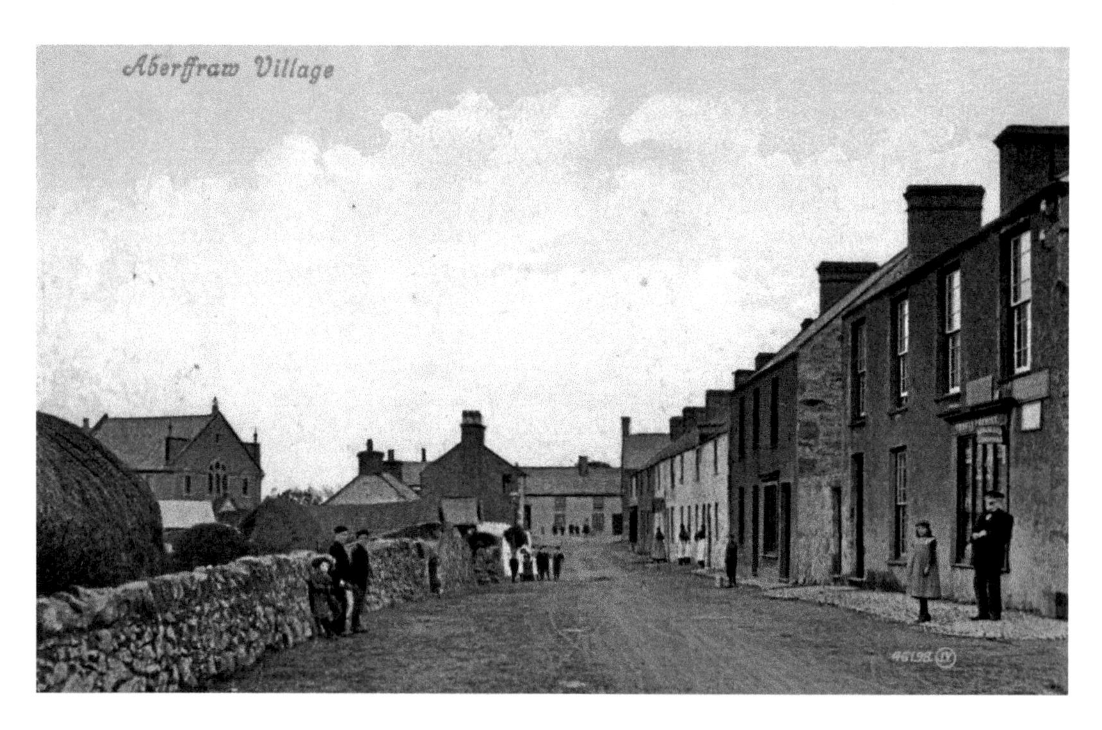

Llewellyn Street, Aberffraw, 1904

Aberffraw's Wesleyan Methodist chapel can be seen in the distance in the above image. The shop at the right was a chemist's shop and post office, called Medical Hall, owned by John Henry Thomas, who took it over from his father, Henry Parry Thomas. Along with the shop and house next door, it was demolished in the late 2000s and now awaits rebuilding. The buildings along the rest of the street were also torn down around 1979, but were rebuilt to look similar to the original buildings. (AA WSJ-1-95)

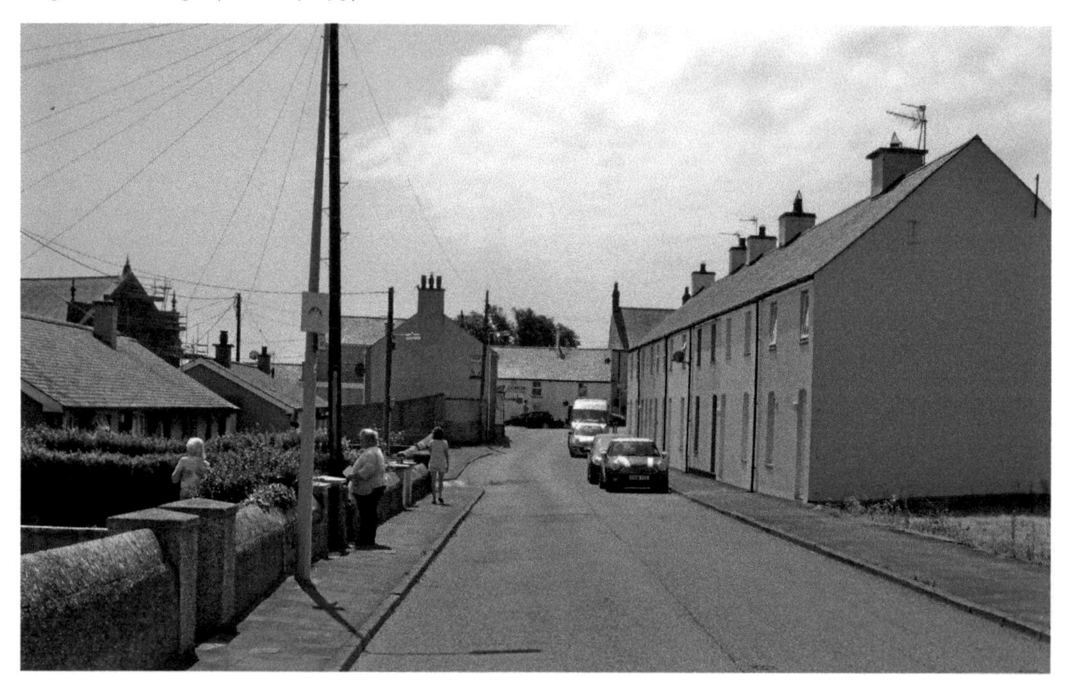

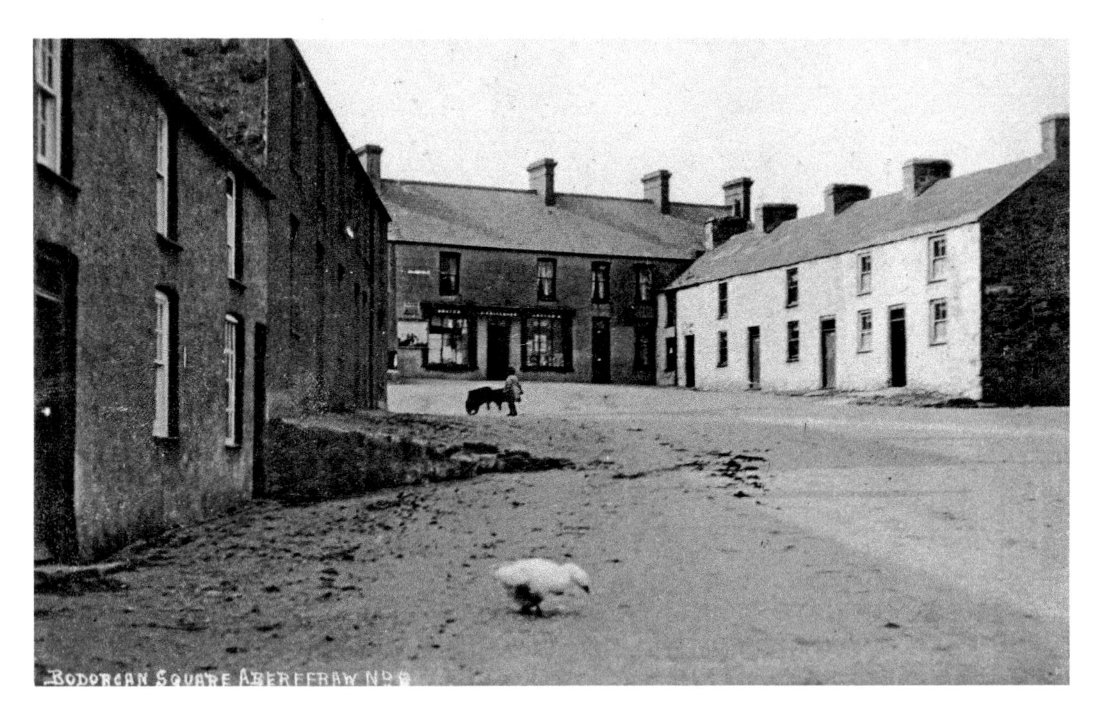

Bodorgan Square, Aberffraw, Early Twentieth Century
The heart of Aberffraw was originally called Dinorban Square, after Lord Dinorban of Llysdulas. It was renamed Bodorgan Square, after the estate of the local Meyrick family, in the 1900s. The shop at the end is Plas Coch, the drapery and grocery store owned at the time by John Pritchard. Shortly after this, the post office also moved there from Medical Hall. Today it is still the post office and main grocery shop. (AA WSJ-1-10)

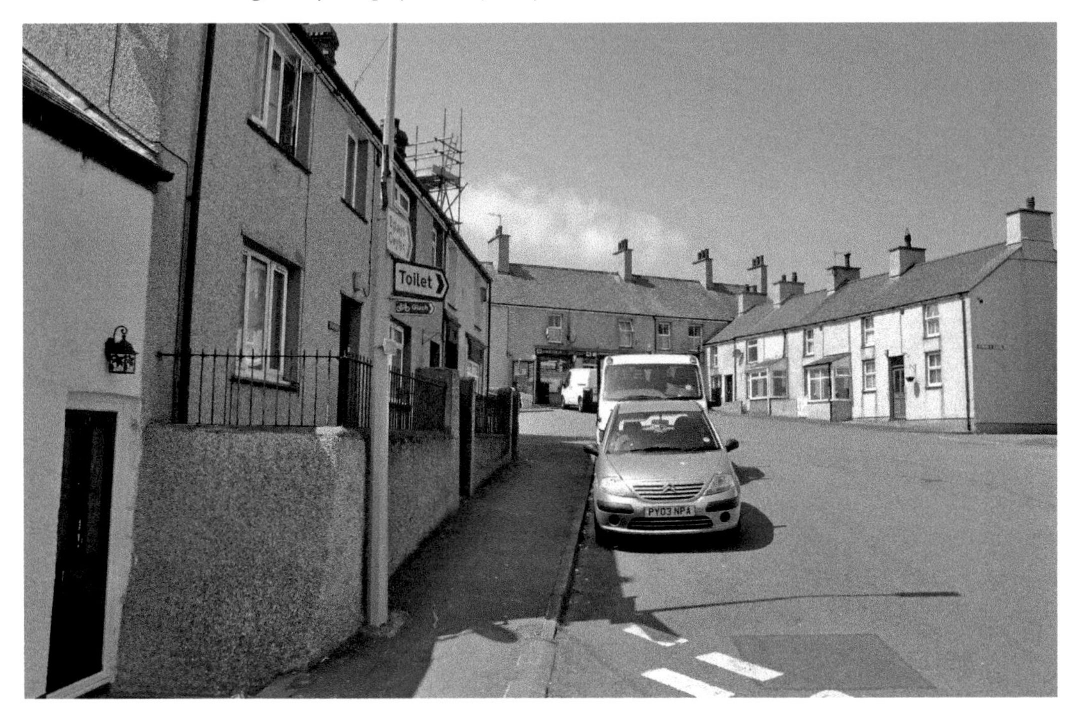

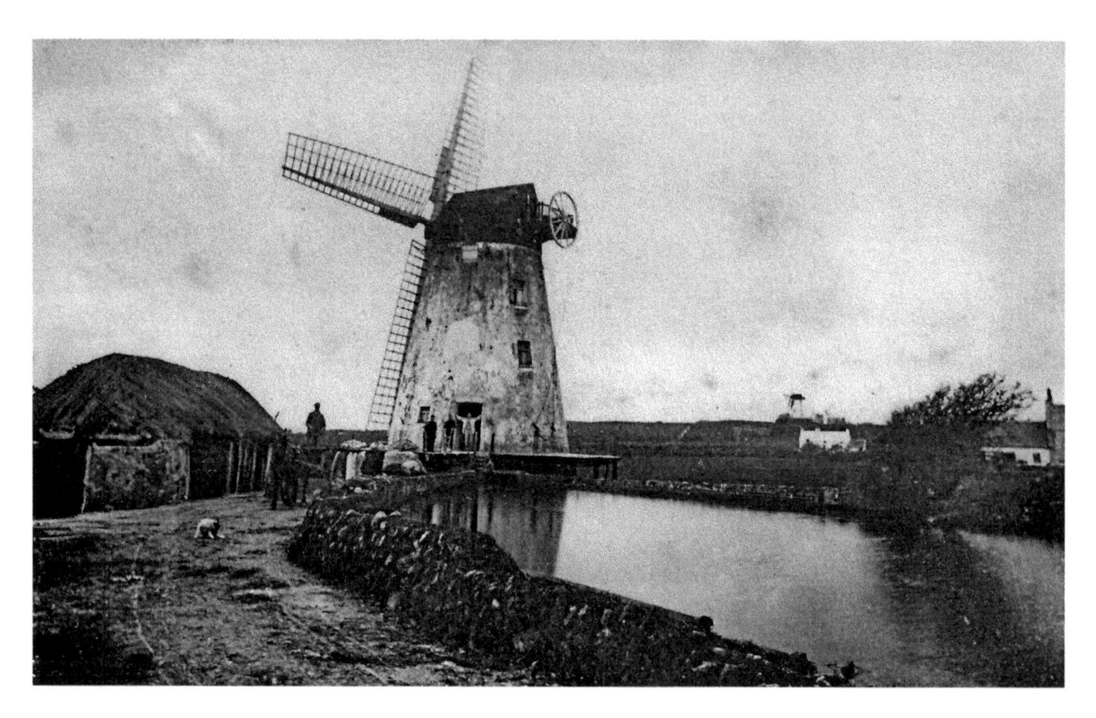

Melin y Bont Windmill, Bryn-Du, Llanfaelog, 1908

There were once almost fifty windmills ('melin' in Welsh) on Anglesey, which harnessed the strong winds off the Irish Sea to grind grain or power other machinery. This one was also called Melin Isaf ('lower mill') to distinguish it from the one in the distance (Melin Ucaf, 'upper mill'). It was unique in that it also had a water wheel, so it could continue working when the wind was low. Like many other old windmills on Anglesey, both of these have been converted into dwellings.

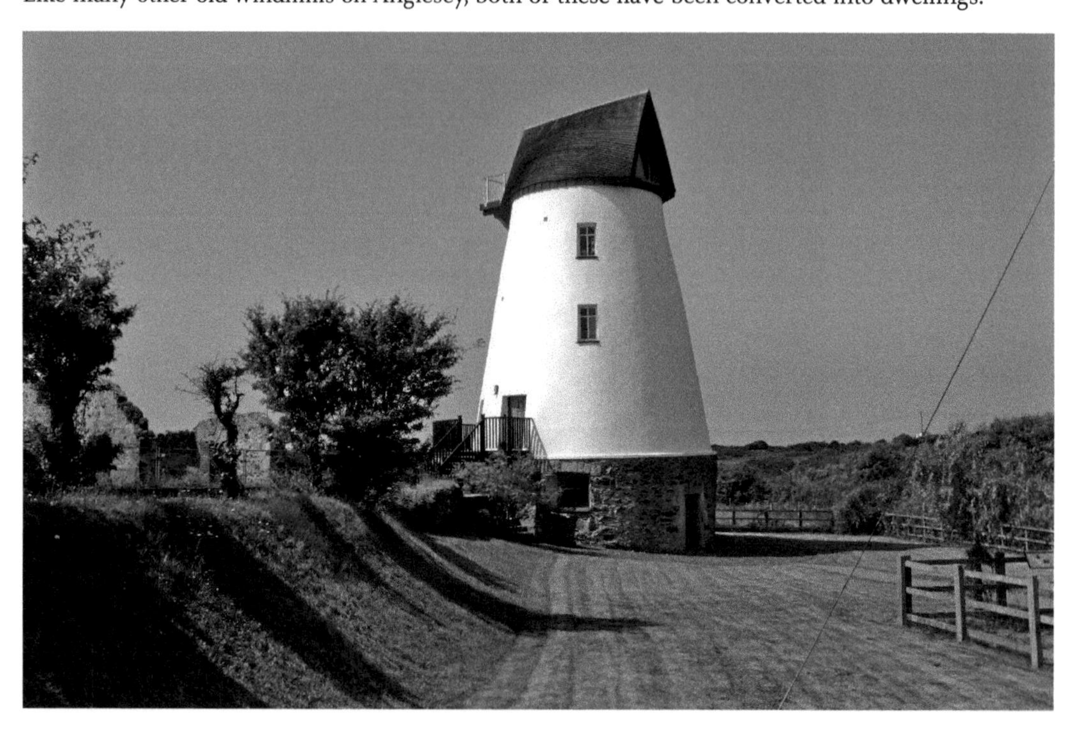

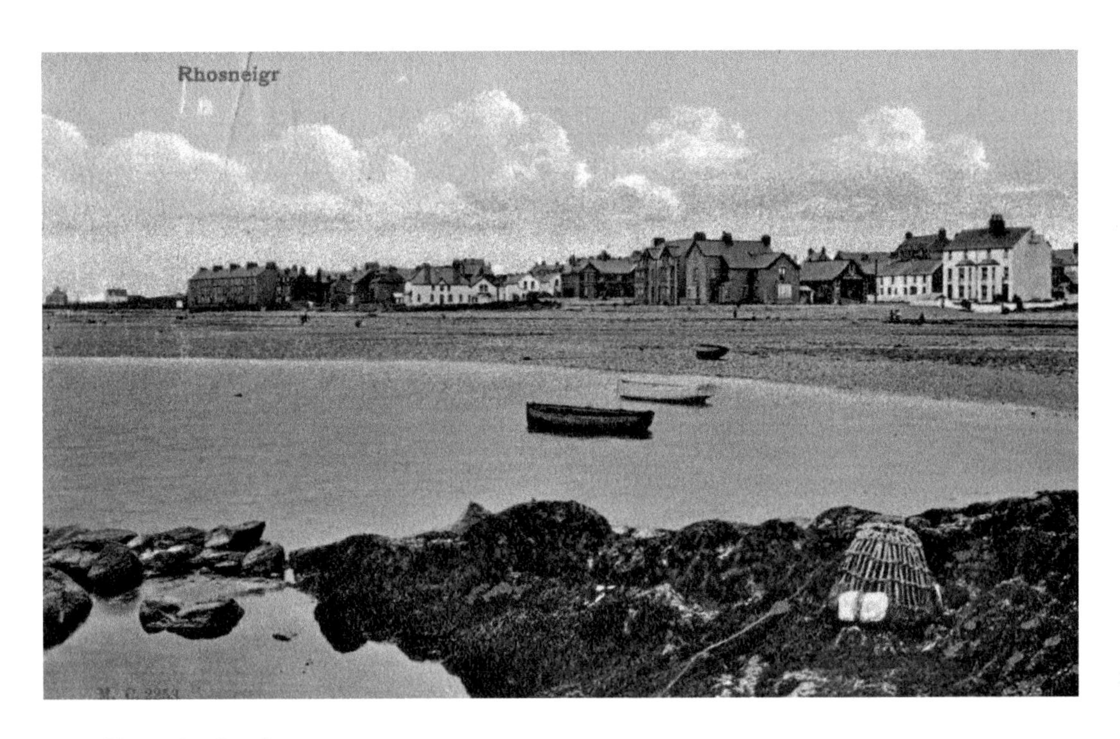

Rhosneigr Beach, *c.* 1910s

In the late nineteenth century, Rhosneigr was a sparsely populated fishing village, with just a few houses and a coastguard station. However, the opening of a railway station in 1907, and the Edwardian taste for seaside holidays, saw the village expand rapidly. Numerous guest houses and holiday homes sprang up along the central Town Beach, from where visitors could enjoy the four miles of beaches along this stretch of the coast. (AA WSJ-8-60)

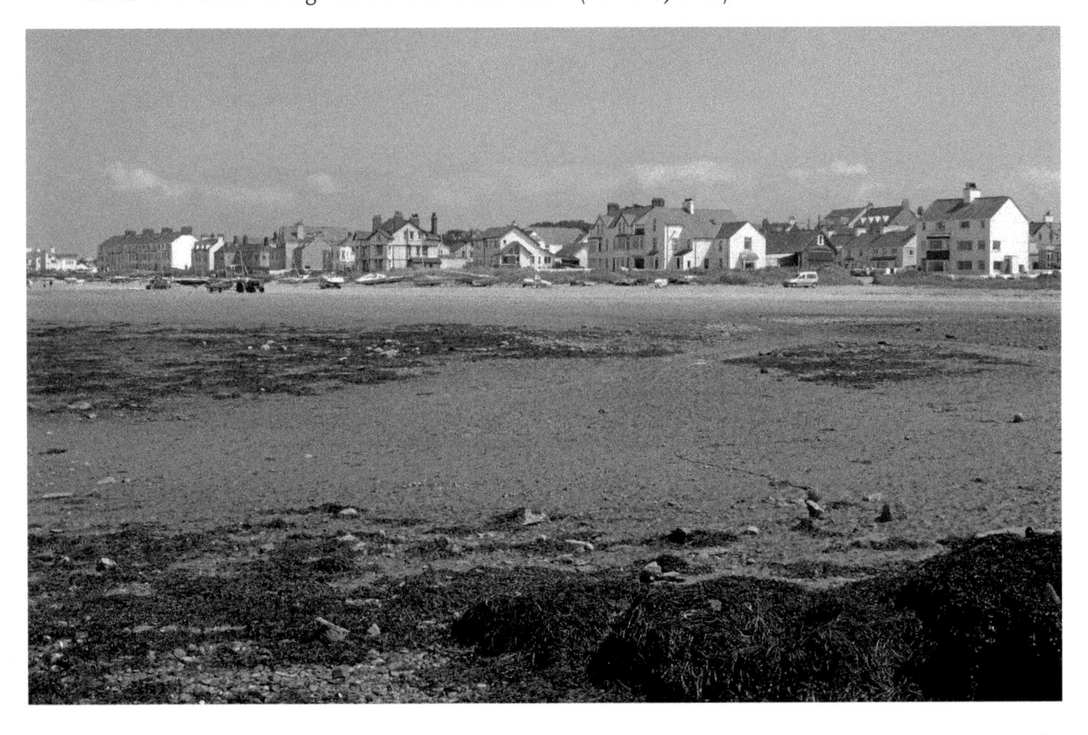

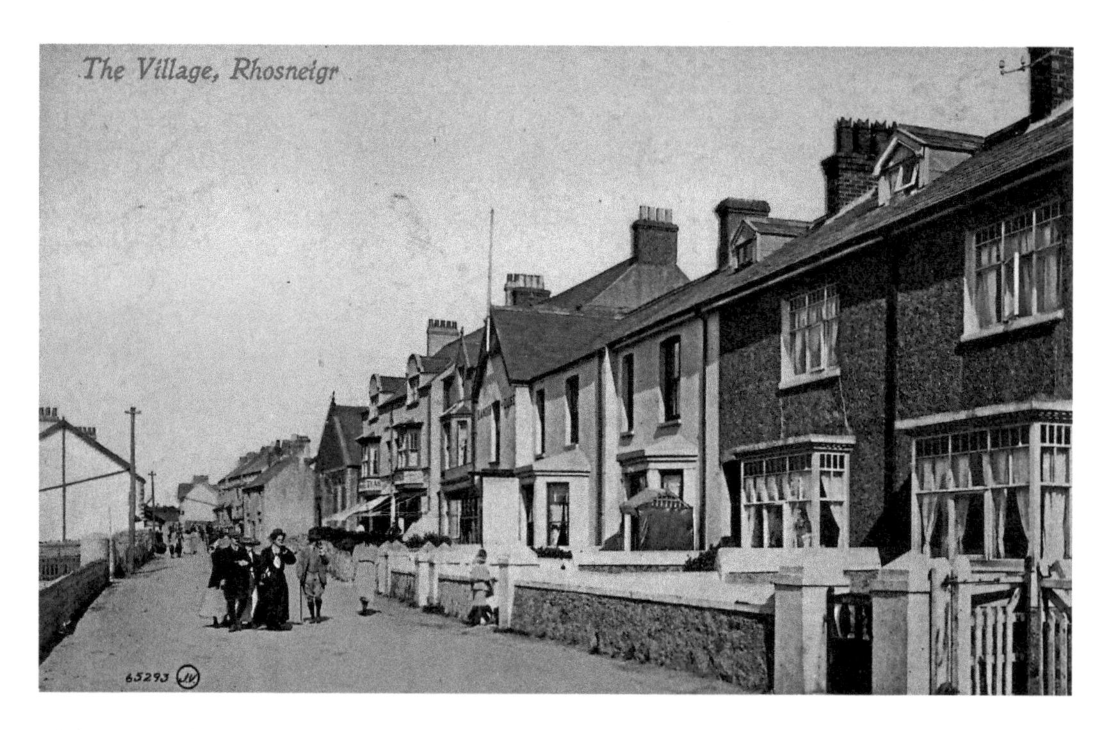

High Street, Rhosneigr, 1910

The High Street, running parallel to the Town Beach further inland, also saw a great deal of new house building at this time. The above photograph shows the Paran Calvinist Methodist chapel (the dark-faced building just behind the people), which once was the only building along that side of the road. The chapel was rebuilt in 1887, based on an 1850 building that replaced an earlier one from 1827. The white buildings include Bangor House (the post and telegraph office) and a café and tea room.

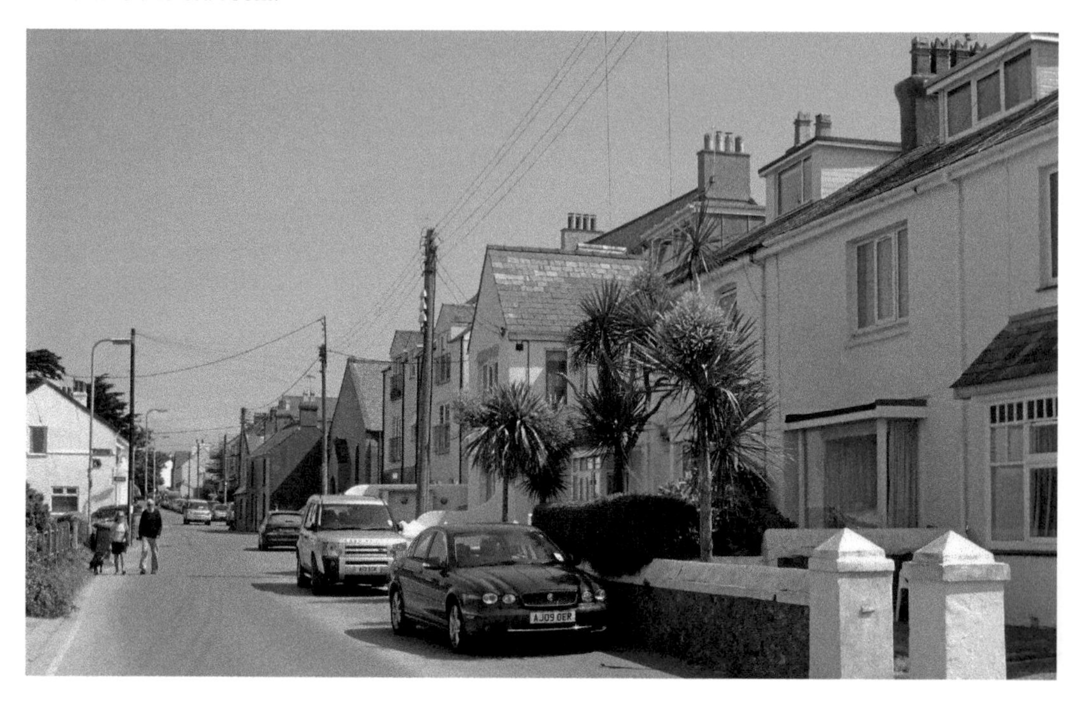

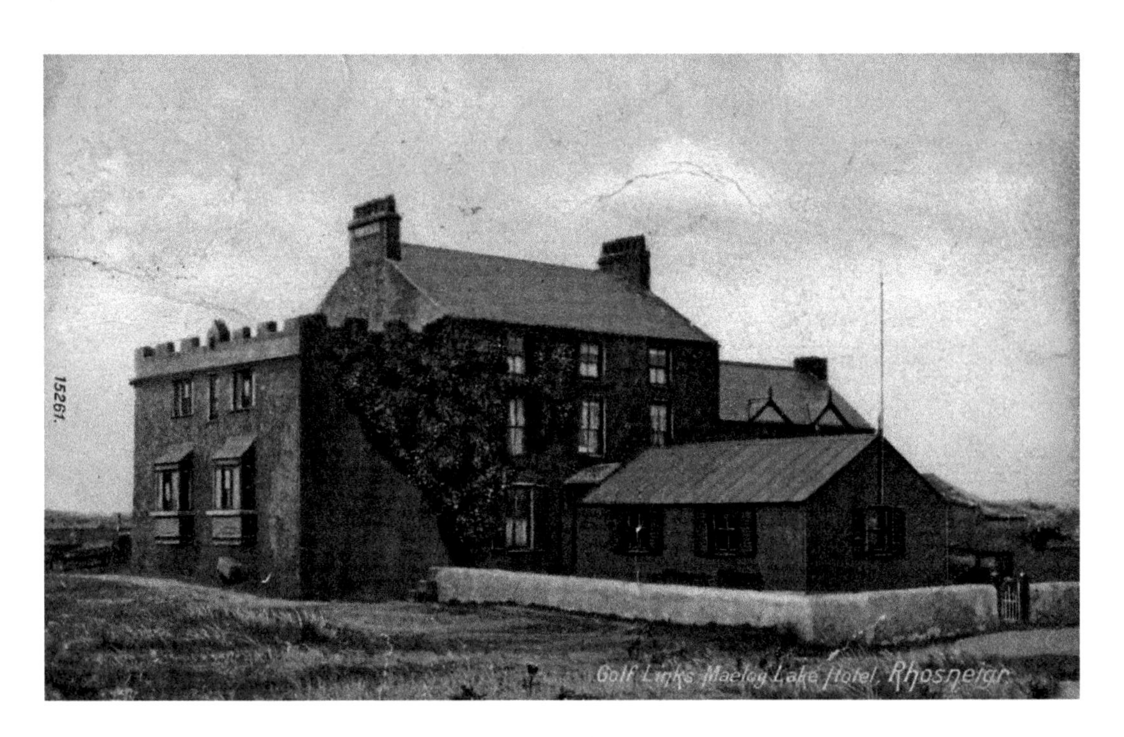

Maelog Lake Hotel, Rhosneigr, Early Twentieth Century

When building of this hotel started in 1863, it aroused opposition among local Temperance campaigners to the extent that it was set alight during construction. It finally opened in 1865 and served Rhosneigr until 2010, when it was closed and demolished. The owners replaced it with an attractive modern building that houses the Oyster Catcher restaurant. It also is home to a chefs' academy that provides valuable training and work experience to the young people of Anglesey. (AA WSJ-8-50)

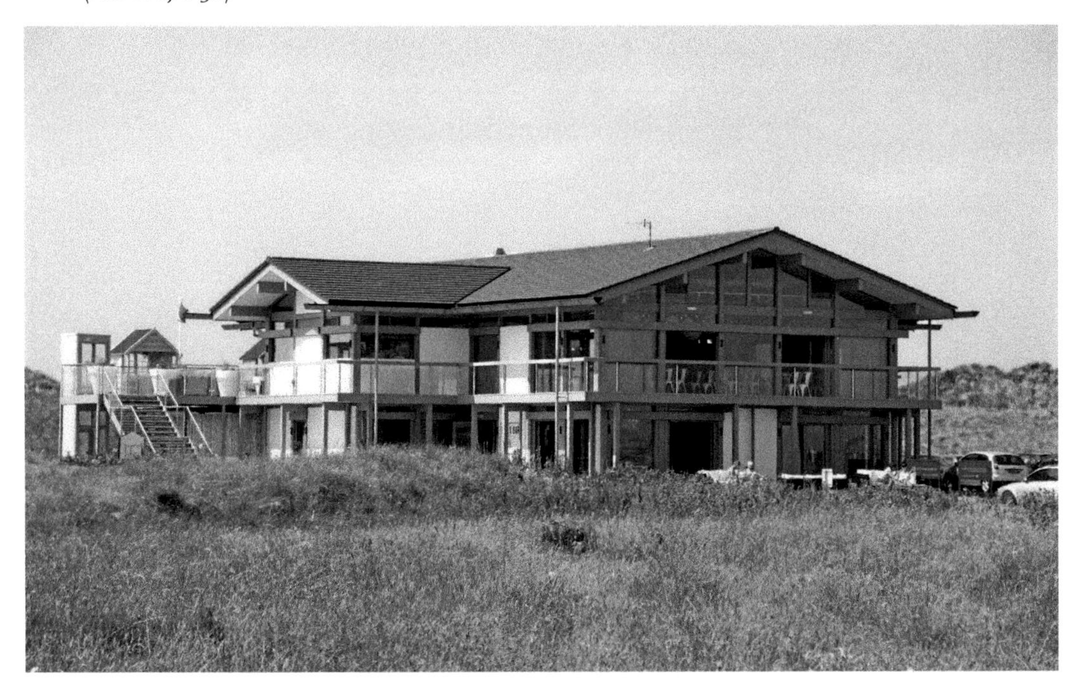

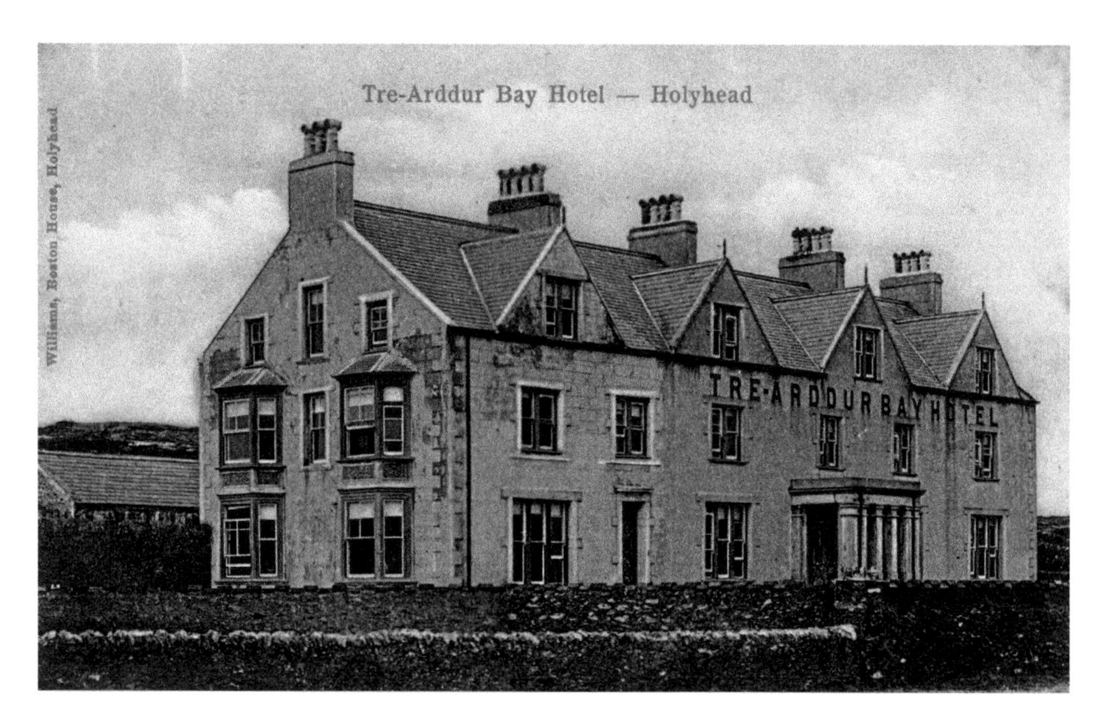

Trearddur Bay Hotel, Early Twentieth Century

This hotel has had many additions and refurbishments, but you can still see the old building peeking out of the middle. Built in the late nineteenth century, it was originally the summer residence of Sir Henry Grayson, a wealthy Liverpool shipbuilder. It was converted to a hotel before 1900. Grayson later built a much larger house, Ravenspoint, across the bay. It also became a hotel, but has since been demolished. (AA WSD-327)

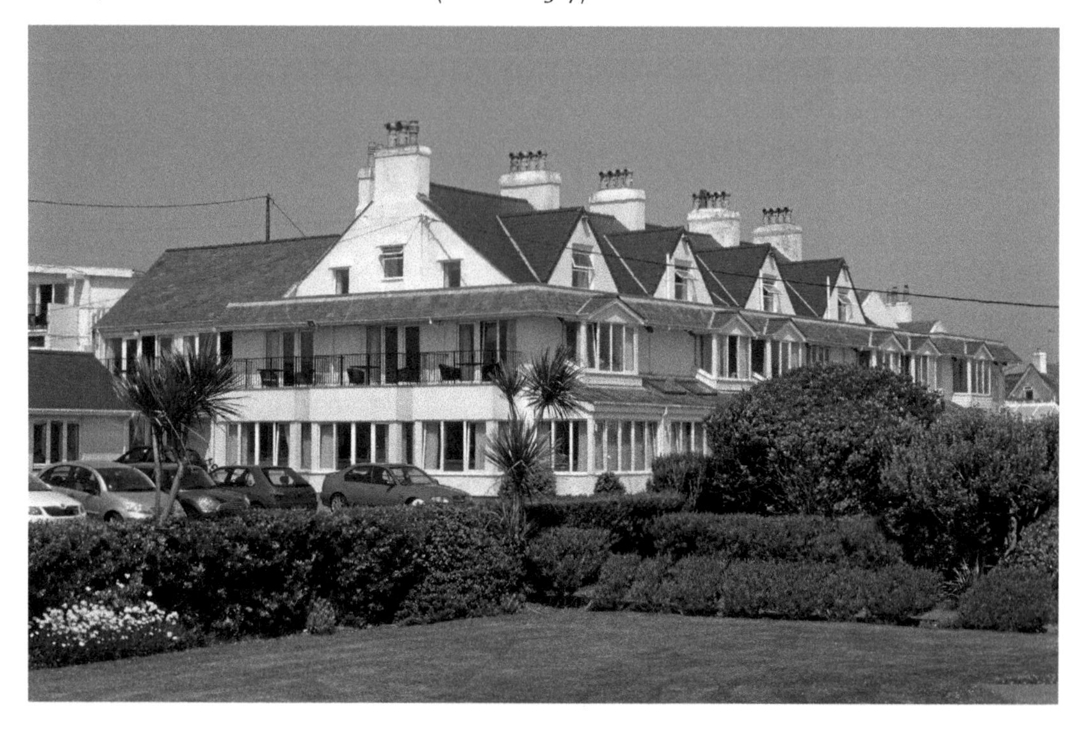

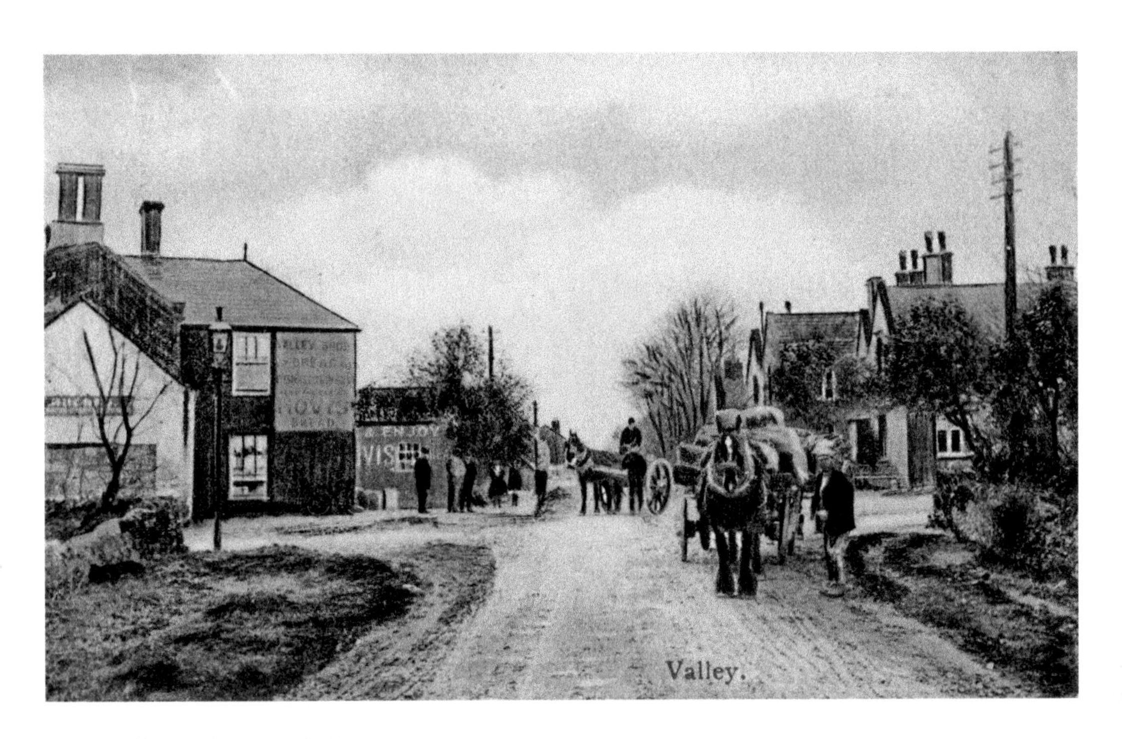

Valley, Early Twentieth Century

Before the new dual carriageway bypassed Valley village, all traffic to Holyhead and Holy Island passed through this junction. The road straight ahead leads to Four Mile Bridge, whereas to the right is the way to the Stanley Embankment, built in 1822 by Thomas Telford. Valley Shop, the main general store run by John Hughes at this time, stands on the left, across the road from the Valley Hotel. (AA WSJ-14-14)

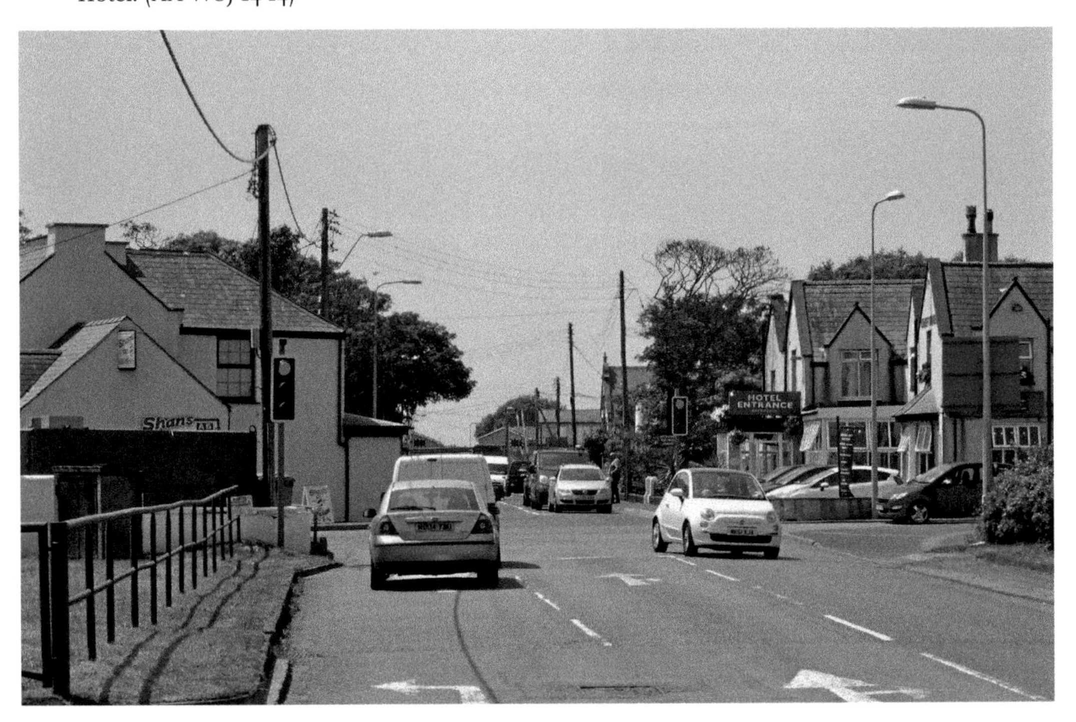

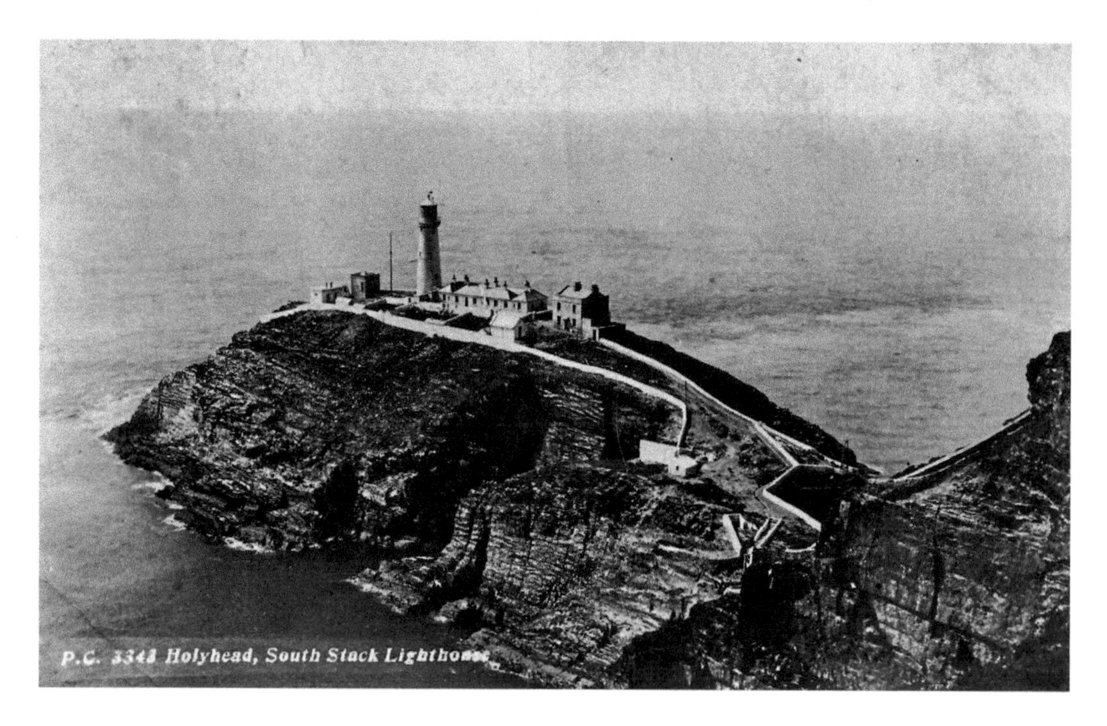

South Stack Lighthouse, *c.* 1908

The lighthouse tower on South Stack was built in 1808, but the surrounding buildings came and went depending on the needs of the keepers. The most noticeable difference between these photographs is the two-storey house to the right. This was built in 1886 to house the telegraph station operators, but fell into disrepair when the staff was evacuated during the First World War. It was demolished in 1923, but the smaller building behind it was preserved. The main building by the tower was reroofed in 1937/38, and the old fog signal and telegraph outlook buildings to the left have now been replaced with the new fog signal, built in 1964.

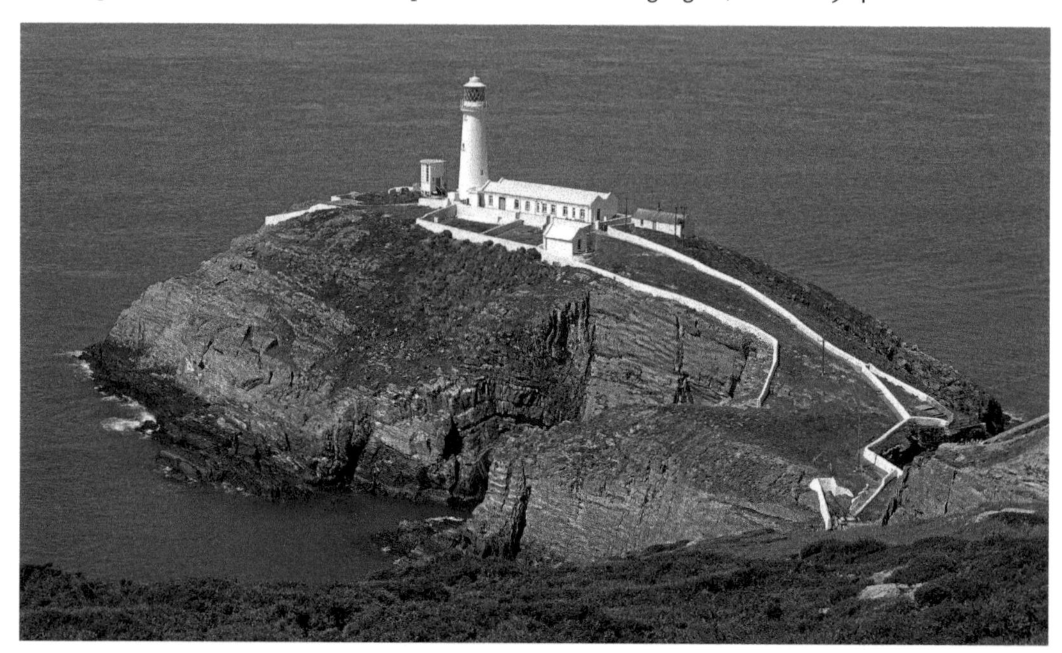

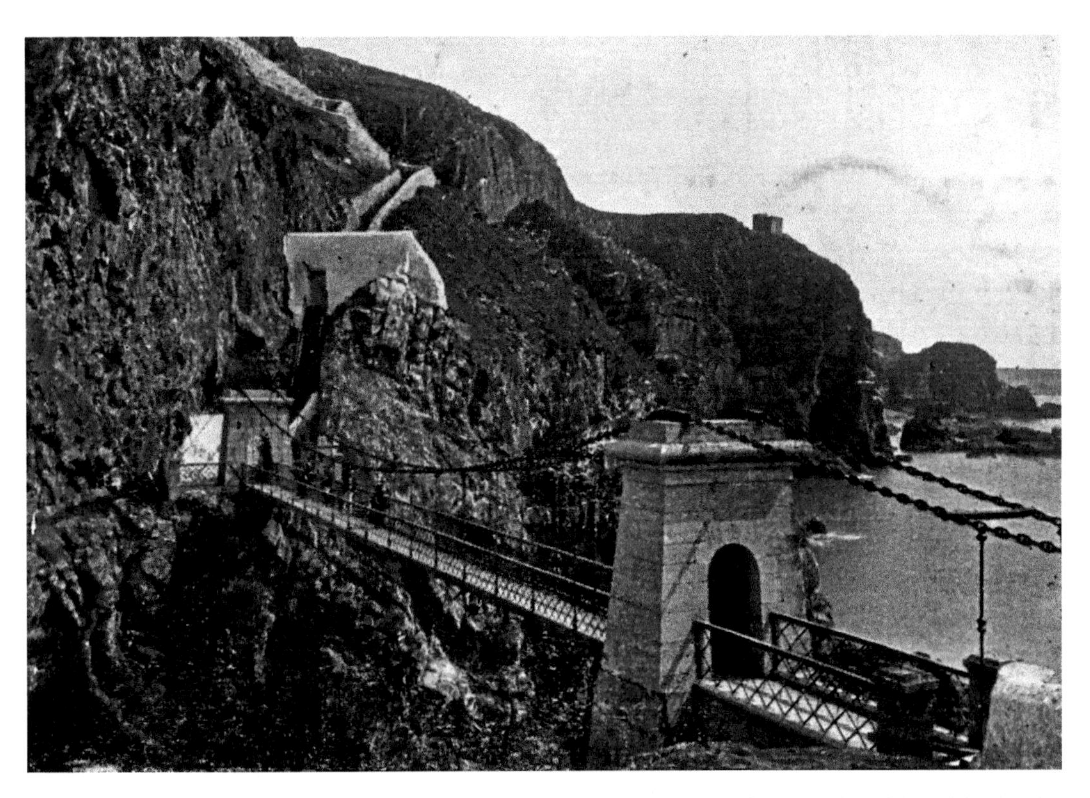

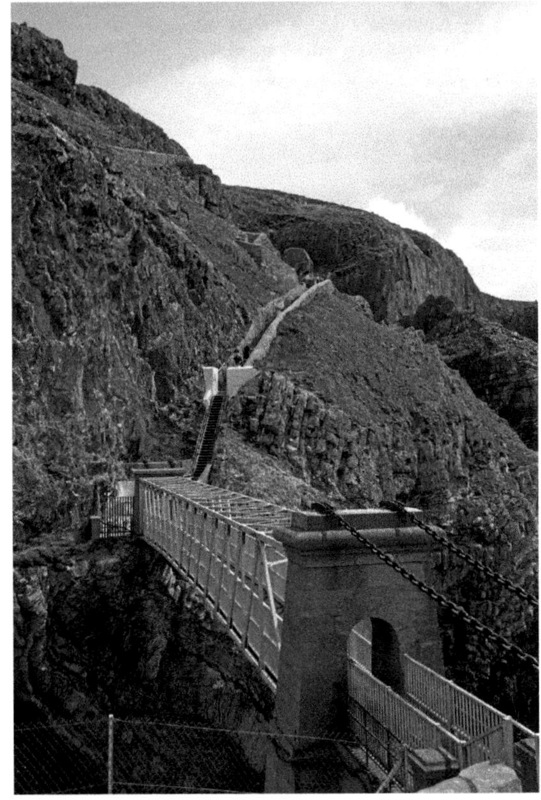

South Stack Suspension Bridge, *c.* 1903
After descending 400 steps down the cliff face, visitors to South Stack must cross a bridge to the island. Before 1827 the keepers used a rope bridge but, inspired by the recently opened Menai Bridge, the Holyhead harbourmaster Captain Hugh Evans commissioned this iron suspension bridge. In the 1960s, it was replaced with an aluminium truss bridge, but this deteriorated rapidly. It had to be rebuilt again in 1997 so the island could be opened to the public.

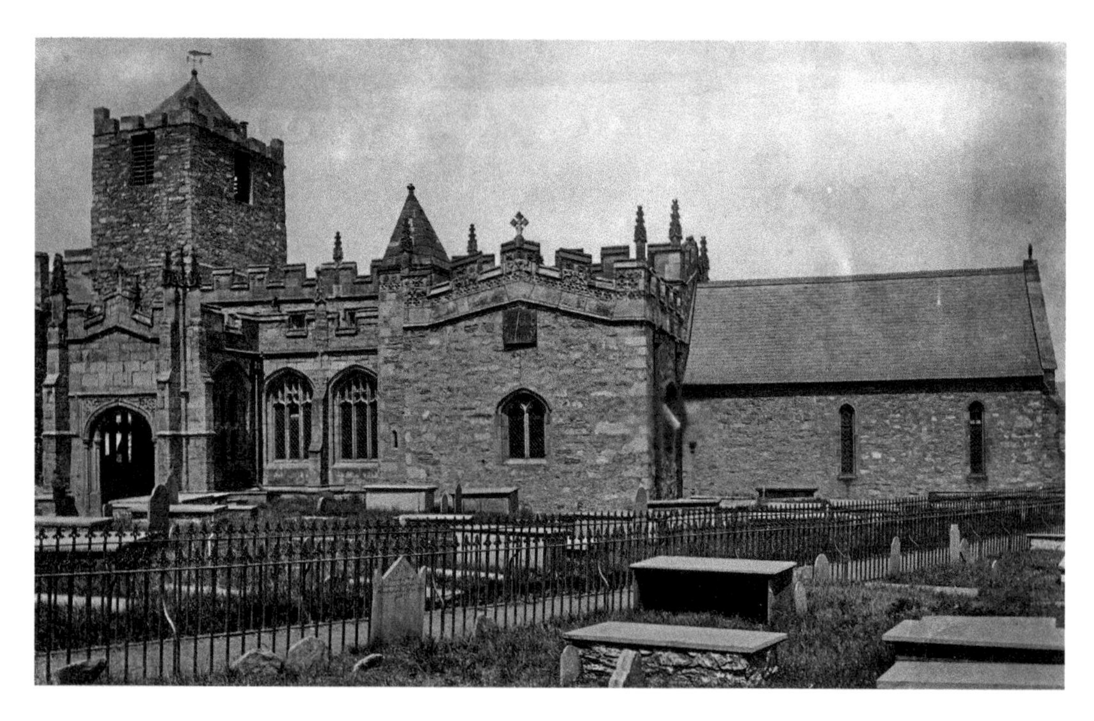

St Cybi's Church, Holyhead, 1891

Sited within the walls of a Roman fort, St Cybi first established a church here around AD 550. The oldest part of the current building is the chancel, on the right above, which dates from the thirteenth century. Most of the rest was built in the fifteenth and sixteenth centuries, with the tower being added around 1625. In the 1650s, it was occupied by Cromwell's army, who added 17 feet to the tower, to be used as a lookout. They also destroyed many of the windows, tombs and statues inside. (AA WSD-93)

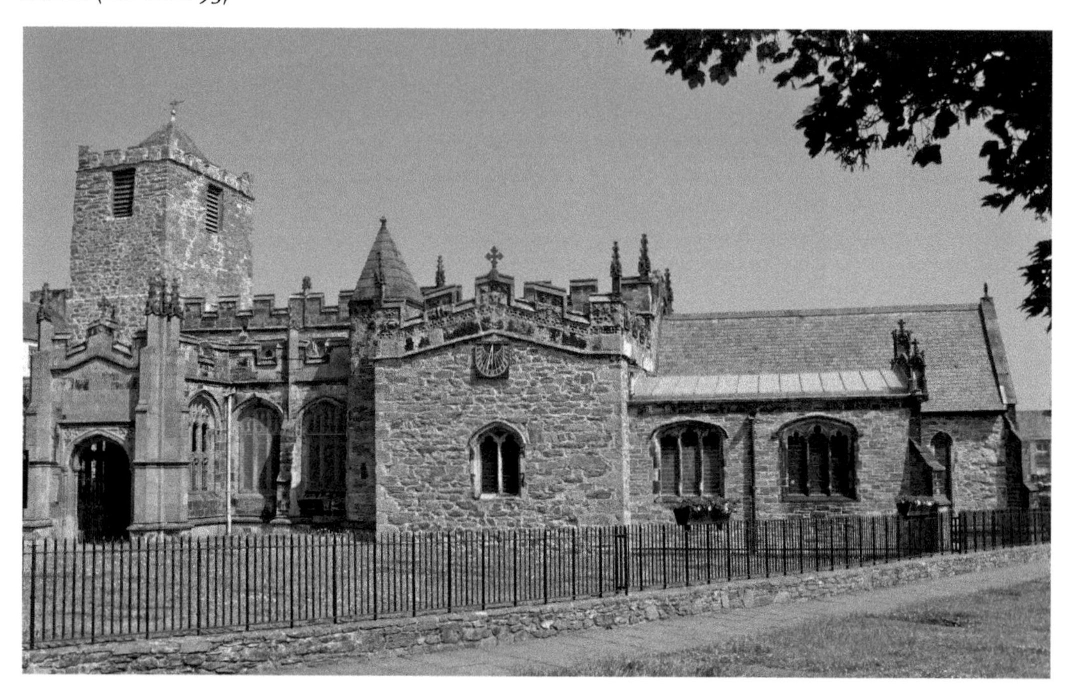

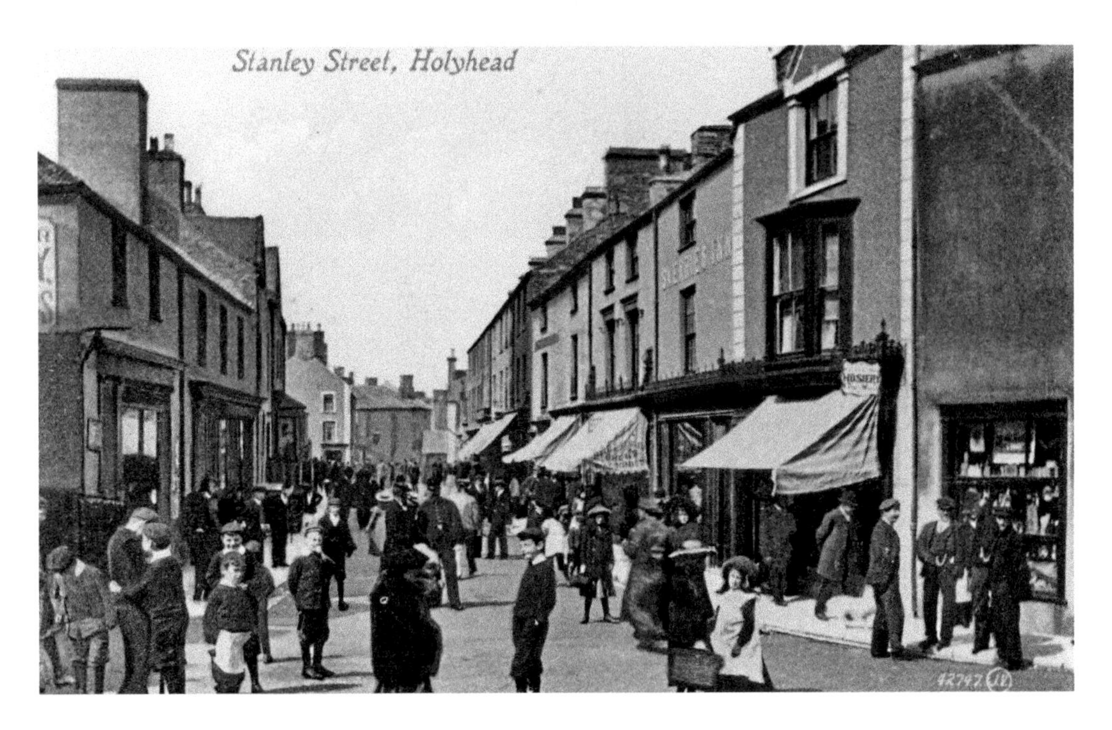

Stanley Street, Holyhead, 1904

Named after the Stanleys, the local landowning family, this street was one of the busiest shopping areas in Holyhead at the turn of the twentieth century. The Market Hall, built in 1855 by Hon. W. O. Stanley, is set back from the street down the road on the left, and the streets leading up to it are lined with shops, pubs and the post office. The Skerries Inn, just on the right, was run by Richard March at the time, and is still open under that name today. (AA WSD-188)

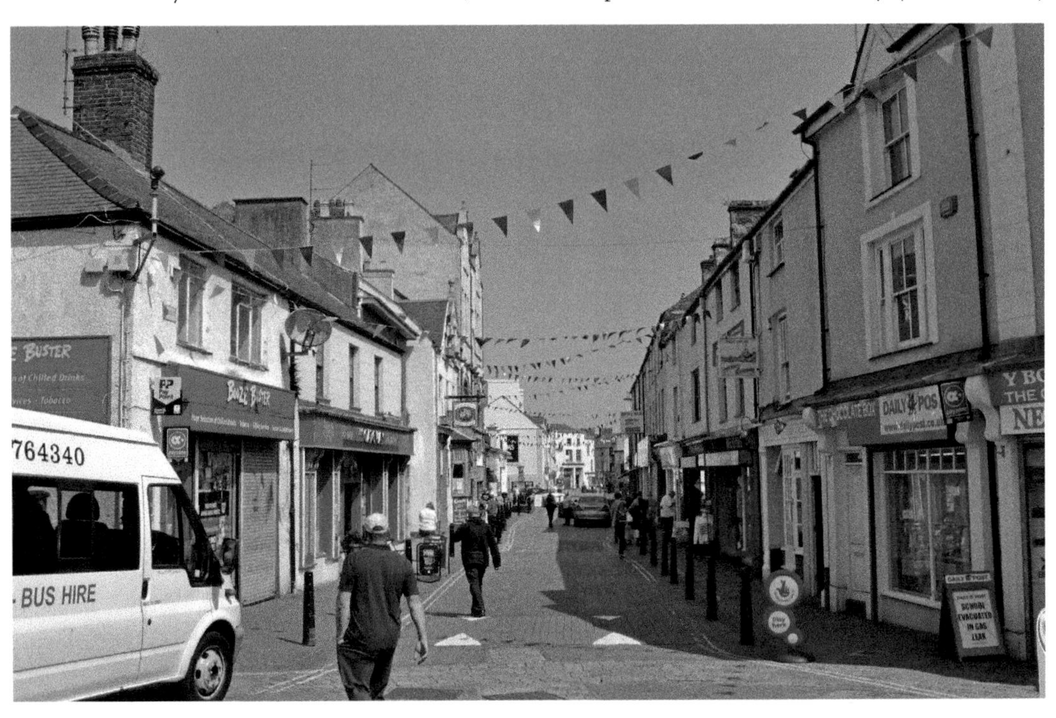

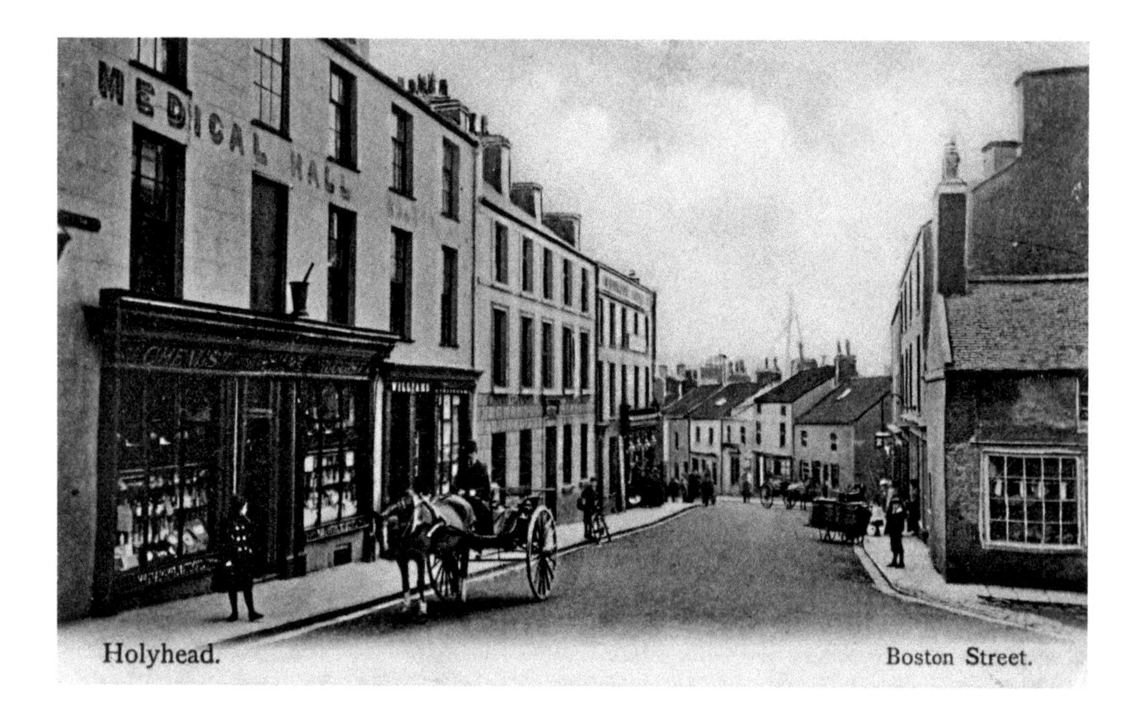

Boston Street, Holyhead, *c.* 1906

Past the Market Hall, the road turns down Boston Street towards the harbour. The top end is dominated by Medical Hall. This chemist shop was run by Rowland Williams at this time, who took over the business from Theophilus Roberts just a few years earlier. It sold all sorts of proprietary medicines and homeopathic cures. The neighbouring Boston House was occupied by Margaret Williams, bookseller, stationer and postcard publisher – she published the photograph above. She took over the shop from her mother, Emma. (AA WSD-36)

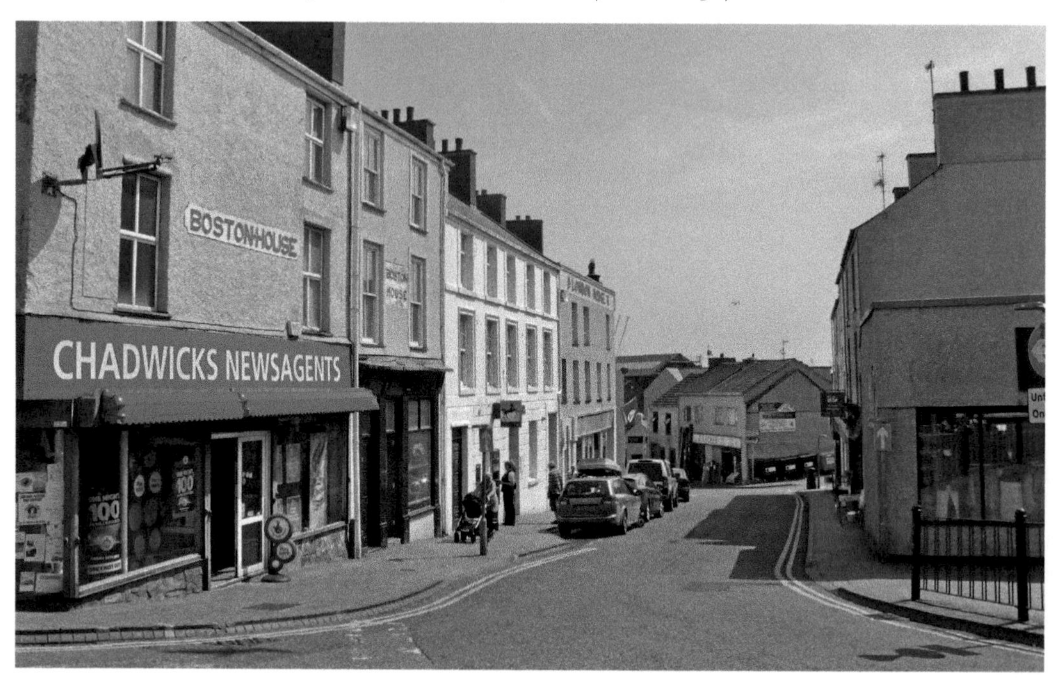

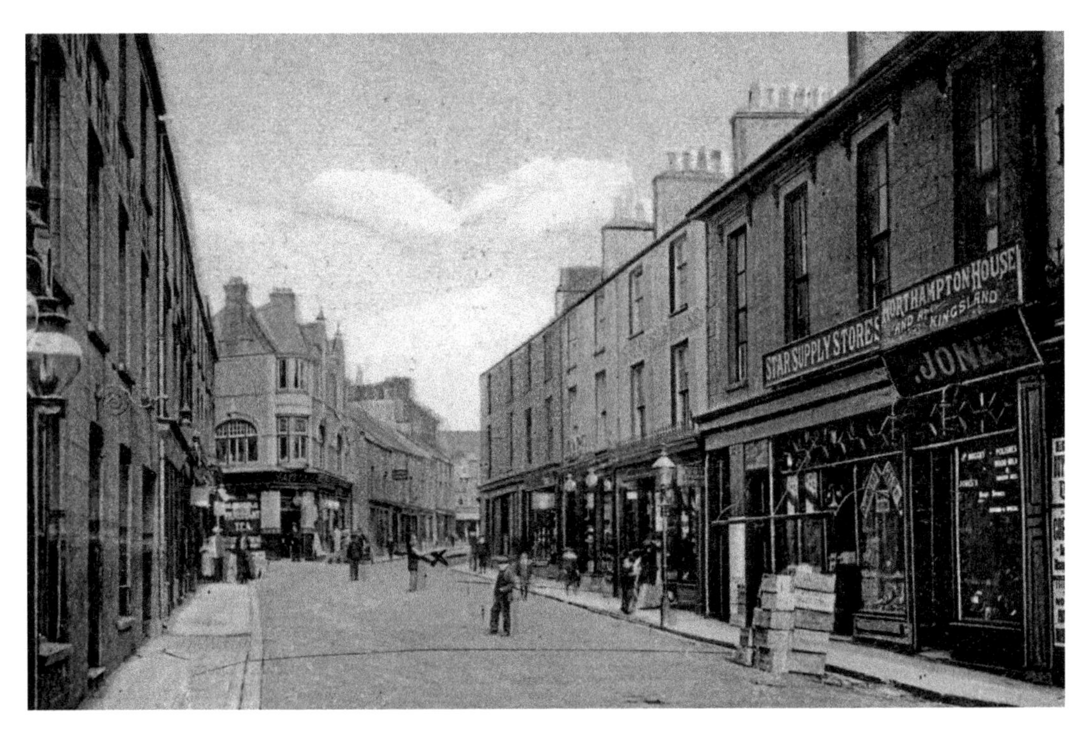

Market Street, Holyhead, Early Twentieth Century

Another main shopping area in Holyhead is Market Street. The Old Market Place, where traders set up their stalls before the Market Hall was built in 1855, is at the far end of this street, near St Cybi's church. Standing prominently at the curve in the road was the Maypole tea shop, run by Joseph Ellis. (AA WSD-242)

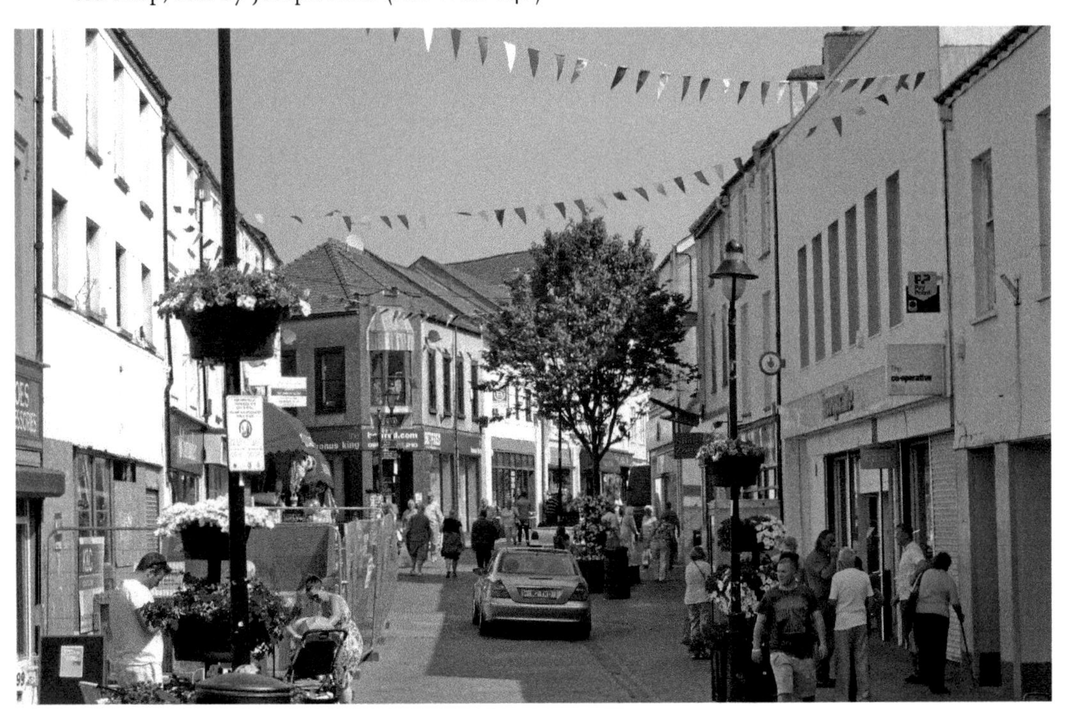

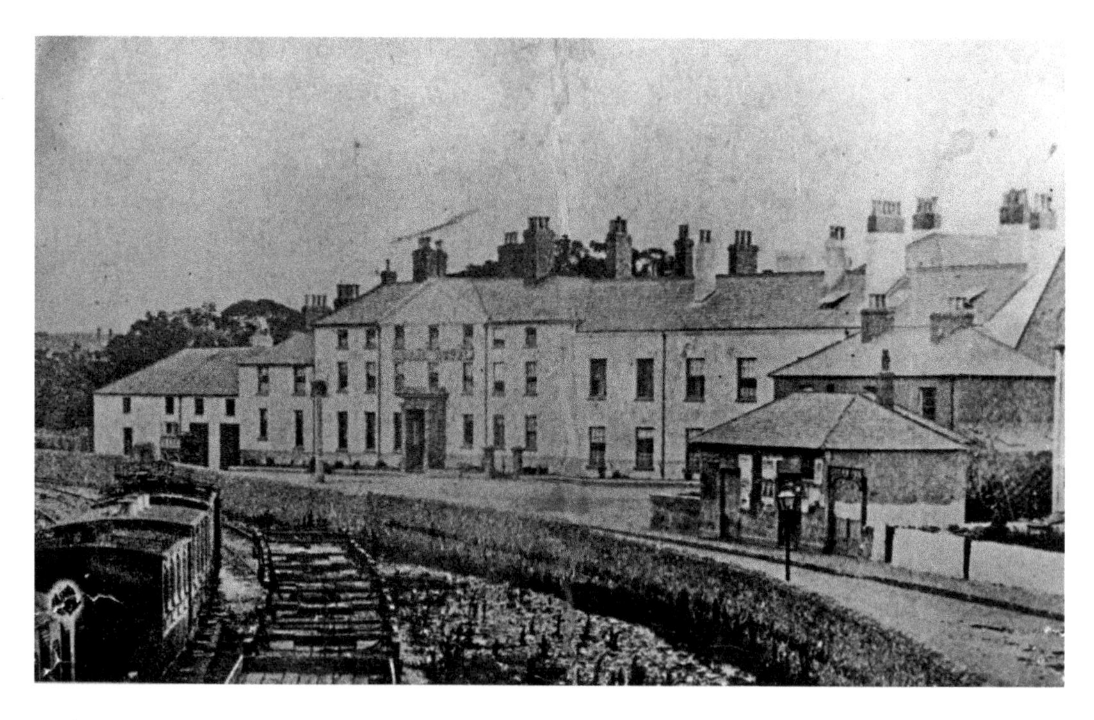

Eagle and Child, Holyhead, *c.* 1880
Built in 1770, the Eagle and Child was the main coaching inn for the port of Holyhead. At the time it would have stood on the edge of the quay, but in the 1870s this part of the harbour was filled in to accommodate the new railway and improved docks. Renamed the Royal Hotel in 1821 after a visit by George IV, it was closed in 1880 and converted into houses. In recent years, part of it was resurrected as the Eagle and Child pub, before being renamed Bar Two. (AA WSD-115)

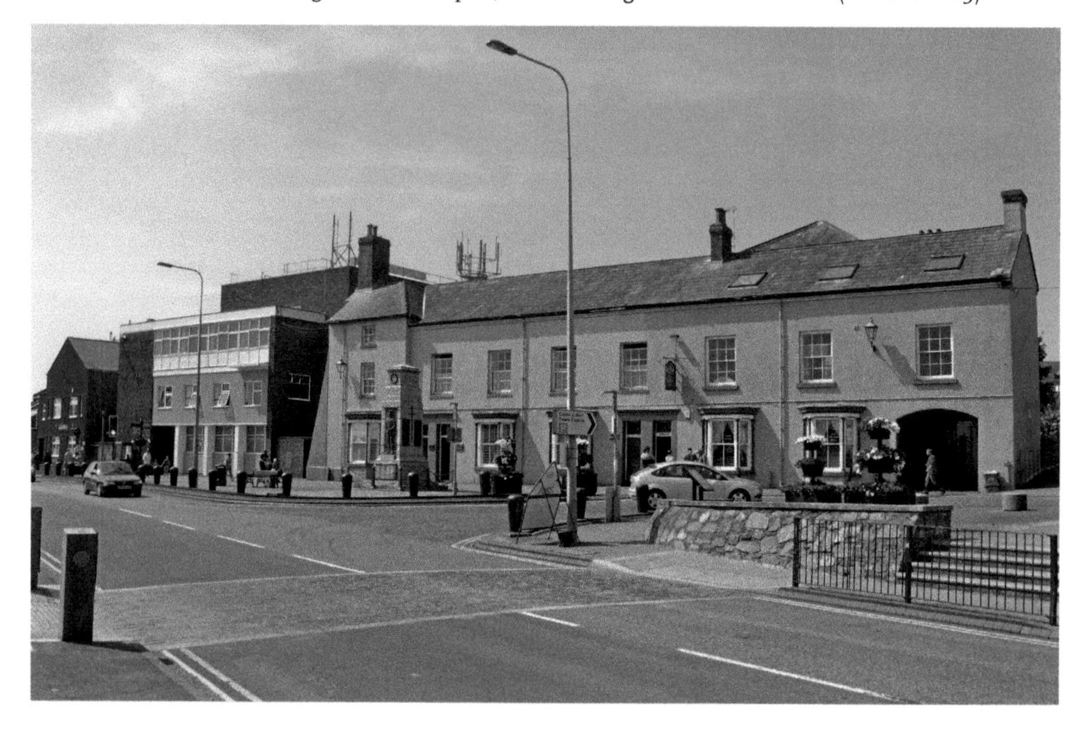

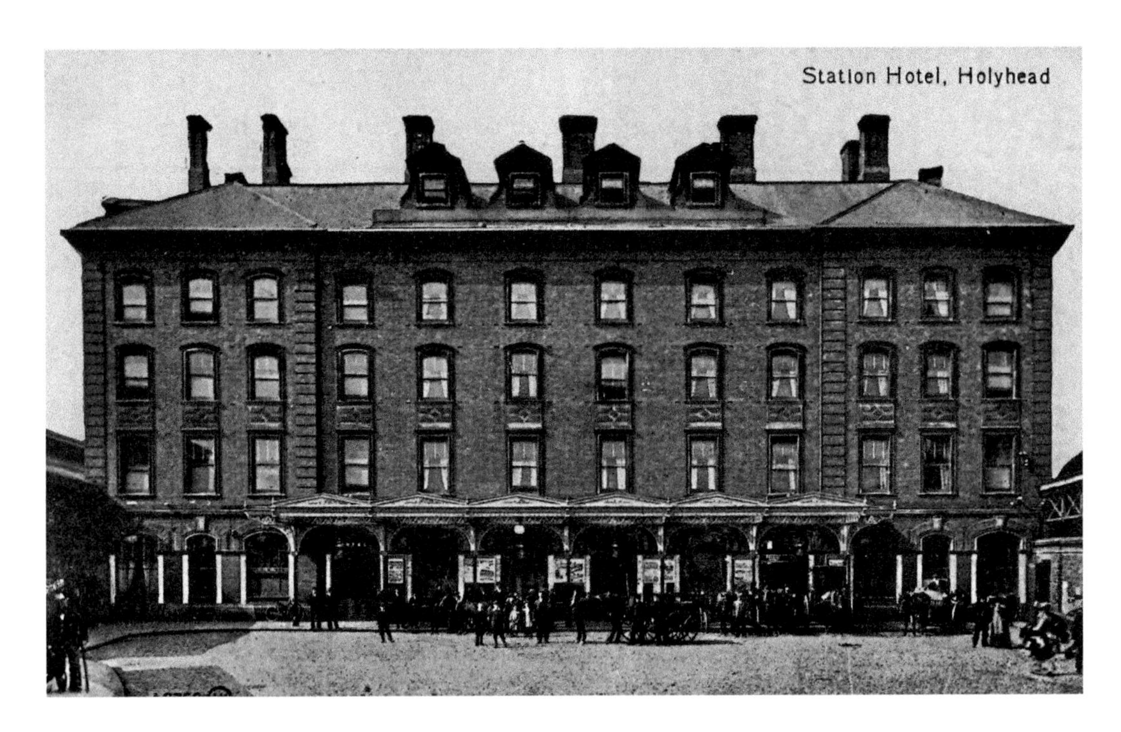

Station Hotel, Holyhead, 1904
With the coming of the railway, the Chester & Holyhead Railway Company bought the Eagle and Child Inn in 1850 to provide accommodation for their passengers. However, increasing passenger numbers meant that a new hotel was needed, so the Station Hotel was built next to the quay and railway station in 1880. It closed as a hotel in 1951, and was used for offices until its demolition in 1979. The current building, housing Stena's ferry operations and the harbour management, was built in 1990.

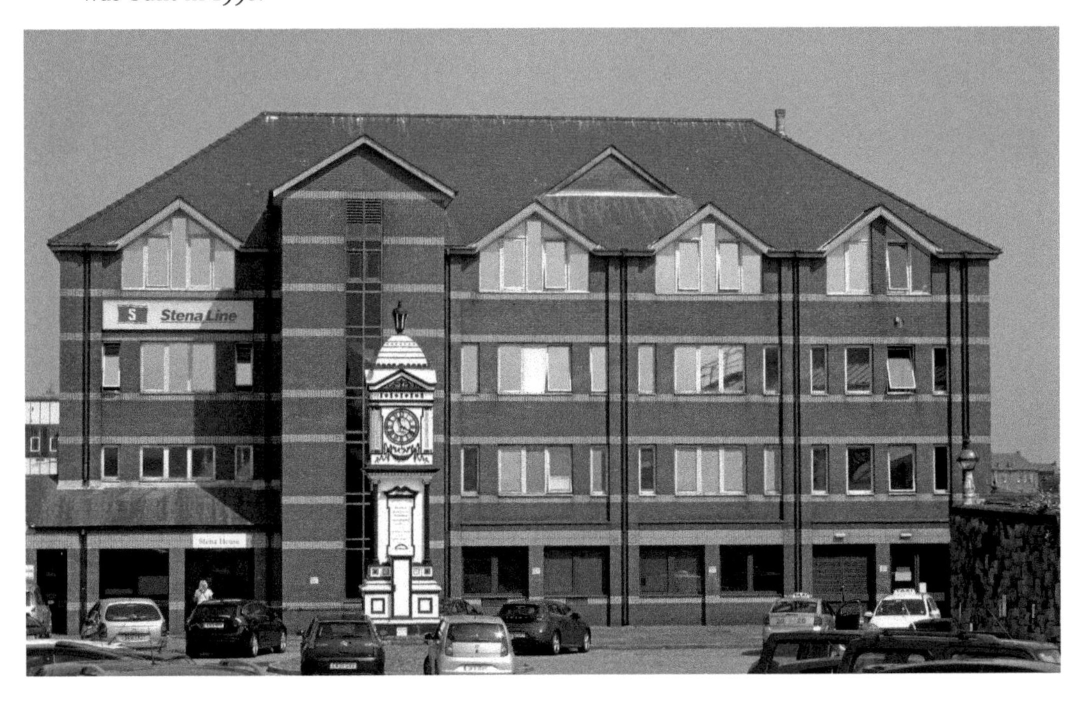

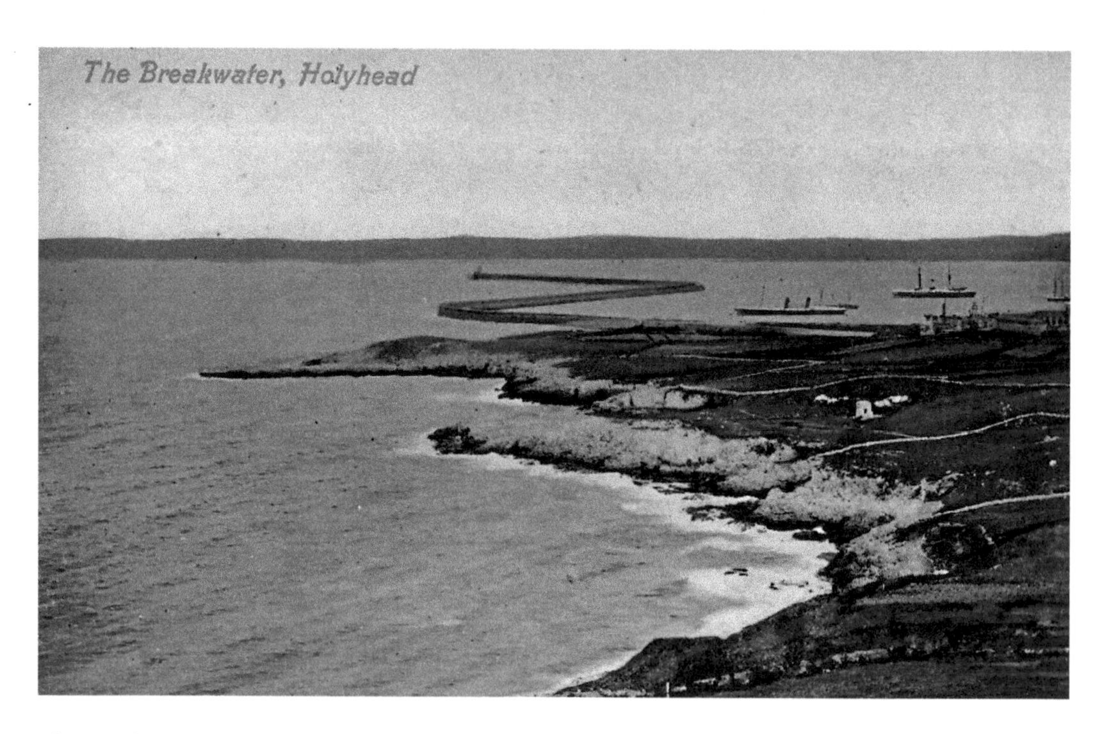

The Breakwater, Holyhead, *c.* 1908

Increased traffic through Holyhead port after the union of Great Britain and Ireland required many harbour improvements, including a breakwater. It was initially planned to have two, with another one further east at Salt Island, but that was abandoned. Work on the breakwater started in 1845 with the building of a railway from a nearby quarry. Initially, the breakwater consisted of just the L-shaped portion, but it was soon extended to the current full 7,860 feet, making it the longest in the United Kingdom. It was finished in 1873.

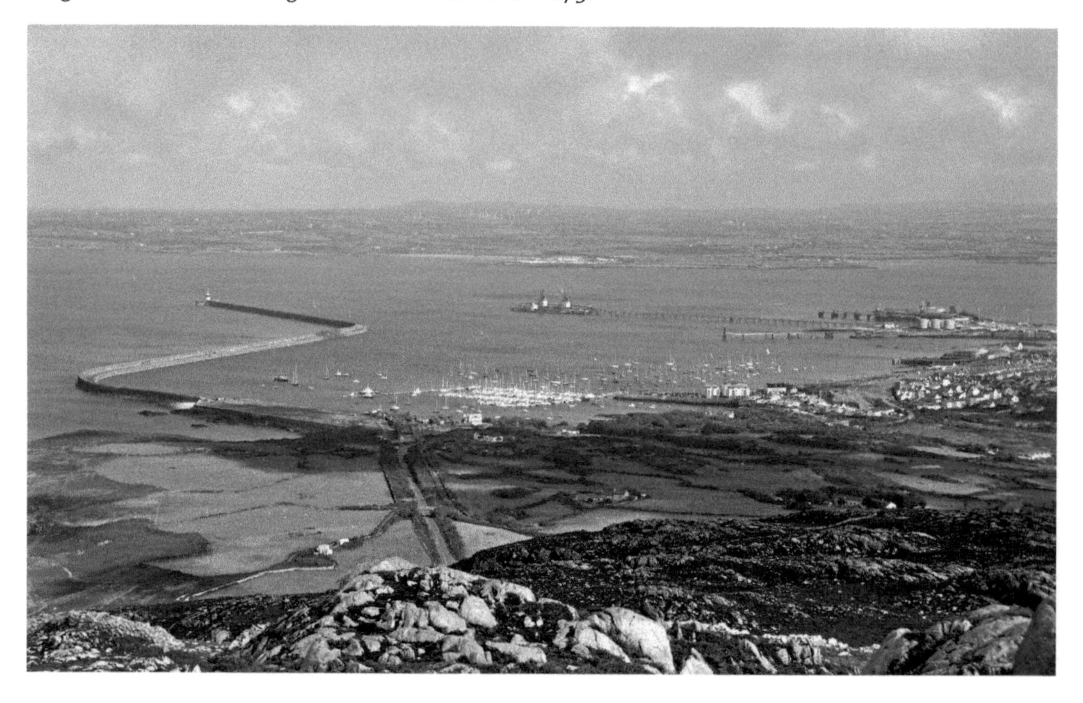

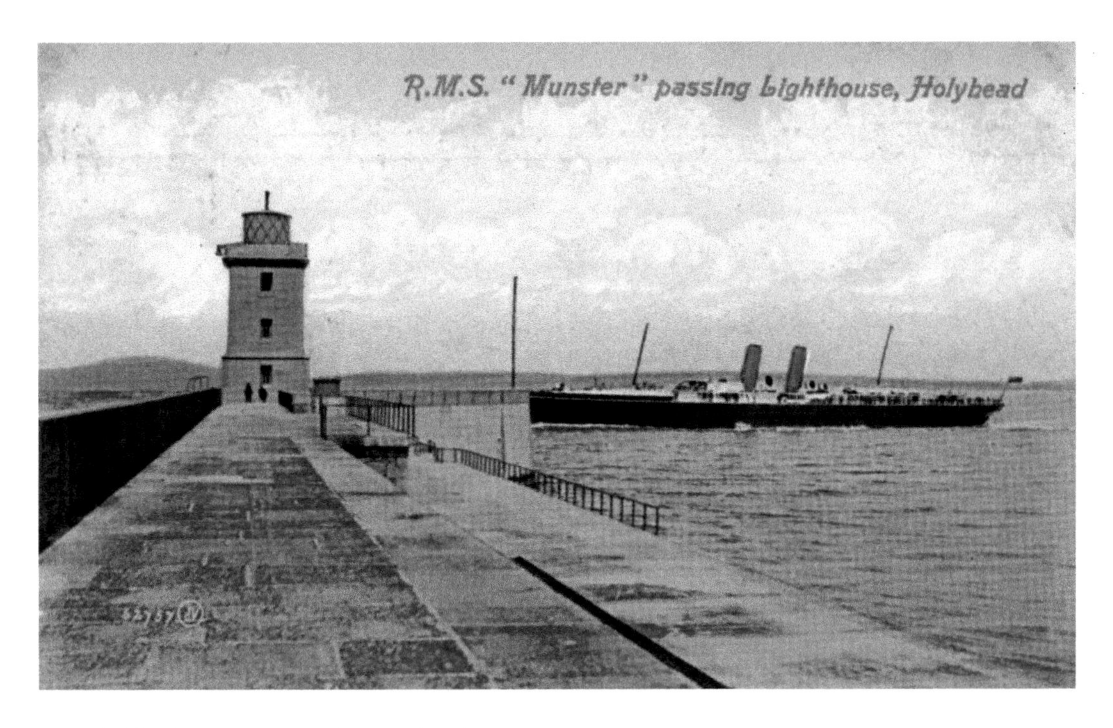

RMS *Munster* from Holyhead Breakwater, 1904

For a century from 1822, mail and passengers were carried across the Irish Sea from Holyhead to Dublin by a series of ships run by the City of Dublin Steam Packet Company. For half of that time, they ran ships named after the four provinces of Ireland. Here, the RMS *Munster*, launched in 1897, sails past the breakwater lighthouse. Today, five ferries cross the Irish Sea daily from Holyhead, including the fast catamaran Stena HSS *Explorer*, shown below. (AA WSD-186)

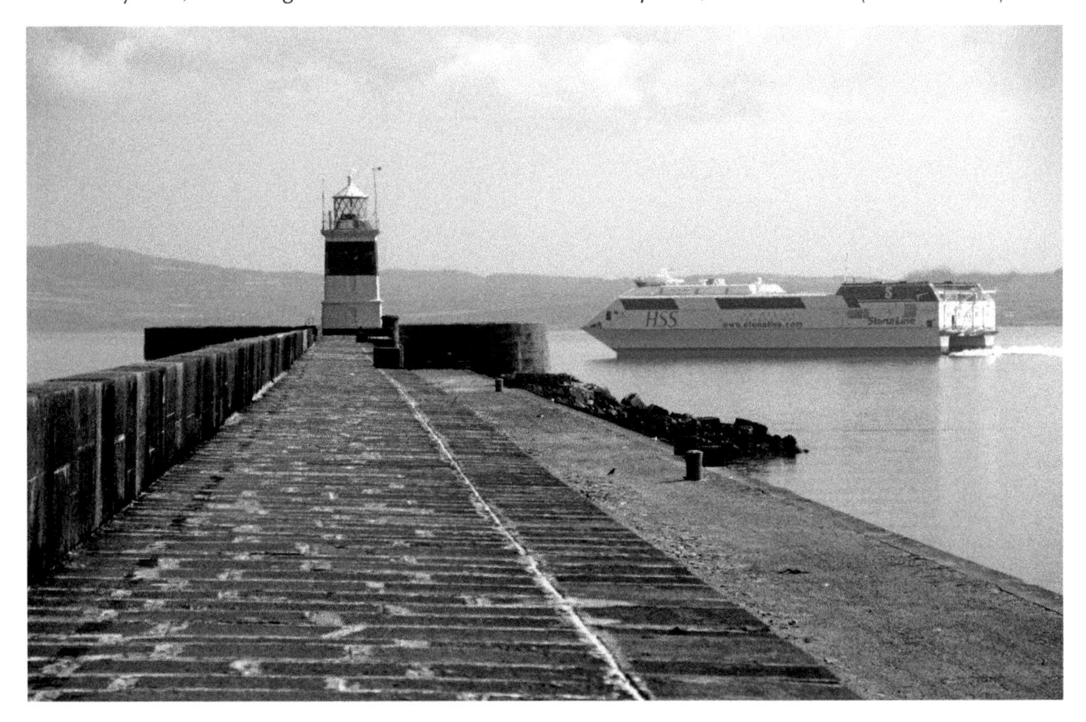

Acknowledgements

The sourcing of old photographs of Anglesey was greatly facilitated by the Anglesey Archives in Llangefni. I am indebted to Hayden Burns and all the archives staff for their friendly assistance during my searches.

I would also like to thank the Menai Bridge Community Heritage Trust who, as well as doing a fantastic job in promoting the heritage of the town and the bridges, also aided me by providing access to some areas of the bridge for photography.

Finally, I thank my wife Catherine Duigan for her support and comments while writing this book, and my son Ciarán Kovach for his interest in the work and for acting as an occasional chauffeur while touring around Anglesey taking photographs.

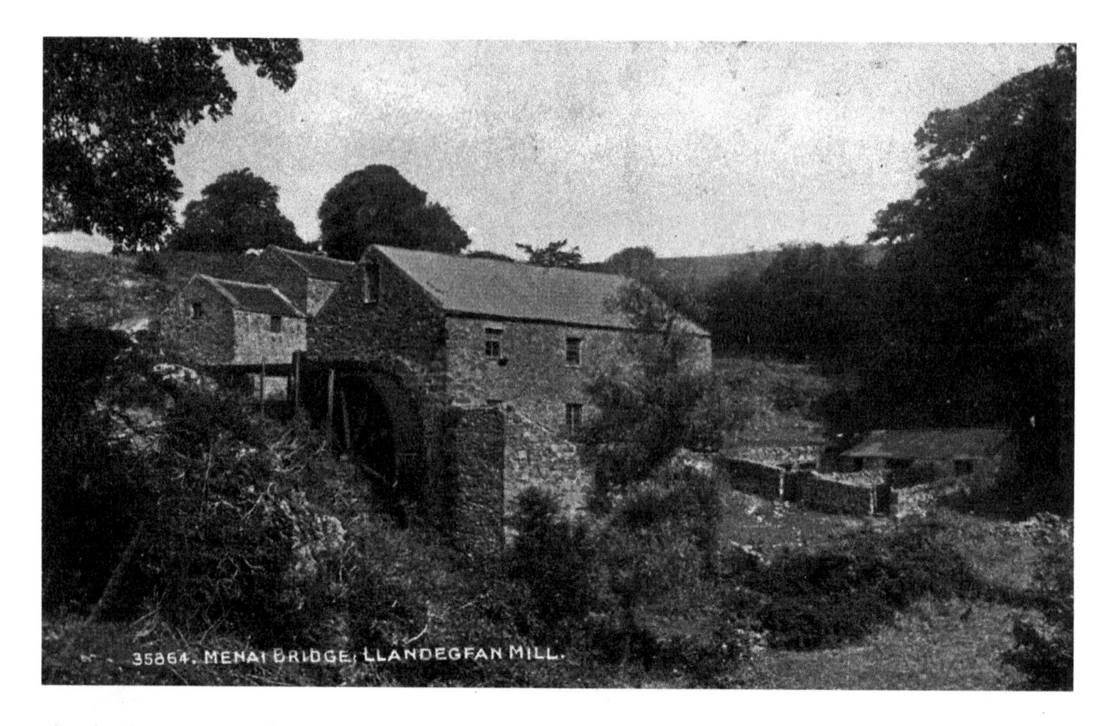

Llandegfan Water Mill, Early Twentieth Century

Also known as the Cadnant Corn Mill, this water mill used the upper Cadnant River, which flows down to the Menai Strait near Menai Bridge, to grind grain to flour. It was built in the early 1800s and was run for decades by David Roberts, before being taken over by William Henry Parry in the 1880s. The mill burned down in 1935, but the cottage behind it remains. Just below this was the Pandy Mill, a fulling mill used for cleaning woollen cloth after it had been woven at the Cadnant Woolen Mill further downstream. (AA WSG-1-4)